For three decades James Dickey has been one of our most popular, most accomplished, and most analyzed poets. Winner of the National Book Award for *Buckdancer's Choice* and author most recently of the critically acclaimed *Strength of Fields* and *Puella,* the multi-talented Dickey remains a major force in American letters today.

Weigl and Hummer, both talented poet-critics in their own rights, have assembled here the best and most representative writings on Dickey and his work. Their cast of contributors includes such well-known poets and critics as Howard Nemerov, Robert Duncan, H. L. Weatherby, Ralph J. Mills, Jr., Joyce Carol Oates, Laurence Lieberman, and Dave Smith. They gauge the measure of Dickey's achievement, pinpoint his failures and successes, illuminate Dickey's philosophy and aesthetics, and suggest the directions his poetry might (or even should) take in the future.

In addition, the book includes two essays by Dickey himself, both of which are central to understanding his work. For anyone who reads, writes, or teaches poetry, this is the best available guide to one of our nation's premier poets.

The Imagination as Glory

The Imagination as Glory:

The Poetry of James Dickey

Edited and with an Introduction by
Bruce Weigl and T. R. Hummer

University of Illinois Press
Urbana and Chicago

Library of Congress Cataloging in Publication Data

Main entry under title:

The Imagination as glory.

  Bibliography: p.
  1. Dickey, James—Criticism and interpretation—Addresses,
essays, lectures. I. Weigl, Bruce, 1949- II. Hummer, T. R.
PS3554.I32Z72 1984   811'.54   83-5108
ISBN 0-252-01101-5

Acknowledgments

The editors wish to thank the following for permission to reprint essays which they originally published:

"Poems of Darkness and a Specialized Light," by Howard Nemerov, *Sewanee Review*, 71 (1963).

"Oriented by Instinct by Stars," by Robert Duncan, first appeared in *Poetry*, was copyrighted in 1964 by the Modern Poetry Association, and is reprinted by permission of the editor of *Poetry*.

"The Way of Exchange in James Dickey's Poetry," by H. L. Weatherby, *Sewanee Review*, 74 (1966).

"The Poetry of James Dickey," by Ralph J. Mills, *TriQuarterly*, 11 (1968).

"Harmony with the Dead: James Dickey's Descent into the Underworld," by David C. Berry, *Southern Quarterly*, 12 (1974).

"A Special Kind of Fantasy: James Dickey on the Razor's Edge," by N. Michael Niflis, *Southwest Review*, 57 (1972).

"Out of Stone, into Flesh: The Imagination of James Dickey," by Joyce Carol Oates, *Modern Poetry Studies*, 5 (1974).

"James Dickey: The Deepening of Being," by Laurence Lieberman, *Unassigned Frequencies: American Poetry in Review, 1964–77*. Urbana, Ill.: University of Illinois Press, 1977.

"*The Moiling of Secret Forces: The Eye-Beaters, Blood, Victory, Madness, Buckhead and Mercy*," by Herbert Leibowitz, *New York Times Book Review*, 8 November, 1970.

"Shamanism toward Confessionalism: James Dickey, Poet," by Linda Mizejewski, *Georgia Review*, 32 (1978).

"The Strength of James Dickey," by Dave Smith, first appeared in *Poetry*, was copyrighted in 1981 by the Modern Poetry Association, and is reprinted by permission of the editor of *Poetry*.

"The Energized Man," by James Dickey, first appeared in *Billy Goat*.

The editors wish to give special thanks to Dave Smith, in whose seminar at the University of Utah this book was conceived and whose continuing support and direction has been indispensible.

Contents

BRUCE WEIGL
and
T. R. HUMMER

Introduction

FOR THOSE WHO HAVE LIVED years with James Dickey's poetry, who have returned to it again and again with growing conviction about its value and its stubborn, lasting power, it is easy to forget how mysterious a universe Dickey projects. His continual transformations, his capacity for engaging the fundamental forces of the world, his invocation of heroes and antiheroes have become so much a part of our way of thinking that we can lose sight of how original and richly strange Dickey's vision actually is. For this reason among others, it is both refreshing and revealing to review the critical response to James Dickey's poetry.

Randall Jarrell, in his essay "The Age of Criticism," gives us the simplest and fullest possible definition of the role of the critic when he writes: "What *is* the critic anyway? So far as I can see, he is an extremely good reader. . . ." Jarrell's essay reminds us that poets write for audiences, for readers, the best of whom approach what they read openly, allowing themselves to respond, in spite of whatever erudition they may possess, with humanity. It is gratifying to discover how many such readers James Dickey has earned over the years. There are so many, in fact, that it seems safe to assume some special quality in the work itself attracts good readers, or even plays a part in creating them. The abundance of fine Dickey criticism can only be a tribute to the poetry itself.

There is one important constant throughout Dickey's poetry: energy. No poet since William Blake has been so concerned with the poem as a generator, repository, and conductor of energy. Dickey's poems are almost always either explicitly or implicitly

I

projections of what he calls the "energized man," the "fully awake man," who utilizes "a hundred percent" of his faculties. Dickey himself, as he readily admits, is not this ideal man—no one is. But his poems body forth at least the possibility of such a man. Further, the poems are designed to seduce the reader into participating momentarily in a more "energized" life.

"Strongly mixed emotions are what I usually have," Dickey writes in *Babel to Byzantium*, "and what I usually remember from the events of my life. Strongly mixed, but giving the impression of being one emotion impure and overwhelming—that is the condition I am seeking to impose on my readers." Dickey wants to change the reader; he wants to use the poem as a medium through which the reader is raised or torn out of himself into a larger, more "energized" state of being. Presumably, this energized state is something the reader could not enter into without the mediation of the poem. This is a poetry that forces the reader to know he is in the presence of a "kind of truth at which I could not have arrived by myself, but its truth is better than the one I had believed" *(Babel to Byzantium)*.

Dickey is not talking here about intellectual awakening alone. He hopes "to get the reader more and more into the actions and happenings of the lines and less and less to stand off and make moral or aesthetic judgements" *(Babel to Byzantium)*. He wants to jar the reader emotionally, intuitively, and even physically, out of complacency into involvement.

Dickey describes the converse of this "energized" condition in his essay, "The Energized Man":

> The main feeling I have as I live longer and longer is a sense of purposelessness, of drift, of just getting along from day to day, of using only those faculties which we must use in order to earn a living. . . . One gets the impression of moving among a vast number of well-meaning zombies; one moves among them, also, as a kind of well-meaning zombie with regrets. The enormous discomfort that settles on Americans as they grow older . . . is that their lives—their *real* lives—seem somehow to have eluded them: to have been taken away from under their very noses.

To help restore the full lives that are rightfully ours, Dickey wants to use poetry as a means of combatting this malaise. In this respect,

Dickey resembles no one more than those among the British Romantic poets who labored to harness poetry as a means of changing men's mental conditions, to purge them, to undistort them so they could see themselves and the world clearly and rightly.

In his "Preface to the Lyrical Ballads," William Wordsworth provides an illuminating parallel to Dickey's description of "well-meaning zombies"; he writes that "a multitude of causes unknown to former times are now acting with a combined force to blunt the discriminating powers of the mind, and unfitting it for all voluntary exertion, to reduce it to a state of almost savage torpor." Wordsworth wants his poetry to reverse this condition, and though he is modest in his estimate of how much good his own poetry can do, he expresses faith that the body of all great poetry can and does contact "certain inherent and indestructible qualities of the human mind." For Wordsworth and for Dickey as well, poetry is something that has a *real effect* in the world. The poem is, as Dickey writes, "something that matters."

It is this design on the reader, this sincere effort to infuse the poem with transforming energy, that critics have responded to in Dickey's work since the beginning of his career. In a 1963 review of Dickey's first book, *Drowning with Others*, Howard Nemerov strips the critical act bare to reveal the reader's entry into Dickey's projected world—the initial repulsion, the grudging acceptance, the whole-hearted embrace—all stages of the subtle but irresistable seduction.

"Dickey's intention," Nemerov writes, "seems often enough this, a feeling one's way down the chain of being. . . . Salvation is this: apprehending the continuousness of forms, the flowing of one energy through everything." From the start, critics have recognized and praised Dickey's metaphysical ambitiousness and the transforming, healing, and life-affirming impulse behind it. "The poet," Robert Duncan writes, "uses the poem to induce flight," and his review of Dickey's *Two Poems of the Air* illustrates the attracting power of Dickey's opening up of form to include the growing chaos of his imagination. The insights of these early reviews are echoed and amplified by later essays, and their essential correctness is underscored by the direction of Dickey's later work.

H. L. Weatherby's seminal essay, "The Way of Exchange in James Dickey's Poetry," clearly reveals Dickey's stark originality.

Weatherby focuses on Dickey's willingness to violently alter the reader's perceptions as the personae attempt to *exchange,* to break down barriers and enter new realms of experience. Weatherby aptly proclaims this double vision of exchange as something both new and very old:

> . . . the paradox of motionless motion, the still point of the turning world, the perfect union of man and his opposites . . . is what poetry always tries to express. . . . But the effort to resolve these paradoxes through the process of exchange . . . may very well be unique with Dickey. If that is true it may be safe to say that he has achieved a new way of doing what all poets do . . . to throw a light on the world which will show it as the poet knows it must be.

Weatherby puts his finger on the basic impulse behind Dickey's work throughout: the obsession with transformation, the desire to move constantly from one state of consciousness to another as if it were possible, through this shifting, to defeat temporality. Furthermore, Weatherby makes the significant observation that the exchange is not always successful in the poems and calls into question the consequences of Dickey's method: "The way of exchange is as dangerous a thing aesthetically as it is spiritually. . . . By staring intently in a certain light you may eventually see your world as you know it must be, but you may also break under the strain of staring."

Dickey's long poem, "The Firebombing," compels critics to question the relationship between the success or failure of the exchange and the success or failure of the poem itself. The poem's terror arises from the inability of its speaker to make an essential, human connection with his victims of twenty years past. Part of the critical problem seems to lie with some readers' unwillingness to make a distinction between Dickey and the poem's persona, hence refusing to see the moral pain the persona suffers as a consequence of his realization that he cannot connect with the victims of his bombing.

Thus, Ralph J. Mills, Jr. can say on one hand that "Dickey's imaginative processes free the body of its earthly ties and permit it a kind of infinite capacity for extension," while saying of "The Firebombing" that it presents "events and details . . . dramatized

4

without ever arousing a commensurate moral—which is to say, human—awareness." In the same vein, D. C. Berry writes that "Dickey has no feeling for those whom he killed in the war . . . he is without feeling, lacking even shame, able only to recall the aesthetic aspect of the killing." Such an *ad hominem* reading blurs the dramatic dimension of Dickey's exploration of exchange. "The Firebombing" is in fact a moral drama in which the persona plays out his failure to make a human connection and to redeem himself in his own eyes. The assumption that Mills, Berry, and a number of other readers make is that a failure of the exchange is a failure of the poem. Clearly "The Firebombing" is morally disturbing, but whether Dickey's point of view represents a moral collapse of the persona, or an imposed moral distance, or both, the knot of ambiguities generated is compelling.

"The Firebombing" is symptomatic of a shift in the direction of Dickey's poetry. As N. Michael Niflis puts it, Dickey becomes "gravely concerned with the terrible conflict which exists between man's basic, driving biological needs and the controls of society. . . . Dickey would reconcile the basic drives with the intellect. But he admits himself that he does not know how this can ever be done, how the man-made obstacles can be overcome." Dickey forces us to the limits of our moral defenses where we may recognize the possibility of moral man committing immoral acts; by entering the arena of moral speculation with his vision of solitary man in collision and collusion with society, Dickey expands his range infinitely. He also becomes a center of critical controversy. Although Dickey continues to employ what Berry calls the "Orphic configuration" where "the living and dead share one space," he can also, as Joyce Carol Oates says, narrate from "the inside of our fallen, contaminated, guilt-obsessed era, and he speaks its language."

The publication of Dickey's *Poems 1957–1967* was an event that called for critical reassessments. In eloquent responses, Oates and Laurence Lieberman help put Dickey back into perspective as a poet/performer who creates composite beings who encompass all of our pathological extremes. Oates cautions us not to blame the poet for the sins of the personae and the characters of the poems; for Dickey,

The process of increasing self-consciousness, as image after image is explored, held up like a mask to the poet's face, absorbed, and finally discarded, comes to seem a tragic movement, as every existential role in the universe must ultimately be abandoned . . . . Dickey contains multitudes; he cannot be reproached for the fact that some of these aspects of a vast, complex self are at war with the others.

Lieberman goes even farther in reconciling the moral stance of "The Firebombing" with the rest of Dickey's canon. He acknowledges Dickey's intimate participation in the poem but says, "The writer has attempted the impossible, and he admits it. He is not ready for self-forgiveness yet, because he is not yet able to feel a guilt commensurate with his crimes. Perhaps he never will be ready." Lieberman, like Oates, acknowledges the inevitable discomfort that a poem like "The Firebombing" produces, but as an antidote to the horror of that side of Dickey's vision, "the dramatic confrontation between self and its guilt," Lieberman recognizes the operation of joy: "The poetic vision of James Dickey's fifth volume of poems, *Falling*, contains so much joy that it is incapable of self-pity or self-defeat."

Not everyone was so enthusiastic about the new work, however, and in long poems such as "Falling," and "May Day Sermon to the Women of Gilmer County, Georgia, by a Woman Preacher Leaving the Baptist Church," critics discovered a new point of controversy. Coincident with Dickey's leap into the public eye following the publication of his novel *Deliverance* and the subsequent appearance of the movie based on that novel, there began a series of attacks on Dickey which have not yet abated: personal and professional accusations of egoism, publicity-baiting, spectacularism, and inflation. In fact, such admonitions had appeared in the criticism before. Mills, after calling "Falling," and "May Day Sermon . . ." "drawn out, repetitive, over-written, blurred, and diffuse," reinforces his warning with a word of caution from the public side: "Large reputations—we know it as a commonplace—can be exceedingly dangerous in the pressures they bring always to be new and inventive . . . in order to maintain one's laurels . . . and a poet of Dickey's strengths can be damaged as easily as can a lesser one."

Many critics felt a falling off in *The Eye-Beaters, Blood, Victory, Madness, Buckhead and Mercy*, a move away from the mythic and dramatic contours of *Poems 1957–1967* in favor of something more like confessionalism. Herbert Leibowitz's review of *The Eye-Beaters* is typical of the mixed reviews the book occasioned. Leibowitz finds "a stagy, unpleasant hysteria" in these poems, "a spirit of religiosity, as though they were infected by the diseases and blindness that afflict the poet and the people in his poems." Liebowitz had admired what he calls Dickey's "gambling with unbalance" in the earlier work; now he believes Dickey's voice has degenerated into "sheer bravado." At the same time, Leibowitz can call the title poem "brilliant, harrowing," revealing the "will of the imagination" as "godlike."

With the publication of *The Eye-Beaters* and even more with *The Zodiac* (not to mention such hybrids as *Jericho* and *God's Images*), Dickey's poetry became an acute problem to his critics. Earlier writers like Weatherby, Mills, and Niflis were never carping; they addressed Dickey's work more like well-wishers speaking to someone on the verge of a dangerous journey. And as Leibowitz's qualified unhappiness shows, some of Dickey's later, more hostile critics did not simply pounce on him; they stood by, appalled and dispirited by what they saw as the failure of one in whom they had placed a vital hope. But the criticism, even when negative, continued to be balanced and cautiously hopeful.

Linda Mizejewski says of *The Zodiac* that it "illustrates all the hazards of confessionalism . . . the problem of justifying interest in the detailed personal problems of the speaker . . . the problem of how to make the imagination transcend intense subjectivity so that there is a resolution in the art, if not in the troubled mind, of the poet." After a careful and regretful examination of *The Zodiac,* Mizejewski looks back nostalgically at Dickey's earlier poetry, wishing for the old magic, the shamanism, the bravura of a poem like "The Performance." "And this is the Dickey we hope to see again in his future work," she writes, "the master performer who can avoid the confessional poet's trap of becoming too entangled in experience to use the magic and artifice of Prospero and Oz."

Jane Bowers-Martin voices a similar regret in her essay on *Jericho* and *God's Images.* What we value in Dickey, she says, is "his creative lying that makes him successful at giving his reader a transcendent experience." The indirect method of *Jericho* and *God's Images,* unlike the active, "energized" thrust of the earlier books, "cuts Dickey off from what he is best at. He cannot give us a new experience; he cannot lie to us. So he must be content to serve as a sort of tour guide. . . ." These two books leave critics longing for Dickey's familiar mysteries of exchange and ritual magic.

Dave Smith's essay on *The Zodiac* and *The Strength of Fields* is a cautious reassessment of Dickey's work. Beyond the explosive magic, Smith identifies a strong contemplative streak in Dickey's poetry, a side of Dickey that has always been operative but that was overshadowed by more active elements. "Dickey's poetry has been as much sorties in epistemology and ontology as in the spoors of the dark woods. Because the search for the energizing Truth was always doomed, as Dickey's poems know, he has been a poet for whom 'the embodiment of that Truth,' or style, was very nearly all there could be."

Viewed in this way, Dickey's stylistic evolution away from the narrative becomes, for Smith, inevitable, and a poem like *The Zodiac* is "important as an impressive failure and as a transitional poem" in which here is so much plainly good and true writing" despite its failings that "I am tempted to feel it is impertinent to cavil."

As for the poems in *The Strength of Fields,* Smith tells us that Dickey is still in his heroic role, but now the role is contemplative rather than wholly dramatic. In the title poem

> Dickey skates the thin ice of fear and trembling, courageously and believably assuming the role of the Chosen Man doomed to bring back from the pyschic underworld the secret of life's fertility and renewal. There is no dramatic occasion or plot to save the presiding ghost of the monomyth's rite of passage but the poem has the force of the private man's public declaration of faith in the earth and the dead. . . . Straight through Dickey speaks with the power of a man who has seen beyond the surfaces of things and, as hard as it is to say it, he redeems us.

The notion of a poetry that strives to utilize all of the poet's energy, enabling him to deliver himself from "drift and inconsequence" into a world "where things are seen and known and felt . . . for their own sake" is an aesthetic that most Dickey critics attempt to embrace. The voice of the "energized man" creates an inclusive structure wherein all of man's emotions and perceptions can be released. Whether this drama of the "energized man" portrays a stewardess falling to her death over the wheat fields of Kansas or a man trying to enter the spirit of animals, Dickey always strives for a vital, charged poetry that is happening "at that level of personality where things really matter," to reach a possible connection, "a divine intermediary" between the world and the poet.

The whole range of Dickey criticism points towards the affirmative myth to which Dickey has devoted his profession: the myth of the "energized man," the man in touch with the transmogrifying power of the imagination. As Lieberman says, "One of Dickey's most sustaining and pervasive faiths is his absolute belief that the human imagination can save us from anything." For Dickey, it is the imagination alone which "is capable, finally, of providing something worth living for, not only in our own case, but sometimes in the case of others.

In assembling this survey of Dickey criticism, we've kept several purposes in mind. First, we wanted to present a history of critical response to Dickey's poetry; we wanted our selection to reveal readers' initial reactions to Dickey, and the continuing critical exegesis of the unfolding of Dickey's canon. For that reason among others, we have included criticism of all sorts, ranging from short reviews to extended studies. Though these various critical modes differ in depth and intensity, they are of equal value in what they contribute to our understanding of the dynamics of Dickey's relationship to his audience over the course of a long and tumultuous career. Shifts in the chronological order have been made to accommodate a balanced presentation of critical themes.

Second, we wanted to present the most important and at the same time the most characteristic statements within the body of Dickey criticism. We felt compelled to reprint certain familiar essays, such as H. L. Weatherby's "The Way of Exchange in James Dickey's Poetry" and Laurence Lieberman's "The Deepening of Being," because they are central to an understanding of the evolution and scope of Dickey criticism. Likewise, we present Joyce Carol Oates's essay in its entirety because it is such a significant summation of the phase in Dickey's career that many critics argue is his zenith.

Apart from the valuable bibliography prepared by Dennis Vanatta, our selection ends with two small pieces written by Dickey himself, both originally written and delivered as addresses. Since

Dickey has been such a vocal critic, it is appropriate for us to include his voice among the others. At the same time, it should be kept in mind that these pieces in no way represent final statements. Dickey's own gesture in writing an afterword to the new Ecco Press edition of *Babel to Byzantium* testifies to his willingness to change his mind while refraining from interference with his own earlier positions. Dickey is willing to quarrel with himself, good-heartedly but seriously. We should regard "The Imagination as Glory" and "The Energized Man" not as statements to which Dickey is forever committed, but as indications of phases in his evolution as a writer.

When Randall Jarrell writes in "The Age of Criticism" that "critics exist simply to help us with works of art—isn't that true?" he does more than ask a self-evident rhetorical question; he issues a challenge. We have tried to respond to that challenge by assembling the most helpful criticism, the criticism which clarifies, and so leads the reader back to the poetry itself.

HOWARD NEMEROV

Poems of Darkness
and a Specialized Light

COMING TO KNOW an unfamiliar poetry is an odd and not so simple experience. Reviewing it—conducting one's education in public, as usual—helps, by concentrating the attention; perhaps, though it is a gloomy thought, we understand nothing, respond to nothing, until we are forced to return it actively in teaching or writing. It is so fatally easy to have opinions, and if we stop here we never reach the more problematic, hence more interesting, point of examining our sensations in the presence of the new object.

The following notes have to do with coming to know, with the parallel development of sympathy and knowledge. Undoubtedly they raise more questions than they can answer; and they may strike the reader not only as tentative but as fumbling and disorganized also, for the intention is to record not only what happened but something as well of how such things happen.

The situation of reviewing is a special case, narrower than merely reading, and nastier, certainly at first, where one's response is automatically that of a jealous cruelty. Hmm, one says, and again, Hmm. The meaning of that is: How dare anyone else have a vision! One picks out odds and ends, with the object of making remarks that will guarantee one is A Critic. Little hairs rise on the back of the neck. One is nothing if not critical. For instance:

> I spooned out light
> Upon a candle thread . . .

Triumphant sneer. Surely this is too ingenious by far? Has he no self-control?

But already I have suspicions of my behavior. I am afraid that a great deal of literary criticism amounts to saying that mobled queen is good, or bad.

Despite myself, I observe that I quite like Mr. Dickey's characteristic way of going: a line usually of three beats, the unaccented syllables not reckoned, or not very closely reckoned; it offers an order definite but not rigidly coercive, allowing an easy flexibility and variation. Although the line so measured will tend to the anapest often, it doesn't lollop along as that measure usually does, maybe because the poet is shrewd enough not to insist on it by riming:

> The beast in the water, in love
> With the palest and gentlest of children,
> Whom the years have turned deadly with knowledge . . .

All the same—give a little, take a little—an indulgence in riming makes hash of this procedure. Mr. Dickey once indulges, in (mostly) couplets:

> With the sun on their faces through sand
> And polyps a-building the land . . .

And so on. Awful. Enough about that.

2

At a second stage, perhaps a trifle less superficial, I find myself thinking how very strange is the poetry of meditation musing on inwardness, where the images of the world are spells whose repetition designs to invoke—sometimes, alas, only in the poet—a state of extraordinary perceptions, of dreaming lucidities sometimes too relaxed. This poetry has not much to do with the clean-cut, muscular, metaphysical way of coming to conclusions; probably in English Wordsworth is the inventor of those landscapes most closely corresponding to certain withdrawn states of the mind, reveries, day-dreams—the style that Keats, with a sarcasm in which there seems all the same a proper respect, calls the Wordsworthian, or Egotistical Sublime.

One of the qualities of such a poetry—or of Mr. Dickey's poetry, to come off the high horse—is a slight over-insistence on the mysteriousness of everything, especially itself:

> A *perfect, irrelevant* music
> In which we *profoundly* moved,
> I in the *innermost* shining
> Of my blazing, *invented* eyes,
> And he in the *total* of dark. . . .

This is the language of a willed mysticism, and it is hard to see any of the words I have underlined as performing a more than atmospheric function—the poet wants the experience to be like profound, perfect, innermost, etc., and incants accordingly.

Another quality, which I take to be related also to the tonal intention of a grave continuousness, is the often proceeding by participles, as though nothing in the world of the poem ever quite happened but just went on happening, e.g. (from the same poem):

> With my claws growing deep into wood
> And my sight going slowly out
> Inch by inch, as into a stone,
> Disclosing the rabbits running
> Beneath my bent, growing throne,
> And the foxes lighting their hair,
> And the serpent taking the shape
> Of the stream of life as it slept.

The objections of this stage have a perfectly reasonable air of being right: you describe a characteristic, and present evidence to show that this characteristic *is* in the poetry. Surely this is How To Do Literary Criticism? All the same, I am still suspicious, and even beginning to get annoyed, because by this time, in order to say what I have said, I have had to read many of the poems a number of times, and have realized that I care for some of them a good deal. In particular, "The Owl King," from which I have quoted the two passages, looks to me like a moving and thoroughly accomplished performance. Even more in particular, the two passages themselves, when read in their places, look appropriate to what is going forward. I have a residual feeling of being cantankerously right in my objection to the first passage quoted, but would incline to say now that the passage is a weak place in the poet's process, but not destructive of the poem.

3

There does come a further stage, where one begins to understand something of the poet's individuality and what it decrees for him in the way of necessities, his own way of putting together the bones and oceans of this world.

Mr. Dickey's materials have a noble simplicity, a constancy extending through many poems. Merely to catalogue them is no use; to project in a single relation their somewhat delicate developments is perhaps impossible, but I shall have to make some more or less compromised try at it.

My impression of the process of his poetry is that it runs something like this: water—stone—the life of animals—of children—of the hunter, who is also the poet. It is rarely or never so simple as this, yet the intention seems often enough this, a feeling one's way down the chain of being, a becoming the voice which shall make dumb things respond, sometimes to their hurt or death; a sensing of alien modes of experience, mostly in darkness or in an unfamiliar light; reason accepting its animality; a poetry whose transcendences come of its reconciliations. Salvation is this: apprehending the continuousness of forms, the flowing of one energy through everything. There is one other persistently dramatized relation, that of the child to his father; and one that is more autobiographical, that of the poet to a brother who died before he was born. And now to particularize this matter.

These are poems of darkness, darkness and a specialized light. Practically everything in them happens at night, by moonlight, starlight, firelight; or else in other conditions that will make ordinary daytime perception impossible: underwater, in thick fog, in a dream—I note especially a dream of being in a suit of armor—inside a tent, in a salt marsh where because of the height of the grass you "no longer know where you are."

Another term for this situation is blindness: the blind child whose totem, or Other, is the owl king who cannot see by day but for whom, at night, "the still wood glowed like a brain." In another poem the owl's gaze "most slowly begins to create/Its sight from the death of the sun." For this power of creation from within, and for being a hunter, the owl is the magician-poet of an intellectual and "holy" song; in "The Owl King" it is he who for the lost, blind child incarnates the mighty powers of sight, growth, belief, resulting in reconciliation and understanding:

> Far off, the owl king
> Sings like my father, growing
> In power. Father, I touch
> Your face. I have not seen
> My own, but it is yours.
> I come, I advance,
> I believe everything, I am here.

The power of poetry, which is to perceive all the facts of the world as relation, belongs in these poems equally to both parties: to the hunter and his victim; to the child and the father he is trying to become; to the father and the child he was, whom he has lost and is trying to find again. The paradoxical continuousness of all disparate forms one with another, in this generated world, is what Mr. Dickey's poems concentrate on representing, often by the traditional lore of the four elements, as in "Facing Africa," where the speaker and his son look out over the ocean from stone jetties (hence "the buttressed water"), where

> The harbor mouth opens
> Much as you might believe
> A human mouth would open
> To say that all things are a darkness.

Thence they look toward an Africa imagined to "bloom," to be "like a lamp" glowing with flashes "like glimpses of lightning," giving off through the darkness "a green and glowing light." In the crisis of the poem this serial relation of the elements is fused in the imagined perception of the other continent, the alien life:

> What life have we entered by this?
> Here, where our bodies are,
> With a green and gold light on his face,
> My staring child's hand is in mine,
> And in the stone
> Fear like a dancing of peoples.

Perhaps it is central to Mr. Dickey's vision that stone and water are one, the reflected forms of one another.

Possible to continue for a long time describing these complex articulations of simple things. Very little use, though, to a reader who has not the poems to hand. Besides, it must be about time for someone to ask, Well, is it great poetry or isn't it? and someone else to ask, What about objective, universal standards for judging poetry?

About all that I shall say to the reader: If you believe you care for poetry you should read these poems with a deep attention. They may not work for you, probably they cannot work for you in just the way that they do for me, but I quite fail to see how you are going to find out by listening to me.

Probably the reviewer's job goes no further than that. Not to be thought of as malingering, though, I shall make a couple of other remarks.

I have attended to Mr. Dickey's poems, and they have brought me round from the normal resentment of any new experience, through a stage of high-literary snippishness with all its fiddle about "technique," to a condition of sympathetic interest and, largely, assent. There are some brilliant accomplishments here: among them, apart from the ones I have partly described, "Armor," "The Lifeguard," "The Summons." There are also some that sound dead, or (what is effectively the same thing) that I do not much respond to, including some that I don't understand. Where his poems fail for me, it is most often because he rises, reconciles, transcends, a touch too easily, so that his conclusions fail of being altogether decisive; that near irresistibly beautiful gesture, "I believe everything, I am here," may represent a species of resolution that comes to his aid more often than it should. Perhaps he is so much at home among the figures I sort out with such difficulty that he now and then assumes the effect is made when it isn't, quite.

There is this major virtue in Mr. Dickey's poetry, that it responds to attention; the trying to understand does actually produce harmonious resonances from the poems; it seems as though his voyage of exploration is actually going somewhere not yet filled with tourists: may he prosper on the way.

ROBERT DUNCAN

Oriented by Instinct by Stars

I HAVE BEEN DRAWN to the poetry of James Dickey by two poems, "The Being" and "Drinking from a Helmet," which tell of seizures or psychic invasions—"as if kissed in the brain"—where the erotic and the spectral seem to advance an initiation, as if he had passed a shadow-line that gave him a secret commission in poetry; to tell "where I stood, / What poured, what spilled, what swallowed," he resolves in "Drinking from a Helmet," "And tell him I was the man." Not only in daily life or in dream but in the poetic process, in our art, the real strives to reveal itself to us, to awaken us to its orders. Wasn't that "infinite, unworldly frankness, / Showing him what an entire / Possession nakedness is" that James Dickey knows in "The Being" a spirit of the same order, advancing from the imagination of his advancing, as that "glitter of a being / which the eye / Accepted yet which nothing understood" whom Stevens raised in "Chocorua to Its Neighbor"? Wherever the thought of the dead, of animal, human or demonic hauntings—the theme of popular spiritism—comes to him. James Dickey's imagination is stirred. In "Drinking from a Helmet," the poet's prayer "directed to Heaven" goes "through all the strings of the graveyard"; in his earlier "Hunting Civil War Relics at Nimblewill Creek," he tells us, "But underfoot I feel / The dead regroup"; or, in "The Being," the visitant is not a living angel but a fallen or dead angel, for it moves "in the heat from a coal-bed burning / Far under the earth"—so, too, the visitant in Stevens's poem had been of a "fire from an underworld, / Of less degree than flame and lesser shine." I am moved by the suggestion throughout of the mysteries of Orpheus, the poet as hero who would charm the dead and the animal world with his music. In "The Being" he is "Given,

17

also, renewed / Fertility, to raise / Dead plants and sleep-walking beasts / Out of their thawing holes."

In these *Two Poems of the Air*—"The Firebombing" and "Reincarnation"—James Dickey continues in his fascination with the spectral, but he has shifted from the tense verse and concentrated stanza sequence, the direct mode of a poetic experience and commitment, towards a more casual verse following a set story line, allowing even clichés of the supernatural tale: "My hat should crawl on my head / In streetcars, thinking of it, / The fat on my body should pale," the protagonist of "The Firebombing" tells us. The characters of the suburban householder who takes flight in his memory-fantasy of a wartime bombing mission over Japan and the office worker who takes flight in his reincarnation-fantasy as a migratory bird may relate to James Dickey's brief biography given in the Penguin *Contemporary American Poetry:* "He flew in the Pacific during the war and afterwards taught and worked for an advertising agency." But these stories of fantasies are themselves fantasies, where the characters and the things of the suburban world are taken for granted by a mind sophisticated to their advertised values in a commodity world and a wage-slave life "where the payments / For everything under the sun / Pile peacefully up." The firebomber would escape from "twenty years in the suburbs" "Blinded by each and all / Of the eye-catching cans that gladly have caught my wife's eye" into his fantasy of having "secret charge— / Of the fire developed to cling / To everything" and yet picture his victims, as he pictures himself as householder, as "nothing not / Amiable, gentle, well-meaning / A little nervous for no / Reason." We are no longer here in a world like that of Wallace Steven's "Chocorua to Its Neighbor," whose shadow belongs to a poem for "the self of selves" or in the world of James Dickey's "The Being" where he tells us he was true to himself in some way he is not in daily life—"as he / Is only in visited darkness / For one night out of the year." The firebomber and the office worker are not persons of a self but social fantasies of alienation in conformity, of a world like that of Auden's *Age of Anxiety* or Ray Bradbury's fantasy fiction. Here the poet uses the poem to induce flight, as the firebomber induces his fantasy "by whatever means, by starvation visions" or as the officeworker induces his by "a word enabling one to fly / Out the window of office buildings" that "Lifts up on wings of its own / To say itself over and over." The firebomber has no creative freedom but must carry out the bombing mission his fantasy demands; the sea bird must carry out his migration driven by instinct and directed by the stars, stronger than any self-creation; the poet carries out the story-idea his fantasy demands; immune by the superior orders of military command, mating instinct, or the story to tell, from that "kiss in the brain," the angel or messenger brings, from the creative ground of image, meaning and self, the real world is.

H. L. WEATHERBY

The Way of Exchange
in James Dickey's Poetry

AT LEAST ONE WAY OF JUDGING the quality of a poet's work is to decide how close he comes to realizing what he set out to do. In the case of James Dickey the intention is fairly clear—to find some light which is not "too feeble to show/my world as I knew it must be." The complexity arises when we try to show how, and how well, he achieves this.

The passage I have just quoted is from "The Owl King," which appears in the 1958 volume, *Drowning with Others*. It is neither so good a poem nor so good a collection as the subsequent ones, *Helmets* (1962) and *Buckdancer's Choice* (1964), which are our present concern; but in several of these earlier poems we find Dickey developing the images through which in the later poetry he is to go about seeing his world. A poem from the earlier collection which will serve our purposes very well is "A Dog Sleeping on my Feet." Here the situation is a simple one, but one which provides a vehicle for most of Dickey's recurrent themes. A fox hound is asleep on a man's leg, and the man is a poet, writing while the hound sleeps and writing about what is being transmitted from the dog's life into his own. "For now, with my feet beneath him/dying like embers,/the poem is beginning to move/up through my pine-prickling legs/out of the night wood,/taking hold of the pen by my fingers."

The result of this transmission is, we imply, the sort of poem Dickey wants to write, one in which the light is sufficiently strong to see the world as it *really* is. Moreover the poem makes it clear how the poet goes about getting this light, and, in seeing how, we get to the heart of all Dickey's poetry, early and late. The light seems to come from some rather mysterious process of exchange between a man and his opposites. In this poem and a great many others the opposition and exchange is between men and animals, but, as we shall see later, it may also occur between men who are opposed to each other by nationality, between the living and the dead, between men and trees, and even between men and wrecked machinery. However, in each of these instances, the same thing happens which occurs here between a man and a dog. Therefore this poem can be used as a key to what I would regard as the central pattern in all Dickey's poetry. By entering into the dog the poet participates in the dog's experience of the chase:

> Before me the fox floats lightly,
> On fire with his holy scent.
> All, all are running.
> Marvelous is the pursuit,
> Like a dazzle of nails through the ankles,
>
> Like a twisting shout through the trees
> Sent after the flying fox
> Through the holes of logs, over streams
> Stock-still with the pressure of moonlight.
> My killed legs,
> My legs of a dead thing, follow,
>
> Quick as pins, through the forest,
> And all rushes on into the dark
> And ends on the brightness of paper.

Then, when the dog gets up, the poet's hand "shall falter, and fail/ back into the human tongue." Through the dog he has been able to see the hunt as he "knew it must be"—the holiness of the scent, the marvellous nature of the pursuit. In other words, the exhange has produced an immediacy of perception which the poet without the dog could never have achieved.

However, as one can see immediately, there is more to the exhange than that. This experience is by no means a simple matter of a man's projecting himself into the beast for the purpose of understanding. The poem which is the product of the exchange presents not simply a dog's perception but a composite vision which is both human and animal at once. In other words the exchange is literally that—an entrance not only of man into dog, but also of dog into man. Dickey is careful never to let this fact out of our sight; the dog's immediate participation in violent scent and movement is fixed and stilled by his participation in the man's intellect. Notice, for instance, that the streams are "stock-still with the pressure of moonlight." In fact all the movement of the poem is motionless; the rushing in the dark ends in absolute, white stillness "on the brightness of paper." Moreover, the dog's running legs are the poet's "killed legs," asleep where the dog is sleeping on them; and this joint participation in sleep is itself important. For the exchange to become possible the opposites, the man and the dog, must die to each other. The dog must give up his immediate perception to the man and the man must give up his power of reflection, his power to fix and see, to the dog, so that in the giving and taking, the mutual surrender, a new and otherwise impossible point of view can be created.

What this new point of view sees is by no means new; in fact the paradox of motionless motion, the still point of the turning world, the perfect union of man and his opposites, the *me* and the *not me*, is what poetry always tries to express. Even Dickey's images, in this poem at least, are not very original. The still stream reminds one of Wordworth's stationary blasts of waterfalls in Simplon Pass; the chase motionless on white is reminiscent of Keats's urn; and the terms in which Dickey presents the paradoxical relationship between animal life and rational death suggest Yeats's Byzantium poems. But the effort to resolve these paradoxes through the process of exchange which we have just examined may very well be unique with Dickey. If that is true it may be safe to say that he has achieved a new way of doing what all poets do or try to do in one way or another, for Simplon Pass, the urn, and Byzantium are all efforts to throw a light on the world which will show it as the poet knows it must be.

I like the owl's metaphor of a light in which to see what *really* is (and it is significant that the owl courts the child in order to see). There are certain days, usually in April and May, when the quality of light is different from what it is at any other time, and in this new quality you can see details of leaves, or houses, and of the contours of land which you have never noticed before. As a result you feel that you have discovered the way things *really* are, as you always knew they must be—what a magnolia tree you have looked at all your life actually is. It is as if you have discovered a new landscape superimposed upon the old one, at once identical with the old one and yet at the same time more nearly coherent and intelligible and consequently more satisfying than the old one. It is this second and fuller vision of the superimposed landscape which Dickey achieves in his exchanges. Take, for instance, one more poem from *Drowning with Others,* "The Heaven of Animals." Here, through the same exchange between bestiality and reason that occurs in "A Dog Sleeping on my Feet," the animals become what we always knew they must be. In "the richest wood, the deepest field" the hunters hunt to perfection "with claws and teeth grown perfect,/more deadly than they can believe." And their prey also fulfill themselves, knowing "this as their life,/their reward: to walk/under such trees in full knowledge/of what is in glory above them,/and to feel no fear,/ but acceptance, compliance." That is, we infer, what a forest really is like, but it can only be seen as that—in fact it can only become that—in Byzantium, or at the "still point," or at the point of exchange, of composite vision, in mutual surrender between man and the animals.

The poems in *Helmets* (1962) touch the exchange again and again. Take, for instance, "Approaching Prayer." To "fall to my knees/and produce a word I can't say" the poet must have all his reason "slain." It is again the process of death by which the speaker in the earlier poem enters the dog and allows the dog to enter him. In "Approaching Prayer" there is actually a physical "putting on" of the beast. The son dresses in his father's old hunting sweater, straps the spurs of gamecocks on his heels, and places on his head the head of the boar he himself has shot in his "own best and stillest moment." Now, in the exchange, that still moment becomes a moment of "murderous stillness" in which the poet is able to use the "images of earth/almightily," in order "for something important to be." He is able to see himself shooting the boar through the eyes of the boar who is being shot, and in so doing the killer and the killed change places, are united, and are enabled by the union to play their respective parts perfectly. Both are able to participate in the glory of killing and in the acceptance, compliance, of the killed. This is the heaven of both hunters and animals.

Or take other instances:

In "Springer Mountain" the hunter strips himself; and in the loss of his four sweaters and dungarees "the world catches fire" from his naked flesh, and he "puts an unbearable light/into breath skinned alive of its garments." Naked like the buck and running with him he is able to think "like a beast loving/with the whole god bone of his horns." By entering into the deer he makes it possible for deer to become what they really are in relationship to men. In the superimposed landscape established by the exhange deer stamp and dream of men

> Who will kneel with them naked to break
> The ice from streams with their faces
> And drink from the lifespring of beasts.

And notice that again the waters from which they are to drink together "stand petrified in a creek bed/yet melt and flow from the hills/at the touch of an animal visage."

In "Chenille," the poems are the bedspreads—not those products of mass manufacture which "hum like looms all night/into your pores" but those made by a "middle-aged man's grandmother" in the "summer green light" of a scuppernong arbor. These embody the composite vision of the exchange; each spread becomes a "heaven of animals"—

> Deer, rabbits and birds,
> Red whales and unicorns,
> Winged elephants, crowned ants:
> Beasts that cannot be thought of
>   By the wholly sane
> Rise in the rough, blurred
> Flowers of fuzzy cloth
> In only their timeless outlines
> Like the beasts of Heaven:
> Those sketched out badly, divinely
> By stars not wholly sane.

The grandmother like the poet has seen what animals *really* are. Moreover, we infer that the rest of us, who are too "wholly sane" to exchange our nature with a dog or a horse, will miss the summer peace of a scuppernong arbor or the winter peace of sleep with our arms around the neck of a unicorn. We shall know instead only the constant hum of factories.

As I have said, however, the exchange need not necessarily be with animals, and in some of Dickey's best poems it is not. In "Cherrylog Road" the man exchanges his life not only with beetles and snakes but also with a woman and even with a junkyard. On account of the sexual exchange between the boy and the girl, snakes and beetles in the wreckage, dying of boredom, come to life again; and of course the act of copulation in which the human beings participate is itself something exchanged with the beasts. However, it is not just the animals in the wreckage but the wreckage itself that participates in man, and he in it. In the act of love the couple is "convoyed at terrific speed/by the stalled, dreaming traffic around us"; the motorcycle becomes "the soul of the junkyard/restored, a bicycle fleshed/with power"; and, on the other side of the exchange, the man, having taken the junkyard into himself, is "wild to be wreckage forever."

"The Driver" is reminiscent of "Cherrylog Road" except that in this underwater junkyard of war machinery we have, instead of animals dying of boredom, dead human beings. Moreover, the exchange which the poet attempts is not with the wreckage but with the dead themselves. The swimmer is "haunted," and that is "to sink out of sight, and to lose/the power of speech in the presence/of the dead." In short, to be haunted is to take upon oneself the condition of the dead, to be possessed by the dead, and that is what the swimmer almost does. He attempts to enter the dead in the same way that he enters the dog, the boar, the deer, the woman, or the wreckage. Again we see Dickey attempting to establish a composite vision, but there are two interesting variations here. In the first place, at the last possible moment, the swimmer refuses the exchange; he leaps "for the sky/very nearly too late, where another/leapt and could not break into/his breath." Moreover, the dead are also incapable of exchange; unlike the buck they do not enter into the experience of the poet. They have failed to "break into/his breath, where it lay, in battle/as in peace, available, secret,/dazzling and huge, filled with sunlight,/for thousands of miles on the water." The boundary between water and air prevents the exchange between the dead and the living; the swimmer can only toy with the possibility.

"The Driver" anticipates a number of poems in Dickey's latest volume in which the exchange does fail. However, in "Drinking from a Helmet," with which *Helmets* closes, the exchange between living and dead is accomplished. A reflection in the water in a dead man's helmet gives the boy back his own face, "in its [the dead's] absence holding/my sealed, sunny image from harm" in the middle of battle. Then, when he puts on the helmet, the dead man's past enters his own experience; so the dead man's image is likewise preserved and with it his family and his past which are, of course, his life—California, the redwoods, a bicycle, and "his blond brother." These are the details of the superimposed landscape; the redwoods and the shelled palm stumps meet in the "rings of a bodiless tree," formed in the water in the helmet.

Buckdancer's Choice contains the best poetry in the three collections. One reason for the improvement is simply Dickey's growing ability to make language do what it is supposed to do. However, in addition to this there is also in this later poetry a new sense of the consequences of the exchange. The dog wakes up and so do the man's legs; at that point the poet returns to human speech. The hunter in "Springer Mountain" gets back finally into his clothes. But to take the exchange seriously is to risk staying under, and the best poems in *Buckdancer's Choice* show an awareness of this risk.

Among the finest of these is "Pursuit from Under," in which the poet, through "the journal of Arctic explorers," is able to experience, in August on his father's farm, "the cold of a personal ice age," the terror of the killer whale who follows always "under the frozen pane,/turning as you do, zigzagging," until he finally shatters through and confronts both the explorers and the poet in their exchange of understanding with "an image/of how the downed dead pursue us." The explorers have had the vision of the snow, the poet the vision of the family field, but in the new landscape of the exchange the explorers know

> That not only in the snow
> But in the family field
>
> The small shadow moves,
> And under bare feet in the summer:
> That somewhere turf will heave,
> And the outraged breath of the dead,

So long held, will form

Unbreathably around the living.

And the poet knows that instead of walking barefoot "so that nothing on earth can have changed/on the ground where I was raised" he will now have to "pitch a tent in the pasture, and starve."

Another sign that Dickey is aware of the danger is the presence in this last volume of a number of poems in which, as in "The Driver," the cost of the exchange makes it impossible. "The Firebombing" is one of these. The poet has dropped napalm on a Japanese village from cold blue heights of "aesthetic contemplation," and isolated in those heights he finds that he cannot enter "the *heart* of the fire." Even at the end of twenty years in his own suburban residence he is still unable "to get down there or see/ what really happened." The reason?—that he has never been able to take upon himself the suffering of the Japanese as he could take upon himself the dreams of a dog or the head of a boar. He cannot imagine at his own "unfired door" a person burning, "with its ears crackling off/like powdery leaves" or "with children of ashes." In fact he can imagine nothing at his door that he hasn't lived with twenty years, and in that fact alone we see the failure of the exchange which is always between opposites—dead men and live men, the suffering and the secure.

"The Shark's Parlor" is another poem about the failure, but this time a comic one. The bloodstain in "our vacation paradise" is somewhat like the personal ice age in the family field, but this time instead of pitching a tent and starving the poet is still using the place for vacations. And that is what you do, I suppose; when you realize that you have not been man enough to stay under or to look the killer whale or the "drowned dead" in the eye, you laugh a little ruefully and cherish the bloodstain you acquired trying.

"The Fiend," if I understand it correctly, is a much more serious poem about the same failure. The voyeur never finally exchanges his nature with the trees from which he peeps. As a consequence he ends in sordid cheapness "like a door-to-door salesman/the godlike movement of trees stiffening with him the light/of a hundred favored windows gone wrong somewhere in his glasses/where his knocked-off panama hat was in his painfully vanishing hair." To exchange life with death is serious enough, but to take upon yourself the "godlike movement" of nature is more serious still. Moreover, if it doesn't work, the failure can in fact produce a fiend. If a man tries to take the natural into himself without in turn giving himself to it, he has not redeemed nature by creating an animal heaven or, in this case, a heaven of trees, but he has brutalized himself instead. There is simply taking, no exchange, which is, interestingly enough, the nature of voyeurism.

I suggested at the outset that at least one way to measure a poet is by how well he has realized his intentions. I suppose at this point it will be perfectly obvious that I think James Dickey is a very fine poet who has attempted to see his world in a remarkable way and has had considerable success in doing so. However, I hold one reservation which seems to me worth stating. The way of exchange is as dangerous a thing aesthetically as it is spiritually, and whereas Dickey's later poems show that he is fully aware of the spiritual danger, I am by no means sure that he has guarded himself sufficiently against the aesthetic. There is always something a little bit staged, exotic, preposterous, and consequently affected about Dickey's situations. All of them lend themselves to parody except those like "The Shark's Parlor" which parody themselves, and if a reader is tempted to giggle when he shouldn't it always means that the poet has fallen short of complete success. I am deeply moved by a poem like "Springer Mountain," but I cannot help being slightly amused at the same time by the softening, middle-aged man's running naked with the buck. In the same way there is something mildly preposterous about putting on cock's spurs and a boar's head in order to pray. As the language in the later poetry grows stronger there is less and less opportunity for the ludicrous, but even here there is sometimes a hint of it— something a little bit silly about pitching a tent in the field and starving with cattle all around.

The reason for this weakness in the poetry is that the kind of vision which Dickey attempts, and in part achieves, requires a great deal of the reader's imagination. By staring intently in a certain light you may eventually see your world as you know it must be, but you may also break under the strain of the staring. According to Christian doctrine, when Nature is redeemed through our Lord's exchange with the dead, men and sharks, lions and lambs, Japanese and Americans, the hunters and the hunted, will all lie down together in a new landscape under a light strong enough and constant enough to show us our world as we have all known always that it must be—and without any strain of staring. Short of that, poetry can, as we know, give us some anticipation of those "other worlds and other seas," but it has been only the very greatest poets—Dante, Spenser, Shakespeare, and possibly Yeats—who have managed it with complete success. Obviously any effort toward this vision that does not take into consideration the aesthetic equivalent of the passion and death is going to wind up sounding fixed and dishonest. For the poet as poet there can be no last-minute leap to the surface for air, no hesitation to undergo his sea change or enter into the heart of the fire. Short of that sacrifice a poetry which attempts such a vision will prove in the last analysis to be affected. That is why most great poetry is tragic, dealing only with the impossibility of the vision.

In his volume of criticism *The Suspect in Poetry,* which was published in 1964 but which contains reviews of contemporary poets published over a period of several years, Dickey sets up a standard of absolute honesty by which poetry is to be judged and according to which he finds most contemporary poetry lacking. Those elements which are "suspect" in poetry are those which readers cannot "believe in as 'reality' "—a "series of unbelievable contrivances, none of which has the power of bringing forth a genuine response." Exactly how unbelievable contrivance can become is amply illustrated by Dickey's examination of people like Allen Ginsberg, Thom Gunn, or Harold Witt, and I think it is indisputable that Dickey himself is considerably above them. On the other hand he has attempted something very difficult, and it seems to me that in doing so he does risk the very contrivance that he warns against. However, I feel sure that he must be aware of the danger himself.

RALPH J. MILLS, JR.

The Poetry of James Dickey

As various poets and critics have been remarking over the past few years, both the mood and the means of much of the important new American poetry has been noticeably changing. While it is difficult in the midst of such movement to predict with anything like accuracy the final course of contemporary poetry's drift and flow, there are certain characteristics which have become rather evident. In a recent essay, "Dead Horses and Live Issues," (*The Nation*, April 24, 1967), the poet Louis Simpson discusses some of them and also indicates the kind of poetry which is currently being rejected. "There is," he says, "an accelerating movement away from rationalistic verse toward poetry that releases the unconscious, the irrational, or, if your mind runs that way, magic. Surrealism was buried by the critics of the thirties and forties as somehow irrelevant; today it is one of the most commonly used techniques of verse." Simpson goes on to specify some of the likely influences to come into play under these circumstances and the dangers of particular sorts of Surrealism, especially the dogmatic irrationalism of André Breton. Then he adds, affirmatively: "Contrary to Breton, poetry represents not unreason but the total mind, including both reason and unreason . . . Poetic creation has been described by some poets—Wordsworth and Keats come to mind—as a heightened state of consciousness brought about, curiously, by an infusion of the unconscious . . . The images are connected in a dream; and the deeper the dream, the stronger, the more logical, are the connections."

If these excerpts from Simpson's essay will not do to describe all the tendencies apparent in American poetry at present (and they were not intended to do so), they have a genuine applicability to

Simpson's own recent work, to the poetry of Robert Bly, James Wright, W. S. Merwin, Donald Hall, and James Dickey—though one must say at once that these poets differ distinctly from one another too. Open this new volume of Dickey's poems [*Poems— 1957–1967*] (which gathers together the larger part of his four previous books and concludes with a book-length section of recent pieces) at any page and you find the artistic realization of Simpson's statement: a poetry which indeed seems composed of "images . . . connected in a dream." Night and sleep, dominated by moonlight (as in Wallace Stevens), moreover, take a prominent place in many of the poems, from "Sleeping Out at Easter" from *Into the Stone* (his first book) to "The Birthday Dream" from the new section entitled *Falling*. But even when he is not directly treating sleep Dickey has a power of imagination that fulfills itself in dreamlike effects. Take, for instance, the initial stanza of "A Screened Porch in the Country." The situation is so ordinary—a group of people sitting inside a lighted porch on a summer night, their enlarged, distended shadows cast outward onto the surrounding grass—and the imaginative rendering of its implications so extraordinary that the reader's habitual way of looking at things, as with Rilke's "Archaic Torso of Apollo," is profoundly shaken. Here, too, one must "change [his] life," or at least his conception of it:

> All of them are sitting
> Inside a lamp of coarse wire
> And being in all directions
> Shed upon darkness,
> Their bodies softening to shadow, until
> They come to rest out in the yard
> In a kind of blurred golden country
> In which they more deeply lie
> Than if they were being created
> Of Heavenly light.

Dickey's imaginative processes free the body of its earthly ties and permit it a kind of infinite capacity for extension. In the passage above a transformation occurs within the poet's vision which locates human bodies in an entirely different dimension; their shadows come to possess their spiritual being or constitute its reflection. The ingredients of the external occasion, as already noted, are commonplace, but Dickey's sudden intense visualization stuns us with the revelation of a hidden metaphysical or religious insight. For the poem proceeds to describe a species of metempsychosis— although, of course, no literal death is involved and the inhabitants of the screened porch are not even consciously aware of the curious spiritual transmigration in which they ae participating with their shadow selves—that brings the "souls" of these people into communion with the world of small night creatures and insects who come only to the edge of "the golden shadow/Where the people are lying." The reader finally gets the haunting feeling of having shared deeply in the life of creation and so loosened the boundaries of the selfish ego. Here are the other three stanzas that complete the poem.

> Where they are floating beyond
> Themselves, in peace,
> Where they have laid down
> Their souls and not known it,
> The smallest creatures,
> As every night they do,
> Come to the edge of them
> And sing, if they can,
> Or, if they can't, simply shine
> Their eyes back, sitting on haunches
>
> Pulsating and thinking of music.
> Occasionally, something weightless
> Touches the screen
> With its body, dies,
> Or is unmurmuringly hurt,
> But mainly nothing happens
> Except that a family continues
> To be laid down
> In the midst of its nightly creatures,
> Not one of which openly comes
>
> Into the golden shadow
> Where the people are lying,
> Emitted by their own house
> So humanly that they become
> More than human, and enter the place
> Of small, blindly singing things,
> Seeming to rejoice

Perpetually, without effort,
Without knowing why
Or how they do it.

This poem provides merely one example—and that not so obvious as might be—of what H. L. Weatherby has called "the way of exchange" and Robert Bly terms "spiritual struggle" in Dickey's poems. Most evident at first in his pieces about animals and hunting, where the poet almost miraculously divides his intuitive powers so as to depict his own inner state in the role of human perceiver or hunter and the sensations of the animal who knows he is pursued, the notion of exchange has far-reaching effects, which include an interpenetration of the worlds of the living and the dead in such poems as "In the Tree House at Night," "The Owl King," "Hunting Civil War Relics at Nimblewill Creek," "Drinking from a Helmet," "Reincarnation (I)," and "Sled Burial, Dream Ceremony." It also, more generally, encompasses the imaginative devices of bodily and spiritual extension, metamorphosis, and metempsychosis of which I have spoken. All of these characteristics, and in addition a preoccupation (strong in his first three books and still present in more recent work) with ritual and archetypal modes of experience, confirm Dickey as a poet who possesses an imagination of a primitive, magical type. Obviously, he is at the same time a modern man of considerable sophistication; but the fact that he hunts with bow and arrow and that he has been a decorated fighter pilot in both World War II and the Korean War indicates something of the broad spectrum of his experience.

The themes of Dickey's best poetry, however, have a timeless aura about them; and while contemporary material and various objects of modern technology necessarily appear in places in his writing, they are simply appropriated and subordinated to the larger concerns at hand. (At any rate, this seems a fair account until we come to some of the poems from *Buckdancer's Choice*—"The Firebombing," for example.) Thus in "Hunting Civil War Relics at Nimblewill Creek" the poet and his brother, who has a mine detector to locate buried metal, "mess tin or bullet," find that this mechanical instrument becomes the means for entering into a state of near-mystical communion with the soldiers who died on this battle ground. As his brother listens through the ear-phones of the detector, Dickey sees his face transformed by a new awareness, strange and awesome, of the way of communication he has unwittingly opened up with the past and the dead; and the brother's expression, in turn, communicates that awareness in all its uncanny force to the poet until, he, too, has been captured by the same experience:

> A faint light glows
> On my brother's mouth.
> I listen, as two birds fight
> For a single voice, but he
> Must be hearing the grave,
> In pieces, all singing
> To his clamped head,
> For he smiles as if
> He rose from the dead within
> Green Nimblewill
> And stood in his grandson's shape.

Here we are close to the idea of exchange between the dead and the living or a transmigration of souls, though it is viewed in this instance not as a literal fact but an unforgettable moment of perception among the living—the poet and his brother. The end of the poem finds Dickey arrived at the threshold of a profoundly moving recovery of his (and our) human ancestry:

> I choke the handle
> Of the pick, and fall to my knees
> To dig wherever he points,
> To bring up mess tin or bullet,
> To go underground
> Still singing, myself,
> Without a sound,
> Like a man who renounces war,
> Or one who shall lift up the past,
> Not breathing "Father,"
> At Nimblewill,
> but saying, "Fathers! Fathers!"

The details of this passage are enormously evocative. His kneeling posture and his careful excavation of relics imply a reverential attitude towards the dead, who are resurrected, as it were, in the poet's inwardness, in feeling and imagination, to enlarge his own humanity so that it knows no limits but flows outward to merge with the being of every creature and thing, and, beyond them, to touch at times the realm of the supernatural. The act of digging, as the stanza discloses, takes on the aspect of a descent into the kingdom of the dead, and the poet returns with his new knowledge upon him: the revelation which becomes his poem. In his well-known study *The Poetic Image* C. Day Lewis notes that a whole poem may be an image composed of smaller contributing images; and of that larger image he offers a general definition which is surely applicable to the poem we have been discussing and also to a fundamental impulse running through Dickey's finest pieces. "The poetic image," he remarks, "is the human mind claiming kinship with everything that lives or has lived, and making good its claim."

A little further on, to stay with Day Lewis, he says that the poet is "in the world . . . to bear witness to the principle of love, since love is as good a word as any for that human reaching-out of hands towards the warmth in all things, which is the source and passion of his song." Plainly enough, this statement elaborates what its author said about the poetic image, only in this instance he looks behind the work for its underlying (whether conscious or not) intention. James Dickey's poems are truly remarkable in just this respect. "The Owl King," which is too long for discussion here, can be read as a mythic poem of initiation and exchange between human life and the rest of creation basic to Dickey's imaginative sympathies. In "The Salt Marsh" and "Inside the River" the poet submits himself to two different experiences in which his own being is altered by elements of the natural world. The concluding lines of "Inside the River" have again the ritual symbolic significance we grow familiar with in Dickey's work:

> Move with the world
> As the deep dead move,
> Opposed to nothing.
> Release. Enter the sea
> Like a winding wind.
> No. Rise. Draw breath.
> Sing. See no one.

35

RALPH J. MILLS, JR.

The beautiful poem "Drinking from a Helmet" describes the incredible changes that occur when a soldier on some Pacific island (presumably some version of the poet himself, as most of Dickey's speakers appear to be) picks up the helmet of a dead countryman to hold his water ration. First, he sees his own reflection on the water's surface framed by the helmet's edges, so he seems to be wearing, in this mirror-image, with safety what another was killed in. As he continues to drink and then to contemplate what remains of the water, his own reflection is replaced by other sorts of details which in their suggestiveness point the direction the speaker's experience now takes:

> At the middle of water
> Bright circles dawned inward and outward
> Like oak rings surviving the tree
> As its soul, or like
> The concentric gold spirit of time.
> I kept trembling forward through something
> Just born of me.

The next two stanzas are devoted to an evocation of the dead ("I fought with a word in the water/To call on the dead to strain/Their muscles and get up . . ."), but we are told that "the dead cannot rise up" though "their last thought hovers somewhere/For whoever finds it." Dickey does find it; and in the eight stanzas that follow there is an elaboration and intensification of the kind of experience rendered in "Hunting Civil War Relics at Nimblewill Creek." The speaker feels himself "possessed," filled out from within by something "swallowed whole" from the helmet, and attains to a sense of rebirth and immortality: he has absorbed and revivified in some mystical fashion the person of the dead soldier and has obviously been transformed himself in the process. Subsequently, he discards his own helmet and puts on the one he has found:

> Warmed water ran over my face.
> My last thought changed, and I knew
> I inherited one of the dead.

That is to say, the speaker's own thoughts die with his cast-off helmet; he assumes the dead soldier's final thought with his headgear and seems to be baptized with the last of the water into a new life. The inherited thought is really a vision drawn from the deceased's past, apparently the final flash of memory across his dying mind, and shows two boys talking in a forest of gigantic redwood trees. The two closing sections of the poem envisage the speaker's destiny: he will survive the war and journey afterwards in search of the dead soldier's brother to carry to him the experience of possession and the life-concluding memory which the helmet has conveyed:

XVIII
I would survive and go there,
Stepping off the train in a helmet
That held a man's last thought,
Which showed him his older brother
Showing him trees.
I would ride through all
California upon two wheels
Until I came to the white
Dirt road where they had been,
Hoping to meet his blond brother,
And to walk with him into the wood
Until we were lost,
Then take off the helmet
And tell him where I had stood,
What poured, what spilled, what swallowed:

XIX
And tell him I was the man.

The claim of kinship mentioned by C. Day Lewis is powerfully realized in this poem, and the speaker provides a link between the dead and the living, between the lost soldier and his brother, that lengthens out the pattern of relations beyond those of "Hunting Civil War Relics at Nimblewill Creek" by reaching from time past toward time future. (The conditional tense of the final portion, like the significance of the poem's last line, makes for a certain ambiguity with regard to the speaker's actual location in time and his identity, but such indefiniteness does not detract from the reader's impression of temporal movement.) Yet the very strength of the human bonds Dickey creates in this poem leads one to wonder all the more at the moral abyss which separates it from the piece that begins his next volume, *Buckdancer's Choice*.

"The Firebombing," clearly based on the poet's experiences as a night-fighter pilot on bombing missions in Asia during World War II, starts off with noctural recollections, entertained years later in the seemingly secure American suburbs, of what he has done to others—burned them alive with napalm, destroyed their property, killed their animals—and the attempt (not very strenuous, I fear, at least in the context of the poem) to project himself into their place, to suffer and understand, and so in part at any rate to expiate his actions. But in spite of an epigraph from the *Book of Job* ("Or has thou an arm like God?") and another one from the contemporary German poet Günter Eich (untranslated as epigraph, but in Vernon Watkins' version from Michael Hamburger and Christopher Middleton's *Modern German Poetry 1910–1960* it reads: "Think of this, after the great destructions/Everyone will prove that he was innocent"), some lines near the beginning already imply that the effort to awaken such emotions is doomed to failure:

> All families lie together, though some are burned alive.
> The others try to feel
> For them. Some can, it is often said.

The flat, impersonal tone of that last sentence is rather indicative of the results of Dickey's attempt—which purportedly comprises the substance of the poem—to "feel for" his deeds, his victims, because close to the end he can tell us that he is "still unable/To get down there or see/What really happened." We cannot quarrel with the apparent honesty of this statement. If the poet is incapable of entering the experience of his victims, there is little to be done about it—though we may recall, with a start, his amazing imaginative sympathies with the animals he hunts. Yet in a bizzare, contradictory way the bulk of the poem concentrates on the re-creation of its author's feelings and perceptions during a night raid with napalm bombs on Japanese civilian, rather than military, objectives. Again, as in some of the hunting poems, we see the poet dividing himself in imagination between his own consciousness and a simultaneous intuition of the existence of the hunted; but it is here precisely in "The Firebombing" that Dickey's imaginative gift collapses at the moral level. While he offers us dramatic impressions of his flight and weaponry (the headiness of power becomes quite plain—and terrifying) and of the imagined horror and destruction wrought upon the land below and its inhabitants by his attack, he expends poetic energy on the creation of images through which these events and details are dramatized without ever arousing a commensurate moral—which is to say, human—awareness. In other words, the poet would appear to be re-living this segment of his past more for aesthetic than for any other reasons, for the pain and terror of his victims are dwelt on and vividly presented (though without sympathy) even when we are going to be told at the conclusion that he "can imagine/At the threshold nothing/With its ears crackling off/Like powdery leaves,/Nothing with children of ashes . . ." Perhaps I am misjudging Dickey's underlying impulse, but if I am the poem still holds puzzling inconsistencies. Robert Bly, who has written a second essay on Dickey's work, a sharp but not quite just criticism of *Buckdancer's Choice*,[2] notes some instances of rather weak irony and self-criticism in the poem, of "complaint" about the pilot-speaker who can feel no remorse for his actions, but certainly such qualifications are almost unnoticeable. Here is a passage which describes the moment the pilot releases his napalm and the holocaust that follows (something Dickey has no difficulty in imagining). References to "anti-morale" raids, "Chicago" fire, and "all American" fire, while they may be intended to serve an ironical-critical function in their context, are feeble by comparison with the overall effect of a fascinated exulting in destructive force, in the superiority of flight and the malevolent artistry of bombing:

> The ships shakes   bucks
> Fire hangs   not yet fire
> In the air above Beppu
> For I am fulfilling
>
> An "anti-morale" raid upon it.
> All leashes of dogs
> Break under the first bomb, around those
> In bed, or late in the public baths: around those
> Who inch forward on their hands
> Into medicinal waters.
> Their heads come up with a roar
>
> Of Chicago fire:
> Come up with the carp pond showing
> The bathouse upside down,
> Standing stiller to show it more
> As I sail artistically over
> The resort town followed by farms,
> Singing and twisting all the handles in heaven kicking

The small cattle off their feet
In a red costly blast
Flinging jelly over the walls
As in a chemical war-
fare field demonstration.
With fire of mine like a cat

Holding onto another man's walls,
My hat should crawl on my head
In streetcars, thinking of it,
The fat on my body should pale.

The self-reproach of the last stanza above is hollow and meaningless next to the fierce delight on re-living that period of godlike superiority. Perhaps Dickey will not try to prove himself innocent, as Günter Eich's poem suggests men do, and that is fine. But Dickey also departs sharply from the spirit of Eich's conclusion, which states: "Think of this, that you are responsible for every atrocity/Enacted far from you." Further on, he makes other gestures aimed toward compassion and feeling; he remarks that "detachment" and "the greatest sense of power in one's life" should be "shed" (apparently by either one or the other odd means of getting drunk or adopting a severe diet), though in the course of the poem these statements again amount to very little. What is strong, vivid, and passionate in "The Firebombing" springs directly from the occasion which gave the poem its title and from the poet's participation in it; any real concern for the terrible fate imposed upon others seems secondary.

A similar failing is evident in such poems as "The Fiend" and "Slave Quarters," both of which employ speakers whose chief desire is the fulfillment, through a warped masculine sexual power, of their own sick fantasies. The knife-carrying, middle-aged voyeur of the first poem and the lustful slave-owner (whose ghostly body the poet enters and joins with) of the second are victims of their private delusions: neither can escape from his diseased view and both are determined to realize their fantasies as fact, though the realization must inevitably do violence to others. In these poems, then, one finds a sort of lyricism of the perverse with little else to be said for it. But Dickey demonstrates here, as in "The Firebombing," an obsession with power and the imposition of will—and a total insensitivity to the persons who are the objects of its indulgence. Admittedly, "Slave Quarters" is the more ambitious poem and attempts in some ways a more difficult feat of understanding; still it is, for me, imaginatively deficient.

Among the recent poems from the lengthy section entitled *Falling,* I believe we must find notable instances of a diminishing of Dickey's poetic intensity, though such a comment does not everywhere apply. Nonetheless, a regrettable straining after material and effect—perhaps really after novelty—seems to me fatally injurious to most of the longer pieces: "May Day Sermon . . ." "Falling," "Sun," "Reincarnation (II)," and "Coming Back to America." Faults frequently pointed out by Dickey's critics are painfully evident in "Falling" and "May Day Sermon . . .": these poems are drawn out, repetitive, overwritten, blurred, and diffuse; the 'ideas' behind them are contrived, and in the case of "Falling," cannot be sustained even by Coleridge's "willing suspension of disbelief." Finally, except for striking passages or images, these poems become boring.

This verdict should not be taken as wholly negative, however, for Dickey can still write poems with the energy and imagination which distinguishes his finest work from *Drowning with Others* and *Helmets* (by far his best books). "The Birthday Dream," "The Leap," "Snakebite," "Sustainment," "The Head-Aim," and "Deer Among Cattle," as well as others, are examples of good Dickey poems. I quote "Deer Among Cattle":

> Here and there in the searing beam
> Of my hand going through the night meadow
> They all are grazing
>
> With pins of human light in their eyes.
> A wild one also is eating
> The human grass,
>
> Slender, graceful, domesticated
> By darkness, among the bred-
> for-slaughter,
>
> Having bounded their paralyzed fence
> And inclined his branched forehead onto
> Their green frosted table,
>
> The only live thing in this flashlight
> Who can leave whenever he wishes,
> Turn grass into forest,

Foreclose inhuman brightness from his eyes
But stands here still, unperturbed,
In their wide-open country,

The sparks from my hand in his pupils
Unmatched anywhere among cattle,
Grazing with them the night of the hammer
As one of their own who shall rise.

At the top of his form Dickey does reveal a large capacity for feeling, for steeping his spirit in the being of others and in the very life of creation; and we think of the poets with whom his most authentic poems have their affinity: Whitman, Lawrence, Roethke; and among the younger: James Wright, Jon Silkin, Robert Bly, Donald Hall, W. S. Merwin; perhaps some European poets as well. But these affinities are broken in the poems which are morally insensate.

Dickey is a prolific writer, to judge from the size of a decade's production, and he has won sudden fame and publicity. Large reputations—we know it as a commonplace—can be exceedingly dangerous in the pressures they bring always to be new and inventive (the blight of the contemporary painter and sculptor) in order to maintain one's laurels, especially in a culture dedicated to the modish and to consumer consumption of artistic goods; and a poet of Dickey's strengths can be damaged as easily as can a lesser one. I hope that will not happen, for he is, defects aside, a very gifted, truly imaginative poet who has already given us excellent pieces. No doubt his work must alter and grow toward full maturity, but its developments need to derive from inner necessity and not in answer to the external demands of reputation or public role. In any event, this collection of Dickey's poetry is an important book; it merits attentive reading—and its readers will be far from unrewarded.

NOTES

1. "The Way of Exchange in James Dickey's Poetry," *Sewanee Review*, Summer 1966, and "The Poetry of James Dickey," *The Sixties*, Winter 1964 respectively. Readers should also see Norman Friedman: "The Wesleyan Poets II," *Chicago Review*, 19, 1, 1966; and Michael Goldman: "Inventing the American Heart," *The Nation*, April 24, 1967.
2. In *The Sixties*, 9, 1967.

DAVID C. BERRY

Harmony with the Dead:
James Dickey's Descent
into the Underworld

RILKE, IN A SONNET TO ORPHEUS, writes:

Does he belong here? No, out of both
realms his wide nature grew.
More knowing would he bend the willows' branches
who has experienced the willows' roots.[1]

Speaking of this poem, Walter A. Strauss says that "this is the
doctrine of the double realm, life and death. Orpheus, as a result
both of his descent and his dismemberment, is perfectly at home in
both realms and unites them. . . . His being-here and being-
beyond are coextensive because the thread joining them has been
restored. Everything now becomes explicable under the category
of 'der klarste Bezug'—the clearest connections."[2]

Rilke, speaking further of this unity of life and death, says
that "death is that *side of life* which is turned away from us and not
illuminated by us: we must make the effort to muster the greatest
consciousness of our being which is at home in *both of these undifferentiated domains nourished inexhaustibly by both.* . . . Life's
true form extends through *both* domains, the blood of the greatest
circulation courses through both: *there is neither a Here nor a
beyond, but only the great unity.*"[3]

James Dickey connects the world of the dead and the world of
the living, but to say that he realizes a unity in them, each sharing
an undifferentiated domain inexhaustibly nourished by the other,
puts it too strongly. The category of "der klarste Bezug" is closer,

for Dickey connects both worlds, and in doing so is usually renewed, nourished.

"The decisive factor in appraising the nature of the modern Orphic," Strauss tells us, "is not so much in the magical mission of the poet, but in the account and interpretation of his experience as reflected in his poetry—the nature of his Orphic journey, that quest for a dark but 'pure' center. These journeys are made more poignant by the fact that the poets, in their own descent into Hades are directly conscious of their 'ancestor' and model, Orpheus."[4] Such is true in the case of Dickey, as a poem from his first collection, *Into the Stone*, indicates:

ORPHEUS BEFORE HADES

The leaf, down from the branch
Swirling, unfastened, falls;
Halfway from there to the ground
Is hypnotized, and stays.
No leaf is as still as that.
The earth-colored forest sways
Whose leaf is the center of waiting.

A great gray cloud lets fall
Its leaves, like the eyelids of fossils,
To a great stone skin on the ground.
I stand, in the frozen field,
In tow-sacks and burlap arrayed.
My breath disappears overhead
And white is the center of waiting.

The spring comes out of the ground.
A wood shades into the air.
Each bough is as light as a fern.
All of life comes in on a breath.
My eyes turn green with the silence
Of the thing that shall move from the hillside
Where love is the center of waiting.

My tongue is of cloth, and I sing,
As she would be singing, like water,
In a land where the cricket is flaking,
Yet chirrs, on the copper grassblade.
The sunlight is thinking of woman,

And black is the world, in its body,
When flesh is the center of waiting.

> God add one string to my lyre,
> That the snowflake and leaf-bud shall mingle
> As the sun within moonlight is shining,
> That the hillside be opened in heartbreak,
> And the woman walk down, and be risen
> From the place that she changes, each season,
> *Her death, at the center of waiting.*

Orpheus in this poem serves as the Janus-face between the living and the dead, being at the center of both worlds, as the refrain of each stanza insists. Nature, in the poem, responds to Orpheus's impending descent by sharing with him the interface: a falling leaf is hypnotized at a point halfway in its plunge from the branch to the ground; snow is *"the center of waiting"* between the "great gray cloud" and "the great stone skin on the ground"; spring and flesh likewise are centers of waiting. Such a pattern follows the cycle of the seasons, in the order of fall, winter, spring, and summer. Orpheus is the center of this cycle, poised at the edge of time and eternity; he asks to be able to mingle "the snowflake and leaf-bud," to mix life and death. Laurence Lieberman is right in stating that *connect* is the central word in Dickey's *Falling,* as it has been up to that volume.[5] This opinion certainly holds in "Orpheus Before Hades," in which Orpheus is an archetypal symbol of man's desire for union of spirit with spirit.

Crunk points out that Dickey's imagination "seems to flower when he moves among the dead."[6] This "flowering" is found in two different relationships: the dead of Dickey's family, and the dead of World War II. When Dickey descends into the underworld, it is usually to connect with somebody.

The renewal aspect of communion with the dead is evident in one of Dickey's early poems, "The Sprinter's Mother."[7] While the poet is sprinting, his mother seems to rise over the threshold:

> The strings of his teeth ache with her voice
> Opening for him: the turn leans: she is rising
> To touch the flowers: at his shoulder, a body,
> Half, a tinge . . .
>
> .   .   .   .

Her cries are shyly balanced,
As if taken back to blood.
And, panting, blowing, he understands
How it is all proved, by childishness,

.   .   .   .

As she turns
Slowly into his face, not as a heelprint,
But as a held look he lets his breath
Gather to sustain, *and the world*
Flowed together in a new way, trembles,
Comes back at him, touches at his hair.

                                        (Italics mine)

"Poem" *(Into the Stone),* dealing with the continuity between
Dickey's dead uncle and Dickey's son, describes the death of the
uncle:

There were powerful strides in his sighing.
He rose. His body made a centaur of the bed.
    With him, four-square,
Death stood on wooden legs. He swayed about in its form.
He looked for a way out of dying
Like a myth and a beast, conjoined.

In this poem the uncle is the Orphic figure at the interface of life
and death; he is between the continuous time of myth and the
ephemeral time of mortality, both united in one man. Here is
Dickey's description of the uncle's death:

His last long breath, drawn up
All the way from the legs of the bed,
    Like Apollo blew on my mind.
I felt the sun turn mortal in the air.
He fell from his fabulous mount.

Then Dickey becomes the connection between life and death, between the dead uncle and Dickey's son:

Thirty years, more slowly than cancer,
You fall from there, Uncle.
    Upon my growing son,
Unfolding your face in his features.

In such a way the living and the dead share one space.

46

The thread of continuity is even more evident in "The String" *(Into the Stone)*. Again Dickey is the agent connecting both worlds:

> It seems to me that the passing on of the technique of making tricks with string, from the dead through the living brother, who is now a father, to *his* boy, says something about the passing on of whatever one is privileged to pass on through the generations. And the fact that it's a string seemed to me to be indicative of something important and mysterious that passes between the generations, a kind of thread of continuity.
>
> So I wrote the poem and used the refrain, "Dead before I was born," as a death bell tolling. . . . But the obsessive fact in the protagonist's mind is that he had a brother who died before he was born, and his way of communicating with his dead brother is to show string tricks to his own son. [8]

The poem itself is written in language as straight-forward as this comment upon it, yet only in the poem does one feel the poignancy—without sentimentality—of the tricks, and this poignancy is best seen in a stanza in which Dickey employs two massive physical structures and an ancient philosopher to carry the weight of temporality that anyone in this world has to be aware of.

> The gaze of genius comes back.
> The rose-window of Chartres is in it,
> And Diogenes' lines upon sand,
> And the sun through the Brooklyn Bridge,
> And, caught in a web, the regard
> Of a skeletal, blood-sharing child
> *Dead before I was born.*

Like the brilliance of the window, the lines upon the sand, and the sun through the bridge, the "communication" is only momentary; but in being able to be passed on, it becomes a ritual, an act forever available, yet one never present except through ceremony.

Also found in *Into the Stone*, "The Underground Stream" is a poem in which Dickey tries to exorcise his memory of the dead brother. Dickey, in this case, tries to break the thread of continuity, which he so strongly feels. Lying near a well, he imagines his brother:

> The tall cadaver, who
> Either grew or did not grow,
> But smiled, with the smile of singing,
> Or a smile of incredible longing
> To rise through a circle of stone,
> Gazing up at a sky, alone
> Visible, at the top of a well,
> And seeking for years to deliver
> His mouth from the endless river
> Of my oil-on-the-water smile,
> And claim his own grave face
> That mine might live in its place.

Ironically, the dead brother has the smiling face, Dickey the grave one (*grave* as the face of one buried, *grave* as a description for solemnity); Dickey would have the roles reversed, himself with the smiling face, the dead brother with the grave. One reason Dickey had the *grave* face is that he suspected that the only reason he had been born was to replace this brother, Eugene, who at six years of age died of spinal meningitis.[9]

But *Drowning with Others* reflects the fact that Dickey was unsuccessful in breaking this continuity with the dead brother. In "In the Tree House at Night" the dead brother's spirit is felt so strongly that Dickey's sense of identification is threatened:

> I stir
> Within another's life. Whose life?
> Who is dead? Whose presence is living?
> When may I fall strangely to earth,
>
> Who am nailed to this branch by a spirit?
> Can two bodies make up a third?

The two bodies Dickey is referring to are his and that of his brother Tom; the spirit is Eugene, though Dickey does not make these identifications in the poem, where his question is "Who am I?" Once more this sharing of life with the dead provides an Orphic or energizing, nourishing effect:

> as my dead brother smiles
> And touches the tree at the root;
>
> A shudder of joy runs up

> The trunk; the needles tingle;
> One bird uncontrollably cries.

In "Armor" *(Drowning with Others)* the reason Dickey dons the armored suit is because

> There is no way of standing alone
> More, or no way of being
> More with the bound, shining dead.

And Dickey's reason for joining the dead is to look for the being he thinks that he was "in a life before life"—in the life of the brother Dickey feels he was born to replace. Having assumed his dead brother's *being,* he then hangs the armor in a glade and enters his "own life," where a "night nearer death" he breathes through his sides "like an insect," his closed hand lying like the dead. Again, as in "The Underground Stream," Dickey seeks to exorcise this brother's spirit in order to escape fulfilling his brother's role. He leaves the armor in the glade so that he "might be naked on earth"— have his own life. The problem he then confronts is that of wondering who he shall be when he dies. Such is the result of moving between two supposedly mutually exclusive worlds, the living and the dead. After this poem there are no others in which Dickey deals with the consummation of oneness he and his dead brother attained.

Considering now Dickey's connection with the war dead, he "contacts" his forefathers as a result of going underground in "Hunting Civil War Relics at Nimblewill Creek" *(Drowning with Others).* While his brother Tom moves the detector over the terrain, Dickey says that he feels underfoot

> The dead regroup,
> The burst metals all in place,
> The battle lines be drawn
> Anew to include us
> In Nimblewill,
>
> And I carry the shovel and pick
>
> More as if they were
> Bright weapons.

Dickey notices his brother Tom, who smiles

> as if
> He rose from the dead within
> Green Nimblewill
> And stood in his grandson's shape.

And what follows is that energizing, what Rilke calls nourishing, response:

> No shot from the buried war
> Shall kill me now. . . .

And he falls to his knees to work the pick,

> To go underground
> Still singing . . .
> Without a sound,
> Like a man who renounces war,
> Or one who shall lift up the past,
> Not breathing "Father,"
> At Nimblewill,
> But saying, "Fathers! Fathers!"

Descent, contact with the inaccessible, celebration: the three Orphic themes are united in this poem.

In "The Island" *(Drowning with Others)* Dickey appears in the role of Rilke's Orpheus:

> A light come from my head
> Showed how to give birth to the dead
> That they might *nourish* me.
>
> (Italics mine)

Between Dickey and the dead soldiers there is an exchange:

> Each wooden body, I took
> In my arms, and singingly shook
> With its being, which stood for my own
> More and more, as I laid it down.

More than empathy is expressed, for there is a movement toward a fuller identity or fuller consciousness:

> At the grave's crude, dazzling verge
> My true self strained to emerge
> From all they could not save
> And did not know they could give.

After covering and currying the graves, Dickey says that "a painless joy" came to him and that he

> Kicked off his old fatigues,
> Saluted the graves by their rank,
> Paraded, lamented, and sank
> Into the intelligent light,
> And danced, unimagined and free.

As in "Hunting Civil War Relics at Nimblewill Creek," the themes of descent, contact, and celebration are again united.

"A View of Fujiyama After the War" *(Drowning with Others)* is also life-enhancing. The scene is deceptively peaceful:

> It could be a country where no one
> Ever has died but of love.

But we find that Dickey is there awaiting "someone to come from the dead / Other side of the war to this place." He waits, wondering if the dead man should pass by if such a one could

> know that to live at the heart
> Of his saved, shaken life, is to stand
> Overcome by the enemy's peace.

Not overcome by violence, which toppled the island in World War II, but overcome by the peacefulness which has come to the island—at the interface of violence and peace—Dickey pauses at the threshold of life and death as if both were in adjacent rooms, separated only by a swinging door.

In "Horses and Prisoners" *(Helmets)* Dickey again fulfills the role of Rilke's Orpheus, the role, according to Rilke, being that of

> one of the staying messengers
> who still holds far into the doors of the dead
> bowls with fruits worthy of praise.[10]

"Horses and Prisoners" portrays harmony with the dead, renewal, and joy:

> my mind like a fence on fire,
> Went around those unknown men:
> Those who tore from the red, light bones
> The intensified meat of hunger
> And then lay down open-eyed

> In a raw, straining dream of new life.
> Joy entered the truth and flowed over
> As the wind rose out of the grass
>
> Leaping with red and white flowers:
> Joy in the bone-strewn infield
> Where clouds of barbed wire contained
> Men who ran in a vision of greenness,
> Sustained by the death of beasts,
> On the tips of the sensitive grass blades,
> Each footstep putting forth petals,
> Their bones light and strong as the wind.

The last two lines further reveal Dickey's relationship to Rilke's Orpheus:

> the dead . . . who invigorate the earth.
> What do we know of their share in this?
> It has long been their way to marrow the loam
> through and through with their free marrow.
>
> . . . .
>
> Are *they* the masters, who sleep with the roots,
> and grant to us out of their overflow
> this hybrid thing made of dumb strength and kisses?[11]

The petals in Dickey's poem, on flowers sprung up where the prisoners stepped before they died, incites Dickey's empathy not only with the prisoners but with their horses as well, for he felt his "long thighbones yearn / To leap with the trained, racing dead." To go down for Dickey is to go up; thus, we are not surprised to hear him say, as a result of this transformation, that

> When death moves close
> In the night, I think I can kill it.

He has been strengthened, which is what Rilke claimed was the effect of accepting both sides of life: the living and the dead.

Orpheus only sought contact with Eurydice. He did not wish to take her place, to share her consciousness. "Drinking from a Helmet" *(Helmets)* offers a variation of this theme, for in this poem consciousness is shared with the dead.

> On even the first day of death
> The dead cannot rise up,

But their last thought hovers somewhere
For whoever finds it.

Dickey finds this thought when he puts on the dead man's helmet, and again there is a sense of renewal, of defiance to death:

In the brown half-life of my beard
The hair stood up
Like the awed hair lifting the back
Of a dog that has eaten a swan.
Now light like this
Staring into my face
Was the first thing around me at birth.
Be no more killed, it said.

(Italics mine)

And we hear Dickey say:

Warmed water ran over my face.
My last thought changed, and I knew
I inherited one of the dead.

The thought he inherited was that of

two boys facing each other,
Quietly talking,
Looking in at the gigantic redwoods,

. . . .

The smaller one curled catercornered
In the handlebar basket.

Dickey says that he will return to the surviving brother and will inform him of what has transpired; from the dead to the living, Dickey is again the agent of continuity.

There are two war poems, however, in which Dickey is unable to descend into the realm of the dead. In "The Driver" *(Helmets)* Dickey tries to assume the consciousness of the soldier who once drove a now rusted and sunken halftrack. Dickey descends

Ten feet underwater . . .
Getting used to the burning stare
Of the wide-eyed dead after battle.

But having noted that he is alive beneath that "lyrical skin that lies /

between death and life, trembling always," he finds it impossible to be that dead driver, even though he has descended to his position:

> "I become pure spirit," I tried
> To say, in a bright smoke of bubbles,
> But I was becoming no more
> Than haunted.

Failing to become "spirit," he rises to the surface

> Very nearly too late, where another
> Leapt and could not break into
> His breath.

The other war poem in which Dickey is unable to make contact with the dead is "The Firebombing" (*Buckdancer's Choice*). In this poem Dickey has no feeling for those whom he killed in the war:

> My hat should crawl on my head
> In streetcars, thinking of it,
> The fat on my body should pale.

But he is without feeling, lacking even shame, able only to recall the aesthetic aspect of the killing. And it is not the killing for which he seeks absolution, but

> this detachment,
> The honored aesthetic evil,
> The greatest sense of power in one's life,
> That must be shed in bars, or by whatever
> Means, by starvation
> Visions in well-stocked pantries.

His failure is one of imagination, being

> unable
> To get down there or see
> What really happened.

Again he is unable to descend:

> It is that I can imagine
> At the threshold nothing
> With its ears crackling off
> Like powdery leaves,
> Nothing with children of ashes, nothing not
> Amiable, gentle, well-meaning.

It is only for his own that Dickey can truly descend, for the members of his family and for his fellow soldiers; he cannot enter the realm of the deceased enemy.

When he descends into the realm of his dead family it is usually for the sake of continuity, as in "Poem" and "The String," though in this regard we see him descend in "The Underground Stream" and in "Armor" to break this thread of continuity. Though he rises nourished from such an encounter, it is not expressed with the intensity of the celebration we see in the war poems, where the descent is employed to renew his life and to salute death. Except in "Drinking from a Helmet" the theme of continuity is not as important as that of descending into the underworld and encountering those who dwell there. In the war poems exploration is enough. In encountering the dead Dickey seems to realize *life* most intensely. The way up, as Heraclitus tells us, is the way down; or as the Biblical paradox puts it: to find your life you must lose it: an Orphic configuration, which Dickey follows.

NOTES

1. Rainer Maria Rilke, *Sonnet to Orpheus*, trans. M. D. Herter Norton (New York: Norton, 1942), p. 27.
2. Walter A. Strauss, *Descent and Return* (Cambridge: Harvard Univ. Press, 1971), p. 186.
3. Strauss, p. 167, citing Rainer Maria Rilke, *Brife II: 1914–1926*, trans. Walter A. Strauss (Wiesbaden: Insel-Verlag, 1950), pp. 480–481.
4. Strauss, p. 10.
5. Laurence Lieberman, rev. of *Poems 1957–1967*, by James Dickey, *Hudson Review*, 20 (August 1967), 514.
6. Crunk, rev. of *Drowning with Others*, by James Dickey, *The Sixties*, 7 (Winter 1964), 42.
7. James Dickey, "The Sprinter's Mother," *Shenandoah*, 6 (Spring 1955), 17–18.
8. James Dickey, *Self-Interviews* (New York: Dell, 1970), p. 89.
9. Dickey, *Self-Interviews*, p. 89.
10. Rilke, *Sonnets to Orpheus*, p. 29.
11. Rilke, p. 43.

N. MICHAEL NIFLIS

A Special Kind of Fantasy:
James Dickey on the Razor's Edge

THE MOST STRIKING CHARACTERISTICS of James Dickey's poems are, I believe, an acute consciousness of being possessed by—or at least identifying with—the dead; an intense identification with animals; the presentation of various experiences of initiation and rebirth; and a fine imagination, shown by originality both in images and in putting ordinary words into new unified combinations. The poems are also extremely heuristic. In them there is much delving into and exploring of the unknown, concerning the self, death, and animals. And I enjoy—as I think the reader must—the taking of these fantastic journeys of exploration with the poet. For the special kind of fantasy found in Dickey's poetry is refreshing.

The identification with the dead is most intense, I think, in his poem "Drinking from a Helmet," and to a lesser degree in "Hunting Civil War Relics at Nimblewill Creek." In the former we find in stanza V: "Like the beards of the dead, all now / Underfoot beginning to grow." Here I immediately think of Walt Whitman's "Look for me under your boot-soles." The likeness is to be expected; I once heard Dickey say that the second greatest American poet is Whitman—the first being Roethke. At any rate, in stanza XII of "Drinking from a Helmet" the persona is seen "Crouching over the dead / Where they waited for all their hands / To be connected like grass roots." Again the preoccupation with the buried soldiers. And in stanza XV we see what is perhaps the strongest plea of the dead to the persona for recognition: "Fresh sweat and unbearable tears / Drawn up by my feet from the field."

This carries the Whitman idea a step farther—the dead don't remain under the "boot-soles," but come right through to possess the man. So, in the following stanza, after he has drunk from the dead man's helmet, we see the identification has been completed:

> I threw my old helmet down
> And put the wet one on.
> Warmed water ran over my face.
> My last thought changed, and I knew
> I inherited one of the dead.

The suggestiveness of "warmed water" is as significant here as the "warmed jewels" are in Keats's "The Eve of St. Agnes." It intensifies the reality and immediacy of the recent wearer. It lets us imagine the helmet still contains some body heat of its last occupant. And in stanza XVIII, where we see the persona return to civilization ("Stepping off the train in a helmet / That held a man's last thought.") still wearing the helmet, the question "Why is he doing this?" arises. This preferring of a dead man's helmet to his own on the part of the persona is psychologically interesting and arousing. It is as if the persona wants somehow both to prolong the life of the dead soldier and to do some kind of weird penance for a strange sense of personal guilt that he has for the other soldier's death. There is a stunning simile in the other poem ("Hunting Civil War Relics at Nimblewill Creek") which almost gives us an explanation for this psychological phenomenon:

> While I stand with
> The same voice calling insanely
> Like that of a sniper
> Who throws down his rifle and yells
> In the pure joy of missing me.

The "sniper" here, of course, is not on the persona's own team, as the original occupant of the helmet was, but still he is a fellow human being with real feelings, as the image clearly shows. This same idea is also beautifully done in Wilfred Owen's poem "Strange Meeting," where we see "the pity of war distilled." But the sniper's feeling does not explain the persona's feeling of guilt— if that is what it is—toward the dead soldier whom he has not personally wronged; he probably doesn't even know him. Perhaps we can explain this feeling by imagining the persona to have reasoned in some such manner as this: I am a human being, a part of the whole family of Man; some of my family are killing each other, therefore I share some of the guilt. The persona, like the sniper in the simile, is an unwilling participant in the killing. His strange attachment to the unknown soldier's helmet, and his appearance in California wearing it, are a kind of personal apology for a public guilt.

Dickey's identification with animals is certainly more intense than the "chameleon" idea of "negative capability" of which Keats speaks. In one of his letters Keats says, "If a sparrow comes before my window, I take part in its existence and pick about the gravel." In his poetry Keats often demonstrates this "negative capability" or sympathetic identification—with animals at least. One example can be found in the first stanza of "The Eve of St. Agnes": "The hare limp'd trembling through the frozen grass." Another example is in stanza 1 of his long poem *The Fall of Hyperion:* "I feel, as vultures feel / They are no birds when eagles are abroad." The identifications with animals which take place in Dickey's poems are, however, much more complex than these from Keats; they are nearer to the kind we see in Walt Whitman's poetry—for example, in these lines: "I think I could turn and live with animals. . . . They bring me tokens of myself. . . . I wonder where they get those tokens, / Did I pass that way huge times ago and negligently drop them?" And certainly, what Whitman says of a stallion—"I love, and now go with him on brotherly terms"—is very similar to the experience we see taking place in Dickey's "Springer Mountain"—that of the poet straining to become a deer, or whatever it is that the deer represents. To some readers this idea is a bit ludicrous, but Dickey is dead serious about his experience. This is one of the best parts of Dickey, because he feels most strongly about it. And we see it working at its best in "Springer Mountain." A hunt is normally a physical experience, but this particular and lonesome hunt becomes rather a kind of spiritual experience to the persona. In fact, I have heard Dickey say, "When I'm in the woods, I don't want anyone within fifty miles of me . . . I love that feeling . . . a man by himself out in the wilderness is a totally different person . . . you can do mad, crazy things . . . and this ["Springer Mountain"] is one poem in which I think I really said it." The character Ed in Dickey's *Deliverance* undergoes an experience which is similar to the one that takes place in this poem.

Dickey is gravely concerned with the terrible conflict which exists between man's basic, driving biological needs and the controls of society. He wants a world, he says, "where the mind and the body can become good friends again"—not the world of D. H. Lawrence, where instinct exists almost alone, but one more like that of which Arnold dreamed, a world in which "there would be no quarrel between desire and intelligence."

It is easy to see, simply by looking around us, that man's mind has even created institutions to make war on his own flesh. Nevertheless, his biological needs *will be met*. And when a lid of any kind is placed over the bubbling hormones, they soon develop such enormous pressures in mind and body that they squirt out at the edges of the lid, taking on various and distorted forms, as we see they have in Dickey's poem "The Fiend." And in that poem all nature is in sympathy ("the smallest root responds") with the virile man outside the building, while the men inside are "indifferent" and "plainly unworthy for what women want"—also an unnatural condition. These are two extremes: the erotically dead men inside; the wild man outside. Both are deviations from the natural. We see a similar idea in Robinson Jeffers's poem (Jeffers is another poet whom Dickey admires a great deal) "Roan Stallion," where we see another unnatural relationship between man and woman. We see the man, in the love act, trying to imitate the stallion's breeding of the mare. And later in the poem we see the woman trying to imitate the mare with the stallion.

What I am saying, then, is that Dickey's animal poems represent much more than a simple identification with animals; the animals represent nature, undistorted—and man today seems to be as far from natural responses as east is from west. Dickey would reconcile the basic drives with the intellect. But he admits himself that he does not know how this can ever be done, how the man-made obstacles can be overcome. He believes, though, that such an accomplishment would be a fine thing to be remembered for.

Experiences of initiation and rebirth can also be seen in "Drinking from a Helmet" and "Springer Mountain." In stanza V of the former we see a soldier, initiated by the hell of war, who has been born again: "I stood as though I possessed a trembling man / Exactly my size, swallowed whole," and, in stanza VIII, "I kept trembling forward through something / Just born in me." In "Springer Mountain" we see the persona "releasing his body" to climb the mountain on his "painfully reborn legs." He had come to hunt but, instead, imagines himself becoming a deer: "My brain dazed and pointed with trying to grow horns."

The persona strips away his civil flesh and begins a wild, dancing chase, naked through the wood, suggesting an experience that is a kind of cross betwen Bottom in *Midsummer Night's Dream* and David in the worship of his God, "deep in the dance / Of what I am and should be." Like Bottom, Dickey's hunter is shaken and confused by his "most rare vision," for when he dresses again he puts his sweaters back on "inside out" suggesting again rebirth and renewal. Moreover, when he leaves the woods, he is as unwilling to live away the experience as Gulliver was when he returned from the land of the Houyhnhnms. As Gulliver tried to imitate the gait and gesture of the noble Houyhnhnms, so this hunter tries to keep wearing some venison flesh, for he does not follow a path from the wood; instead he follows "hoof-tracks" out. What a nice stroke of the poet here! And it is typical of Dickey's imagination, an imagination which is full of fantasy and at the same time full of method. There is a unity and a logical progression of images, one image requiring, supplying, and enhancing another.

In the first stanza of his poem "Slave Quarters" Dickey speaks of "my imagining loins." This tells us at least two things about Dickey: he is the persona of his poems; and he is very conscious of his obligation as a poet to present imaginative work to his reader, to present, as Pope put it, "What oft' was thought, but ne'er so well expressed." We can see his strange yet very sensitive imagination working well in "Springer Mountain." There we see this nice image: "The sun comes openly in / to my mouth and is blown out white" (this is also an example of how Dickey gets extra mileage from words with line-breaks). This image is as commendable as Dickinson's "little tippler / Leaning against the sun." Another example of the fruit of Dickey's "imagining loins" is seen when the persona removes his "tense bow off the limb." The "tense bow" shows his ability to select common objects from the immediacy of the action to be used as images which empathize with the tone of the performance. When he says "My crazed laughter pure as church-cloth," I again think of the influence and confidence of Whitman, e.g., "The scent of these arm-pits aroma finer than prayer."

A further example of Dickey's fresh imagination is in his poem "The Performance." There we see Donald Armstrong's face described: "blood turned his face inside out." Another good example is in stanza II of "Drinking from a Helmet": "a graveyard / Was advancing after the troops." What is so stunning to me about these images is the fact that they are so literal and yet contain so much power. It is Dickey's fresh way of seeing and describing the near and mundane things that makes his images staggeringly powerful. His remarkable power seems to lie not necessarily in an ability to manufacture images but in an ability to *select* images, as I have said, from the immediate environment of the persona's activities—images which will fit naturally, giving off a kind of vibrating sympathy to the poem's performance.

In *Self-Interviews* Dickey says something that casts a good deal of light on how his imagination works:

> There's a razor's edge between sublimity and absurdity. And that's the edge I try to walk. . . . If you insist on literal interpretations of a lot of my poems, of *course* they seem farfetched. They're meant to seem farfetched. My only regret is that I did not make them more far-fetched than I did.

I believe therein lies at least one secret to the greatness of Dickey's imagination—his letting go. By that I mean that he tries to imagine what an experience might be like if certain things were to occur, then writes about that experience. It does not matter to him at all that the experience may be an impossible one, one that could never really happen as he imagines it. One thinks, for example, of poems like "The Underground Stream," "The Sheep Child," or "The Owl King."

In spite of all the strengths I have mentioned, there are ways in which it seems to me Dickey could improve his work. He pushes to the limit of his perceptions, and while this is certainly commendable, it would be better if the reader were unaware of the pushing. Dickey relies excessively, I think, on the use of adverbs—"Springer Mountain" is an example—when he could perhaps find more exact diction, so that fewer of them would be necessary. I can feel his pushing when I see the adverbs piling up. Similarly, he could achieve his experiences of identification while using a bit less of his own anatomy in his poems. His poems are filled with his own body and limbs. I know that these anatomical interventions are necessary for his purpose; but I do think that the same end could be reached if they, with the adverbs, were fewer in number. If he doesn't make these changes, surely someone will accuse him of excessive narcissism and perhaps even parody him for it. I am convinced, however, that these anatomical intrusions are not at all what narcissism denotes, or even connotes.

These, then—an identification with the dead and animals, initiation and rebirth, and a unique, forceful imagination—are the outstanding characteristics of Dickey's poetry. It is not yet certain whether the identification with the dead or the identification with animals will become the stronger and more lasting element in his poems. But I feel it will be the latter. For as Dickey has said in *The Suspect in Poetry*, ". . . what we need most [in poetry] is the simple belief that a human being has said something because it matters." And this identification with animals—or what they represent—matters a great deal to him. In line with this are his tastes in criticism which ". . . are actually quite simple. [He wishes] merely to be able to feel and see and respond to what the poet is saying, and with as much strength and depth as possible."

I hope the best of Dickey's poems are yet to come. With the exception of "The Eye-Beaters" and one or two others, the poems in his most recent book are not, in my opinion, as good as his earlier poems. He has had remarkable success, however, with his first novel, and he still has a great deal of energy, a tremendous capacity for work, and a youthful look about him. He could produce good material for many years yet. I hope he will. But even if he does not, he has written great poems. They will survive our time. I genuinely believe, so help me, that Dickey is our greatest American poet. And I bar none—not Roethke, not Whitman, not Frost, not Dickinson, not Robinson, not Jeffers, not Stevens. Dickey gives us experiences we have never seen before in poetry, and his poems keep pulling us back again and again for another look at their wealth. His best ones are absolutely permeated with rich images. Such an abundance of richness makes the work of other good poets look somewhat sparse. I believe Mark Schorer was right when he said,

> James Dickey's poetic gift is unique. Perhaps his most striking quality is the way he plunges his reader, with something like aesthetic rudeness, into the heavy stream of experience which is the poem itself. Emerging with a renewed if slightly dazed sense of his own existence, the responsive reader wants only to plunge in again.

Out of Stone, into Flesh:
The Imagination of James Dickey
1960–1970

Despair and exultation
Lie down together and thrash
In the hot grass, no blade moving. . . .

> Dickey, "Turning Away"

A man cannot pay as much attention to
himself as I do without living in Hell
all the time.

> Dickey, "Sorties"

THE REMARKABLE POETIC ACHIEVEMENT of James Dickey is characterized by a restless concern with the poet's "personality" in its relationships to the worlds of nature and of experience. His work is rarely confessional in the sense of the term as we have come to know it, yet it is always personal—at times contemplative, at times dramatic. Because Dickey has become so controversial in recent years, his incredible lyric and dramatic talent has not been adequately recognized, and his ceaseless, often monomaniacal questioning of identity, of the self, of that mysterious and elusive concept we call the personality, has not been investigated.

Yet this is only natural: it is always the fate of individuals who give voice to an era's hidden, atavistic desires, its "taboos," to be controversial and therefore misunderstood. Dickey's poetry is important not only because it is so skillful, but because it expresses, at times unintentionally, a great deal about the American imagination in its response to an increasingly complex and "unnatural" phase of civilization. (To Dickey mental processes have come to seem "unnatural" in contrast to physical acts: hence the "Hell" of the quote from his journal, *Sorties*.) He has said, quite seriously, that "the world, the human mind, is dying of subtlety. What it needs is force" (*Sorties*, Garden City, New York, 1971; p. 85). His imagination requires the heroic. But the world cannot and will not always accommodate the hero, no matter how passionately he believes he has identified himself with the fundamental, secret rhythms of nature itself. One comes to loathe the very self that voices its hopeless demands, the "I" that will not be satisfied and will never be silent. *I myself am hell* is a philosophical statement, though it is expressed in the poetic language of personal emotion.

The volumes of poetry Dickey has published so far—*Into the Stone* (1960), *Drowning with Others* (1962), *Helmets* (1964), *Buckdancer's Choice* (1965), *The Eye-Beaters, Blood, Victory, Madness, Buckhead and Mercy* (1970)—present a number of hypothetical or experimental personae, each a kind of reincarnation of an earlier consciousness through which the "self" of the poet endures. He moves, he grows, he suffers, he changes, yet he is still the same—the voice is a singular one, unmistakable. It asks why, knowing the soul heroic, the man himself is so trapped, so helpless? Dickey's central theme is the frustration that characterizes modern man, confronted with an increasingly depersonalized and intellectualized society—the frustration and its necessary corollary, murderous rage. Dickey is not popular with liberals. Yet one can learn from him, as from no other serious writer, what it is like to have been born into one world and to have survived into another. It might be argued that Dickey is our era's Whitman, but a Whitman subdued, no longer innocent, baptized by American violence into the role of a "killer/victim" who cannot locate within his society any standards by which his actions may be judged. A personality eager to identify itself with the collective, whether nature or other men, can survive only when the exterior world supports that mystical union of subject and object. Dickey speaks from the inside of our fallen, contaminated, guilt-obsessed era, and he speaks its language.

This was not always so: his earliest poems are lyric and meditative. They present a near-anonymous sensitivity, one hypnotized by forms, by Being in which dramatic and ostensibly intolerable truths are resolved by a formal, ritualistic—essentially magical—imagination into coherent and well-defined unities; his later poems submit this sensitivity to a broken, overheated, emotionally and intellectually turbulent world. The "stoneness" of the first volume undergoes an astonishing variety of metamorphoses until, in "The Eye-Beaters" and "Turning Away: Variations on Estrangement," it emerges as stark, isolated, combative self-consciousness, in which "A deadly, dramatic compression/Is made of the normal brow. . . ." The poet begins as Prospero, knowing all and forgiving all, and, through a series of sharply tested modes of perception, comes to seem like Hamlet of the great, tragic soliloquies.

Who can tell us more about ourselves?—about our "American," "masculine," most dangerous selves? Even more than Whitman, Dickey contains multitudes; he cannot be reproached for the fact that some of these aspects of a vast, complex self are at war with the others. He experiments with the art of poetry and with the external world and the relationships it offers him (will he be lover?—murderer?—observer?), but what is most moving about his work is his relentless honesty in regard to his own evolving perception of himself, the mystery of his "personality." He refuses to remain in any explored or conquered territory, either in his art or in his personality. Obsessed with the need to seek and to define, he speaks for those who know that the universe is rich with meaning but are not always able to relate the intellectual, conscious aspect of their natures to it. Thus, the need to reject the "conscious" mind and its public expression, civilization itself, which is so disturbing in Dickey. Indeed, *Sorties* is very nearly a confession of despair—the poet seems unable to integrate the various aspects of his nature, conceiving of the world of the intellect and art as "Hell." "Believe me, it is better to be stupid and ordinary," Dickey tells us early in the book. What such a temperament requires, however, is not less intelligence, but more.

Dickey has not always expressed himself in such extreme terms, and he has been, all along, a careful craftsman, knowing that meaning in poetry must be expressed through language, through a system of mental constructs. In fact, it must be invented

anew with each poem; it must be rigorously contracted, ab-
breviated, made less explosive and less primitive. In an excellent
essay in *The Suspect in Poetry* he cautions young poets against
abandoning themselves to their unconscious "song," which he
defines as "only a kind of monstrousness that has to be understood
and ordered according to some principle to be meaningful."[1] The
unrestrained and unimagined self must be related syntactically to
the external world in order to achieve meaning.

Yet the phenomenal world changes; language shifts, evolves,
breaks free of its referents; and the human ego, mysteriously linked
to both, is forced to undergo continuous alterations in order simply
to survive. In the poem "Snakebite" (1967) the "stage of pine logs"
and the "role/I have been cast in" give way suddenly and horribly to
the dramatic transition from the pronoun "it" to the pronoun "me"
as the poet realizes he is confined in his living, breathing, existential
body: he is not playing a role after all. If he wants to survive he will
have to drain that poison out of his blood stream. Therefore, one of
the burdens of the poet's higher awareness is to discover if there is
any metamorphosis, any possible reincarnation, that is ultimately
more than a mode of perception, *a way of arranging words.* Otherwise we begin to imagine ourselves as totally "estranged." To deny
that estrangement we must deny our very framework of perception—language and sanity and logic—as if, by annihilating the
mental construct of incarnation, we might somehow experience it
on a level far below consciousness. Certainly Dickey has empha-
sized the poem as physical experience; he has set up opposing
pseudocategories of the poetry of "participation" and the poetry of
"reflection" (*Sorties*, p. 59). Such an estrangement rests, however,
upon the metaphysical assumption that man's intellect is an intruder
in the universe and that the language systems he has devised are not
utterly natural, natural to his species. Surely the human invention or
creation of language is our species' highest achievement; some
psycholinguists speculate that human beings are born with a genetic
endowment for recognizing and formulating language, that they
"possess genes for all kinds of information, with strands of special,
peculiarly human DNA for the discernment of meaning in syntax."[2]
Failing to accept the intellect as triumphantly human, rather than
somehow unnatural, the poet is doomed to endless struggles with

the self. The "variations on estrangement" at the end of *The Eye-Beaters* deal with countless battles and meadows strewn "with inner lives," concluding with the hope that the poet's life may be seen "as a thing/That can be learned,/As those earnest young heroes learned theirs,/Later, much later on."

An objective assessment of one's situation must be experienced apart from life itself, then. And only "much later on." To use a critical term Dickey appropriated from Wordsworth, he is a poet of the "Second Birth," not one who, like Rimbaud or Dylan Thomas, possessed a natural instrument for poetry but one who eventually reduces the distinction between "born" and "made" poets only by hard work, by the "ultimate moral habit of trying each poem, each line, each word, against the shifting but finally constant standards of inner necessity" (*The Suspect in Poetry*, pp. 55–57). Contrary to his instinct for direct, undiluted self-expression, the poet has tried to define and develop his own personality as a "writing instrument"; he has pared back, reduced, restrained the chaotic "monstrousness" of raw emotion in order to relate his unique experience to common experience. He contradicts Eliot's ideal of an impersonal poetry, yet paradoxically refuses to endorse what he would call the monstrousness of confessional verse: "The belief in the value of one's personality has all but disappeared. . . ."

But what is personality, that a belief in it might save us?

Not a multileveled phenomenon, Dickey's sense of "personality," but rather a series of imagined dramas, sometimes no more than flashes of rapport, kinships with beasts or ancient ancestors—as in the apocalyptic "The Eye-Beaters," in which personality is gained only when "Reason" is rejected in favor of primitive action. The process of increasing self-consciousness, as image after image is explored, held up like a mask to the poet's face,[3] absorbed, and finally discarded, comes to seem a tragic movement, as every existential role in the universe must ultimately be abandoned.

"Intact and Incredible Love"

Dickey has said that the century's greatest phrase is Albert Schweitzer's "reverence for life." This conviction runs through his work but is strongest in the earliest volumes. *Into the Stone* consists of contemplative, almost dreamlike poems that investigate the poet's many forms of love: beginning with the mythical, incantatory dissolution of the individual personality into both "dark" and "light" and concluding with the book's title poem, which emphasizes the poet's confident "knowing" and his being "known" through his relationship with a woman.

"Sleeping Out at Easter" is terse, restrained, as the "Word rising out of darkness" seems to act without the deliberate involvement of the poet. As dawn arrives in the forest, the "Presences" of night turn into trees and "One eye opens slowly without me." Everything moves in its own placid, nonpersonalized pattern, out of darkness and into the sunlight, and the world is "made good" by the springing together of wood and sun. The metamorphosis of Presences into daytime trees is one that could occur without the poet's song, yet the poet voices a total acceptance, as if he knew himself uniquely absorbed in the cycle of night/day, his "magical shepherd's cloak . . . not yet alive on [his] flesh." In other, similarly incantatory poems, the poet lies at the edge of a well, contemplating himself and his smile and the "grave face" of his dead brother, or lies "in ritual down" in a small unconsecrated grove of suburban pines— trying to get back, to get down, beneath both gods and animals, to "being part of the acclaimed rebirth" of spring ("The Vegetable King"). (Years later, when his poetry has undergone tremendous changes, Dickey will deal again with the transformation of a human being into a tree, in "The Fiend," one of his most eccentric poems).

Into the Stone contains a number of war poems, but in spite of their subject they absorb the poet's personality much as the nature poems do, locating in confusion and panic certain centers of imagination, of decision, that the poet is able to recall years later, when "at peace." "The Enclosure" is the first of Dickey's many poems that "enclose" and idealize women: a group of war nurses on a Philippine island are protected by a compound with a wire fence, but the poet imagines them whispering to the soldiers outside "to deliver them out/Of the circle of impotence. . . ." In lines of curious, ceremonial calm the poet declares how, after the war, this vision led him to "fall/On the enemy's women/With intact and incredible love." Of the war poems, the most vivid is "The Performance," which celebrates the paradox of pain and triumph in the memory of David Armstrong, executed by the Japanese; Dickey remembers Armstrong doing a handstand against the sun, and his death by decapitation is seen as another kind of "performance." Even here there is a sense of acquiescence, finality, as if the cycle of nature could absorb this violent death as easily as it could absorb the shapes of trees back into primordial Presences.

The reverential awe of "Trees and Cattle" places the poet's consciousness in a "holy alliance" with trees, cattle, and sunlight, making his mind a "red beast"—his head gifted with ghostly bull's horns by the same magic that allowed Lawrence to imagine his head "hard-balanced, antlered" in "A Doe at Evening"; the sun itself burns more deeply because trees and cattle exist. A miracle of some kind has occurred, though it cannot be explained, and the poet half believes he may be saved from death; as, in a later poem, "Fog Envelops the Animals," the poet-hunter is somehow transformed into the "long-sought invisibility" of pure things or events or processes: "Silence. Whiteness. Hunting." But *Into the Stone* is characterized by passivity and no hint of the guilty, pleasurable agitation of physical life, whether hunting or love; the title poem describes the poet "on the way to a woman," preoccupied with a mystical absorption into the "stone" of the moon. The woman is outside the concern of the poem, undefined, not even mythologized; the poet is not vividly portrayed, as in "Cherrylog Road"; he could be any man, any lover, believing that "the dead have their chance in my body." All is still, mysterious, calm. The poet "knows" his place and his love, quite unlike the moon-drawn men of a later poem, "Apollo," who are seen as floating "on nothing/But procedure alone" and who symbolize "all humanity in the name/Of a new life. . . ." This later poem makes the "stone" of the moon into "stones," breaks up a seamless cosmology into a universe of "craters" and "mountains the animal/Eye has not seen since the earth split" (the earth-moon split an ancient and honored moon theory, of obvious symbolic, if not scientific, value)—not the Platonic oneness of stone, but stones:

> . . . We stare into the moon
> dust, the earth-blazing ground. We laugh, with the beautiful craze
> Of Static. We bend, we pick up stones.
>
> ("Apollo")

A more dramatic sense of self is evident in Dickey's second book, *Drowning with Others*. Here he imagines the torturous memories of a lifeguard who failed to save a drowning child; he imagines himself inside the hunting dream of a dog sleeping on his feet; he contemplates fish in "The Movement of Fish" with the alert, awed scrutiny of Lawrence himself, making a judgment, like Lawrence's, that arises from the distant Otherness of the fish's world, where its sudden movement has the power to "convulse the whole ocean" and teach man the Kierkegaardian terror of the leap, the "fear and trembling" of great depths that are totally still, far beneath the superficial agitation that men see or float upon in their boats.

Yet the hunted/hunting animals of "The Heaven of Animals" are poetic constructions, Platonic essences of beasts wholly absorbed in a mythical cycle of life-death-rebirth: at the very center of nature these beasts "tremble," "fall," "are torn," "rise," and "walk again," like Emerson's red slayer and his perpetual victim. "The Heaven of Animals" is all but unique in Dickey's poetry because the poet himself has no clear position in it, as if its unity of Being somehow excluded an active intellectual consciousness; if we look back at the poem from "Fog Envelops the Animals" and other hunting poems and from Dickey's statements in *Self-Interviews* (Garden City, New York, 1970) about the mysterious "renewal" he experiences when hunting, we can assume that his deepest sympathies are with the predators, but this is not evident from the poem itself, which is one of his finest, most delicate achievements. The owl of "The Owl King" is another poetic (and not naturalistic) creature, a form of the poet himself who sits "in my shape/With my claws growing deep into wood/And my sight going slowly out,/ Inch by inch. . . ." Superior forces belong to those who, like the owl, can see in the dark; or to those who, like Dickey himself, possess extraordinary powers of vision[4] that set them apart from other, average men. But the forces are benevolent, godly, and restrained—the owl king participates in a mysterious ceremony with the blind child "as beasts at their own wedding, dance" and is not the symbol of cold, savage violence of the owl perched upon the tent in *Deliverance*, just as the poet-narrator of the volume *Drowning with Others* is not the helplessly eager murderer of *Deliverance*. Here, in the owl king's Roethkian kingdom, all nature is transformed by mind, its brutal contingencies and dreams suppressed, the possible "monstrousness" of its song made into a childlike lyric.

Its final stanzas link it to earlier poems of Dickey's in which tension has been resolved by an act of impersonal, godly will:

> Far off, the owl king
> Sings like my father, growing
> In power. Father, I touch
> Your face. I have not seen
> My own, but it is yours.
> I come, I advance,
> I believe everything, I am here.

Through the child's (blind) acceptance, Dickey accepts the world; just as, in the anguished "The Eye-Beaters," he rejects the world of normal, rational vision, having been shaken by the experience of seeing blind children beat at their eyes in order to "see." In "The Owl King" the transcendent, paternal bird withdraws into the darkness of his own vision, while the lost child's father emerges, "In love with the sound of my voice," to claim his child; both aspects of the poetic consciousness are required if the child is to be saved, cherished, and yet both are dependent upon the child's acquiescence. (Just as, for the hunter, the imagined "acquiescence" of the hunted—the slain—is a ritualistic necessity; see Dickey's attempted justification of his love of hunting in *Self-Interviews*). This poem is a "song of innocence" whose unearthly simplicity—the child moves from tree to tree as if blessing them—will be transformed, years later, into the nightmarish "song of experience" of the crazed blind children in "The Eye-Beaters." Then, the objects of the poet's pity being, in themselves, hopeless, not even human children, beyond all love or language, the poet himself will narrowly escape madness. But this is years later, years deeper into flesh.

Entering History

In his third book, *Helmets,* Dickey begins to move out of the perfected world of eternal recurrence, no longer the awed, alert, but essentially passive observer, now ready to experience history. It is clear that Dickey desires to take on "his" own personal history as an analogue to or a microcosmic exploration of twentieth-century American history, which is one of the reasons he is so important a poet. In his inspired, witty, and ingeniously balanced essay on

Randall Jarrell in *The Suspect in Poetry,* Dickey says he can discover in Jarrell's poetry very little excellence of technique, but he insists that Jarrell's contribution—"that of writing about real things, rather than playing games with words"—is a valuable one. Dickey indicates implicitly that *he* will take on both the challenge of being an artist and a historian of our era, which he has, applying a superior poetic talent to Jarrell's "realm . . . of pity and terror . . . a kind of non-understanding understanding, and above all of helplessness."[5]

Once he is released from the sacred but bloodless cycle of nature, Dickey is concerned with giving life to this "non-understanding understanding" of creatures simpler than himself, or of an earlier form of himself, as in the beautiful, perfect poem, "Drinking from a Helmet." In "The Dusk of Horses" the emphasis has shifted from acceptance to a sharper awareness of distinctions between self and object, the need for the human participant in an action to judge it:

> No beast ever lived who understood
>
> What happened among the sun's fields,
> Or cared why the color of grass
> Fled over the hill while he stumbled,
>
> Led by the halter to sleep
> On his four taxed, worthy legs. . . .
>
>   ("The Dusk of Horses")

In this and similar poems in *Helmets* the graceful fluidity of the lines is like the fluidity of the earlier poems: the god's-eye vision set to music. As the theme of "helplessness" grows, however, Dickey loses interest in well-made and sweetly sounding poetry and pours his remarkable energies into such extravaganzas of shouts and shrieks as "May Day Sermon." And where death might once have been resolved by a mystical affirmation of unity, in the recent poem "Diabetes" it is resolved by a surreptitious drink of beer; in "The Cancer Match," by whiskey.

Throughout *Helmets* there is an increasing growth, as if the subjects long loved by the poet are now shifting out of the hypnosis of love itself, beginning to elude his incantatory powers: coming alive and separate. In a poem reminiscent of Wallace Stevens' "Anecdote of the Jar," Dickey stands by a fence with his palm on

the top wire and experiences a vision or a nervous hallucination of
the disorder that would result if the tension of the wire were broken:

> If the wire were cut anywhere
> All his blood would fall to the ground
> And leave him standing and staring
> With a face as white as a Hereford's. . . .
>
> ("Fence Wire")

The "top tense strand" is like a guitar string "tuned to an E," whose
humming sound arranges the acres of the farm and holds them
"highstrung and enthralled." Suddenly the poet in his human role
must accept a position in nature which is superior to that of trees and
cattle, an intellectual responsibility that will involve both exultation
and the risk of despair. But because of Dickey's hand on this fence
wire,

> The dead corn is more
> Balanced in death than it was,
> The animals more aware
>
> Within the huge human embrace
> Held up and borne out of sight
> Upon short, unbreakable poles
> Where through the ruled land intones
> Like a psalm. . . .

Because of the sensational aspects of some of his later poems,
Dickey is not usually known to have concerned himself so seriously, and so perceptively, with the metaphysics behind aesthetic
action; it is characteristic of his energy and his pursuit of new
challenges that a very few poems about "poetry" are enough for
him. If read in its proper chronological place in Dickey's work,
"Fence Wire" is a moving as well as a significant poem; it is the first
clear statement of the poet's sense of himself as involved responsibly
in history. In his most powerful poems the tension between that
"top thread tuned to an E" and the abandonment to one's own
possible, probable "monstrousness" provides a dramatic excitement
generally lacking in these early, though entirely admirable poems,
and less content with lyric verse itself, Dickey will experiment with
wildly imaginative monologues in which words float and leap all
over the page.

In *Helmets* there is also a new sense of exploration into an

"Otherness," not a declaring of unities, analogues, "correspondences" between all phenomena in nature: Dickey stands "At Darien Bridge" and muses upon the chain-gang workers who built the bridge many years ago, when he was a child; he hopes to see a bird, the one bird "no one has looked for," and the scratched wedding band on his finger recalls the convicts' chains—like them, he longs for freedom, or even death, or at least the ability to believe again in "the unchanging, hopeless look/Out of which all miracles leap." (In contrast to the miraculous vision of "Trees and Cattle.") In "Chenille" he encounters another kind of poet, an old woman who darns quilts endlessly, not ordinary bedspreads of the kind made by machine and sold in the normal world but quilts decorated with red whales, unicorns, winged elephants, crowned ants—"Beasts that cannot be thought of/By the wholly sane." Increasingly, the surreal intrudes into what should be the real, or sane; in "On the Coosawattee" Dickey and his companion on a canoeing trip are shocked to see how the water has been defiled by a poultry-processing plant upstream:

> All morning we floated on feathers
> Among the drawn heads which appeared
> Everywhere, from under the logs
>
> Of feathers, from upstream behind us,
> Lounging back to us from ahead,
> Until we believed ourselves doomed
> And the planet corrupted forever. . . .

Though the two men shoot the rapids and finally escape this horror, the canoeists of *Deliverance* return to experience the river's mysterious dangers and the unhuman ground-bass of sound that becomes "deeper and more massively frantic and authoritative" as they continue—and this time not all will survive, and none will get back to civilization with anything like this poem's triumphant declaration of the human ability to escape other human defilement. In the blaze of noon the canoeists on the Coosawattee River feel

> The quickening pulse of the rapids
> And entered upon it like men
> Who sense that the world can be cleansed
>
> Among rocks pallid only with water,

And plunged there like the unborn
Who see earthly streams without taint
Flow beneath them. . . .

"Cherrylog Road" is the first of the unmistakable Dickeyesque poems: nostalgic and comic simultaneously, demystifying the love so laboriously mystified elsewhere, even naming names ("Doris Holbrook") and giving directions:

Off Highway 106
At Cherrylog Road I entered
The '34 Ford without wheels,
Smothered in kudzu,
With a seat pulled out to run
Corn whiskey down from the hills. . . .

And in this automobile graveyard the boy moves from car to car, delighted to be naming, placing, experiencing, without the need to make anything sacred or even essentially important: from the Ford to an Essex to a blue Chevrolet to a Pierce-Arrow, "as in a wild stock-car race/In the parking lot of the dead. . . ." He hopes his girl friend will come to him from her father's farm "And . . . get back there/With no trace of me on her face"; when she does arrive and they embrace, their love-making takes place in the same "stalled, dreaming traffic" as the hunting of mice by blacksnakes, and beetles soon reclaim the field of the car's seat springs. The narrator leaves on his motorcycle, which is unglamorized, "Like the soul of the junk-yard/Restored, a bicycle fleshed/With power"—an earlier, more convincing version of the spectacular "May Day Sermon."

"The Poisoned Man" deals with the same situation explored in a later poem, "Snakebite" (from FALLING, in *Poems 1957–1967*) in which the victim of a poisonous snake is forced to cut himself with a knife in order to drain out the poison. In the earlier poem a formal, almost allegorical meaning evolves from the terrifying experience; the poet has a kind of vision, feeling that his heart's blood could flow "Unendingly out of the mountain. . . ." "Snakebite" reduces this visionary abstraction to "I have a problem with/My right foot and my life." Aging, the poet is urgently concerned with survival itself; he has called himself a poet of "survival." In another poem about snakes, "Goodbye to Serpents," Dickey and his son observe snakes in a Parisian zoo, and Dickey tries to concentrate on them as he never has in the past. His meditation is so complete that he seems to pass into them, seeing the human world of towers and churches and streets "All old, all cold with my gaze. . . ." and he longs to believe that he has somehow retained, at the same time, his own human presence, the human miracles of "self" and "love." But it is a failure:

> And I know I have not been moved
> Enough by the things I have moved through,
> And I have seen what I have seen
>
> Unchanged, hypnotized, and perceptive. . . .

Unchanged, hypnotized, and perceptive: a strange combination of words. But in the first of Dickey's "reincarnation" poems in a later volume, *Buckdancer's Choice*, he becomes a snake with head "poisonous and poised." Perhaps he is suggesting that the very awe of nature that mesmerized him has prevented his being "moved" humanly by the things he has experienced. The mystic's world of total acceptance has always contrasted sharply with the world of human suffering.

Helmets concludes with one of Dickey's most remarkable poems, the little-discussed "Drinking from a Helmet." The young narrator, in wartime, drinks from a helmet he picked up near his foxhole and sways "as if kissed in the brain," standing

> . . . as though I possessed
> A cool, trembling man
> Exactly my size, swallowed whole.

He throws down his own helmet and puts on the one he has found, an inheritance from the dead. Then he seems to "see" in his own brain the dying man's last thought—a memory of two boys, the soldier and his older brother in a setting of tremendous trees "That would grow on the sun if they could. . . ." Where "Approaching Prayer" traced what seemed to be the poet's conscious effort to imagine a dying hog's experience, "Drinking from a Helmet" seems sheer unwilled vision:

> I saw a fence
> And two boys facing each other,
> Quietly talking,
> Looking in at the gigantic redwoods,
> The rings in the trunks turning slowly

To raise up stupendous green.

. . . .

I would survive and go there,
Stepping off the train in a helmet
That held a man's last thought,
Which showed him his older brother
Showing him trees.
I would ride through all
California upon two wheels
Until I came to the white
Dirt road where they had been,
Hoping to meet his blond brother,
And to walk with him into the wood
Until we were lost,
Then take off the helmet
And tell him where I had stood,
What poured, what spilled, what swallowed:

And tell him I was the man.

The relationship between the two brothers is interesting, because it reverses the relationship of Dickey and his own older brother, who evidently died before Dickey was born. (See "The Underground Stream," "The String," and other poems in which the "tall cadaver" of the brother is summoned up by the poet, who believes himself conceived by his parents "out of grief" and brought to life "To replace the incredible child" who had died. The psychologically disastrous results of such a belief, if sincere, hardly need to be examined; one is always a "survivor," always "guilty," and always conscious of being an inferior substitute for some superior being.) Here, the younger brother has died and Dickey himself will go to visit the surviving older brother, as if, somehow, both he and his older brother were living and able to speak to each other; a life-affirming magic, in spite of a young soldier's death.

Monsters

After *Helmets* Dickey's poetry changes considerably. The colloquial tone and unserious rhythms of "Cherrylog Road" are used for deadly serious purposes as Dickey explores hypothetical selves and the possibility of values outside the human sphere. Where in an early poem like "The Performance" a mystical placidity rendered even a brutal execution into something observed, now most actions, most states of being, are examined bluntly, brutally, emotionally, as the poet subjects himself to raw life without the sustaining rituals of Being.

Dickey has many extraordinary poems, fusions of "genius" and "art," but the central poem of his work seems to be "The Firebombing," from *Buckdancer's Choice*. No reader, adjusted to the high, measured art of Dickey's first three volumes, can be ready for this particular poem; it is unforgettable, and seems to me an important achievement in our contemporary literature, a masterpiece that could only have been written by an American, and only by Dickey.

"The Firebombing" is an eight-page poem of irregular lines, abrupt transitions and leaps, stanzas of varying length, connected by suburban-surreal images, a terrifying visionary experience endured in a "well-stocked pantry." Its effort is to realize, to *feel*, what the poet did twenty years before as a participant in an "anti-morale raid" over Japan during the closing months of World War II. Its larger effort is to feel guilt and finally to feel anything. One of the epigraphs to the poem is from the Book of Job: "Or hast thou an arm like God?" This is Dickey's ironic self-directed question, for it is he, Dickey, the homeowner/killer, the Job/God, who has tried on the strength of vast powers and has not been able to survive them. Irony is something altogether new in Dickey:

> Homeowners unite.
>
> All families lie together, though some are burned alive.
> The others try to feel
> For them. Some can, it is often said.

The detachment is not godly, but despairing. Though he is now Job, he was at one time the "arm of God," and being both man and God is an impossibility. Dickey's earlier war poems always show him a survivor, grateful to survive, rather boyish and stunned by the mystery of a strange rightness beneath disorder; it seems to have taken him many years to get to this particular poem, though its meaning in his life must have been central. Now the survivor is also a killer. What of this, what of killing?—What is a release from the sin of killing? Confession, but, most of all, guilt; if the poet cannot make himself feel guilt even for the deaths of children, how will it be possible for him to feel anything human at all?—

> . . . some technical-minded stranger with my hands
> Is sitting in a glass treasure-hole of blue light,
> Having potential fire under the undeodorized arms
> Of his wings, on thin bomb-shackles,
> The "tear-drop-shaped" 300-gallon drop-tanks
> Filled with napalm and gasoline.

This stranger is, or was, Dickey himself, who flew one hundred combat missions through the South Pacific, the Philippines, and Okinawa and participated in B-29 raids over Japan; but he is only a memory now, an eerily aesthetic memory. He exists in the mind of a suburban husband and father, worrying about his weight and the half-paid-for pantry that is part of his homeowning and his present "treasure-hole":

> Where the lawn mower rests on its laurels
> Where the diet exists
> For my own good   where I try to drop
> Twenty years. . . .

So many years after the event, what remains? He is now a civilian, a citizen, an American who understands himself in ironic, secret charge of all the necessary trivia of unaesthetic life—the purchasing of golf carts and tennis shoes, new automobiles, Christmas decorations—that he knows as the "glue inspired/By love of country," the means by which the possibly atomistic or death-bound ego is held fast in its identity. Though the wonder remains, he is far from the moon-hypnotized, somnambulistic rhythms of the past; "The Firebombing" is what Dickey would call an "open poem," one in which a certain compulsiveness in the presentation of the subject matter precludes or makes peripheral an aesthetic response,[6] and the poet's own recollection of his action is mocked, if it must be assessed in stylized terms:

> As I sail artistically over
> The resort town followed by farms,
> Singing and twisting
> All the handles in heaven   kicking
> The small cattle off their feet
> In a red costly blast

Flinging jelly over the walls
As in a chemical war-
fare field demonstration.

Remembering this, he knows that "my hat should crawl on my head" and "the fat on my body should pale"—but one of the horrors of this bombing raid is that it has somehow destroyed a normal human response, as if the "arm of God" the pilot had assumed had also annihilated him. Having shown us so convincingly in his poetry how natural, how inevitable, is man's love for all things, Dickey now shows us what happens when man is forced to destroy, forced to step down into history and be an American ("and proud of it"). In so doing he enters a tragic dimension in which few poets indeed have operated. Could Whitman's affirmation hold out if he were forced to affirm not just the violence of others, but his own? If war is necessary, warriors are necessary; someone must sacrifice his cosmic love; and not only is the traditional life-praising song of the poet savagely mocked by his performance as a patriot in wartime, but the poet cannot even experience his own deeds, for he has acted as a machine inside a machine. In "The Firebombing" everything must remain remote and abstract, not experienced in any vital way. The Machine Age splits man irreparably from his instinctive need to see, to feel, to *know* through the senses. The Whitmanesque affirmation of man is difficult to sustain if the poet can see the objects of his love only from a great height, through an intellectual telescope. When Whitman feels he is "on the verge of a usual mistake" ("Song of Myself," stanza 38), it is only an emotional mistake; he could never have considered the nihilism of a self without emotions, in which his inventiveness could really attach itself to nothing because it could experience nothing.

After this dreamlike unleashing of "all American fire," the poet states flatly that *death will not be what it should*—a counterstatement, perhaps, to Schweitzer's *reverence for life*. This is the poet's unique vision:

Ah, under one's dark arms
Something strange-scented falls—when those on earth
Die, there is not even sound;
One is cool and enthralled in the cockpit,
Turned blue by the power of beauty,
In a pale treasure-hole of soft light

> Deep in aesthetic contemplation,
> Seeing the ponds catch fire
> And cast it through ring after ring
> Of land. . . .
>
> .   .   .   .
>
> It is this detachment,
> The honored aesthetic evil,
> The greatest sense of power in one's life,
> That must be shed in bars, or by whatever
> Means, by starvation
> Visions in well-stocked pantries. . . .

These "visions" will inspire in the poet wilder and wilder imaginings in his own creative life and an abandonment of the ego as "home-owner" in favor of the ego as "hunter" or "primitive." The mechanized State tempts one to an aesthetic evil, and so perhaps salvation may be found in a pre-aesthetic, prehistorical animality that will seize upon possible rites (the structural basis of *Deliverance*) in order to exorcise the despairing and suicidal violence of the animal self. Whether Dickey's themes are explorative rather than absolute, whether his work traces an autobiographical query or a record, the function of his poetry seems to be the demonstration of the failure of such a vision. And yet it is certainly tempting to take on the viciousness—and the innocence—of the animal, to take for our totems owls, snakes, foxes, wolverines, and to reject forever the possibilities of detachment and evil that are inherent in civilization.

Like Dostoyevsky, Dickey considers the helplessness of the *killer*. But, unlike Dostoyevsky, he cannot imagine a transformation of the killer into a higher form of himself: the mysterious process by which Raskolnikov grows and by which Smerdyakov can be seen as a rudimentary form of Father Zossima. But Dickey cannot operate through metaphor, as Dostoyevsky did, for he was the man, he did these things, *he* and no one else. Though his poetry charts a process of wonders, a changing of selves, finally he is only himself, a particular man, trapped in a finite and aging body with memories that belong to him and not to the rest of us, not to any liberalized concept of the guilt we all "share." (Like Marcuse, Dickey could probably feel no more than scorn for the "repressive tolerance" of some aspects of liberalism.) If made general and universal, in order to be shared, is guilt itself not made an aesthetic event?—a luxury?—a perversion?

But the narrator of the poem cannot concern himself with such abstractions:

> All this, and I am still hungry,
> Still twenty years overweight, still unable
> To get down there or see
> What really happened.
>
> . . . .
>   . . . It is that I can imagine
> At the threshold nothing
> With its ears crackling off
> Like powdery leaves,
> Nothing with children of ashes, nothing not
> Amiable, gentle, well-meaning. . . .

A poetry of Being can move to perfect resolutions, but this poetry of anguished Becoming cannot. ("Some can, it is often said," Dickey has remarked, ironically and sadly.) The narrative and confessional elements of "The Firebombing" demand a totally different aesthetic: the aesthetic-denying open form. No reconciliation of opposites is possible here because the poet cannot reconcile himself to his earlier self. And so what of "Absolution? Sentence?" These do not matter for "The thing itself is in that."

"The Firebombing" is central to an understanding of Dickey's work. It could not have been prophesied on the basis of the earlier, Roethke-inspired poems; but once it appears, unsuppressed, it is so powerful an illumination that it helps to explain a great deal that might remain mysterious and puzzling. *Buckdancer's Choice*, "Falling," and, above all, *The Eye-Beaters* deal with mortality, decay, disease, perhaps attributable in part to the poet's actual aging, but only in part, for the descent into a physically combative and increasingly unaesthetic world is not the usual pattern our finest poets follow, as both Roethke and Yeats, and other poets of the "Second Birth," suggest. Yet the emphasis Dickey places upon mortality, his self-consciousness about it, is a motif that begins to appear even in his literary criticism. How is it possible that the man who believes in nature—in natural processes—should feel uneasy about the natural process of aging? It is a paradox in Hemingway also, but perhaps it is to be understood in Rilke's terms: our fear is not of death, but of life unlived. In an introduction to Paul Carroll's *The Young American Poets* (Chicago, 1968), Dickey makes a statement that totally contradicts the contemplative, balanced criticism of *The Suspect in Poetry* of only four years previous:

> The aging process almost always brings to the poet the secret conviction that he has settled for far too little. . . . The nearer he gets to his end the more he yearns for the caves: for a wild, shaggy, all-out, all-involving way of speaking where language and he (or, now, someone: some new poet) engage each other at primitive levels, on ground where the issues are not those of literary fashion but are quite literally those of life and death. All his lifelong struggle with "craft" seems a tragic and ludicrous waste of time. . . .
>
> (p. 7)

One would imagine, from such remarks, that the speaker is far older than forty-five; "the nearer he gets to his end . . ." is a visionary statement that might be comprehensible in the Yeats of *Last Poems*, but astonishing in a poet who is the same age as the Yeats of *The Green Helmet*. But if a denial of "craft" (or civilization) is needed in order to release spontaneous energy, then one can see why, for Dickey, it must be attempted.

Entropy

Buckdancer's Choice received the National Book Award in 1965, and in 1967 Dickey put together his *Poems 1957–1967* for Wesleyan University Press. The *Poems* do not observe strict chronological order, however, beginning with the demonic "May Day Sermon to the Women of Gilmer County, Georgia, by a Woman Preacher Leaving the Baptist Church," one of Dickey's most flamboyant poems. Clearly, Dickey does not want the reader to enter the world of *Into the Stone* with the innocence he himself had entered it; that celebration of forms is all but outshouted by the eleven-page sermon, which is about violence done to and by a young girl in Georgia, and about her escape with her motorcycle-riding lover, "stoned out of their minds on the white/Lightning of fog"—

> singing   the saddlebags full of her clothes
> Flying   snagging   shoes hurling away   stockings grabbed-off
> Unwinding and furling on twigs: all we know   all we could follow

Them by was her underwear　was stocking after stocking where it tore
Away, and a long slip stretched on a thorn　all these few gave
Out. Children, you know it: that place was where they took
Off into the air　died　disappeared　entered my mouth your mind

It is an incredible achievement, with the intonations of a mad, inspired sermon, the flesh elevated beyond the spirit, but both elevated into myth. It is a myth that transforms everything into it: everything turns into everything else, through passion. The intellect exercises very little control in this "wild, shaggy, all-out, all-involving" work, and though Dickey has expressed doubt over the value of Allen Ginsberg's poetry,[7] one is forced to think of certain works of Ginsberg's and of how, under ether sniffing or morphine injection, Ginsberg wrote all of *Ankor Wat* and that extravaganza "Aether," in which a preaching voice proclaims certain truths to us: "we are the sweeping of the moon/we're what's *left over* from perfection"—"(my) Madness is intelligible reactions to/Unintelligible phenomena"—
　　And—

　　　　What *can* be possible
　　　　in a minor universe
　　　　in which you can see
　　　　God by sniffing the
　　　　gas in a cotton?

　　　　　　　　　　　　　　("Aether," in *Reality Sandwiches*)

　　Dickey is much more violent, more heartless than Ginsberg, of course, since he is driven by energies more archaic than is Ginsberg, who is a philosopher with a respect for the syntax of the imagination if not of superficial grammar; the "May Day Sermon" is at once revenge for and repetition of the helplessness of the bomber pilot, a mythic annihilation of a punishing, near-invisible father, and an escape off into space, the girl's clothing cast off behind her like the airline stewardess' clothing in "Falling." In all the exuberant spurts of language there is violence, but especially here:

　　And she comes down　putting her back into
　　The hatchet　often　often　he is brought down　laid out
　　Lashing　smoking　sucking wind: Children, each year at this time
　　A girl will tend to take an ice pick in both hands　a long pine
　　Needle　will hover　hover: Children, each year at this time

> Things happen quickly   and it is easy for a needle to pass
> Through the eye of a man bound for Heaven   she leaves it naked goes
> Without further sin through the house

After countless readings, "May Day Sermon" still has the power to shock: consider the "needle-eye-Heaven" joke. The maniacal repetitions make one wince ("get up . . . up in your socks and rise"), and the Dylan Thomas-surreal touches sometimes seem forced ("Dancing with God in a mule's eye"), but the poem's shrieking transmutation of murder, nakedness, eroticism, fertility, and poetry into a single event has an irresistible strength: "everything is more *more* MORE." Nature itself becomes active in the process of transmutation as even "peanuts and beans exchange/Shells in joy," and in a poetic sleight of hand reminiscent of Thomas's *Ballad of the Long-Legged Bait* at its apocalyptic conclusion, "the barn falls in/Like Jericho." The countryside itself is speaking through the woman preacher "as beasts speak to themselves/Of holiness learned in the barn." It is mysticism, but existential and ribald, noisy, filled with the humming of gnats and strange prophecies:

> Each May you will crouch like a sawhorse to make yourself
> More here   you will be cow chips   chicken croaking . . .
> . . . .
>   and every last one of you will groan
> Like nails barely holding   and your hair be full of the gray
> Glints of stump chains.   Children, each year at this time you will have
> Back-pain, but also heaven

In "May Day Sermon" Dickey creates a patchwork of images that go beyond the "not wholly sane" images of "Chenille."

However, *Buckdancer's Choice* contains several very personal and moving poems dealing with mortality, the title poem and "Angina" (which deal with Dickey's mother, an invalid "dying of breathless angina"), "Them, Crying," "The Escape," and one that reasserts the mystical possibility of transcending death, its certainties expressed in a steady three-beat line:

> All ages of mankind unite
> Where it is dark enough.
> . . . .
> All creatures tumbled together

86

Get back in their wildest arms
No single thing but each other. . . .

("The Common Grave")

But the most passionate poems are counterstatements concerned with developing images adequate to express horror; in "Pursuit from Under" the poet summons up a terrifying image that does not have its place in his own experience, or even in his probable experience, but is a conscious re-creation of a memory. He is standing in a meadow, in August, and imagines he hears the "bark of seals" and feels "the cold of a personal ice age. . . ." Then he recalls having once read an account of Arctic explorers who died of starvation and whose journal contained a single entry of unforgettable horror:

. . . under the ice,

The killer whale darts and distorts,
Cut down by the flawing glass

To a weasel's shadow,
And when, through his ceiling, he sees
Anything darker than snow
He falls away
. . . .
To gather more and more force

. . . .
. . . then charges
Straight up, looms up at the ice and smashes
Into it with his forehead. . . .

And so the killer whale pursues the poet, even in this familiar meadow in the South, and he thinks of "how the downed dead pursue us"—"not only in the snow/But in the family field." It is interesting to note that Norman Mailer's nihilistic and very deliberately "literary" novel *Why Are We in Vietnam?* also transports its protagonist/victim to the Arctic in order to allow him a vision of God-as-beast; this "vision" is then imposed upon all of American (universal?) experience and can allow for no possibilities of transcendence. If God is a beast (as Dickey concludes in "The Eye-Beaters"), then the beast is God, and one must either acquiesce to Him and experience the helplessness of terror in an ordinary southern meadow, or imitate Him, taking on some of His powers. But, increasingly, the poet reaches out beyond his own geographical and

87

historical territory to appropriate this vision. It demands a distortion or a rejection of naturalistic life; at times, as he admits, a kind of necessary theatricality, as he explains in *Self-Interviews* why hunting is so important to him: ". . . the main thing is to re-enter the cycle of the man who hunts for his food. Now this may be playacting at being a primitive man, but it's better than not having any rapport with the animal at all . . . I have a great sense of renewal when I am able to go into the woods and hunt with a bow and arrow, to enter into the animal's world in this way." And, in *Deliverance*, the experience of "renewal" or deliverance itself is stimulated by a hunt for other men; simple animals are no longer enough, and the whole of the novel is constructed around those several intensely dramatic moments in which the narrator sights his target—a human and usually forbidden target—and kills him with an arrow from his powerful bow. The arrow is at least real; the napalm and gasoline bomb are not, since they are dropped upon abstractions. And, too, the necessary intimacy of the besieged men in *Deliverance* approximates a primitive brotherliness, excluding the confusion that women bring to a world of simple, clear, direct actions. For women, while mysterious and unfathomable, are also "civilization."

But if women are objects, goddess objects, they too can be assimilated into the mystique of primitive power-worship. One of the most striking poems in all of Dickey's work is "The Fiend," which magically transforms a voyeur/lover into a tree, into an omnipotent observer, back into a voyeur again, while throughout he is the poet who loves and desires and despairs of truly knowing his subject; the poem is a long, hushed, reverential overture to murder. Yet the equation of the voyeur with the poet is obvious, and the poem concludes ominously by remarking how "the light/Of a hundred favored windows" has "gone wrong somewhere in his glasses. . . ." Dickey is remarkably honest in acknowledging the value he puts upon his own fantasies, in contrast to the less interesting world of reality. What is important is *his* imaginative creation, *his* powers of seeing. In praise of what a Jungian would call the "anima," Dickey has said in *Sorties* that "poor mortal perishable women are as dust before these powerful and sensual creatures of the depths of one's being" (p. 4). A dangerous overestimation of the individual's self-sufficiency, one might think, especially since there is always the possibility of that interior light going "wrong some-where in his glasses."

In fact, in Dickey's later poems eyesight becomes crucial, aligned with the mysterious grace of masculinity itself. When one's vision begins to weaken, there is an immediate danger of loss of control; conversely, "sight" itself can be rejected, denied, as a prelude to glorious savagery. Or the denial of vision can facilitate a more formal, sinister betrayal, as Dickey imagines himself as, si-multaneously, a slave owner on a southern plantation and the white father of an illegitimate black son and the father-who-denies-his-son, a master driven to madness by his role as an owner, in the poem "Slave Quarters." Dickey's question concerns itself with many forms of paternal betrayal, a betrayal of the eyes of others:

> What it is to look once a day
> Into an only
> Son's brown, waiting, wholly possessed
> Amazing eye, and not
> Acknowledge, but own. . . .

How take on the guilt . . . ? is the poem's central question.

In the section FALLING in *Poems 1957–1967,* Dickey explores further extensions of life, beginning with "Reincarnation (II)," in which the poet has taken on the form of a bird. His first reincarna-tion was into a snake, which we leave waiting in an old wheel not for food but for the first man to walk by—minute by minute the head of the snake becoming "more poisonous and poised." But as a bird the poet undergoes a long, eerie, metaphysical flight that takes him out of mortality altogether—

> to be dead
> In one life is to enter
> Another   to break out   to rise above   the clouds

But "Reincarnation (II)" is extremely abstract and does not seem to have engaged the poet's imaginative energies as deeply as "Reincar-nation (I)" of *Buckdancer's Choice.* It is balanced by the long "Falling," an astonishing poetic feat that dramatizes the accidental fall of an airline stewardess from a plane to her death in a corn field. "The greatest thing that ever came to Kansas" undergoes a number of swift metamorphoses—owl, hawk, goddess—stripping herself naked as she falls. She imagines the possibility of falling into water, turning her fall into a dive so that she can "come out healthily dripping/And be handed a Coca-Cola," but ultimately she is helpless to save herself; she is a human being, not a bird like the spiritual power of "Reincarnation (II)," and she comes to know how "the body will assume without effort any position/Except the one that will sustain it   enable it to rise live/Not die." She dies, "driven well into the image of her body," inexplicable and unquestionable, and her clothes begin to come down all over Kansas; a kind of mortal goddess, given as much immortality by this strange poem as poetry is capable of giving its subjects.

The starkly confessional poem "Adultery" tells of the poet's need for life-affirming moments, though they are furtive and evidently depend upon a belief that the guilt caused by an act of adultery is magical—"We have done it again   we are/Still living." The poem's subject is really not adultery or any exploration of the connections between people; it is about the desperate need to prove that life is still possible. *We are still living:* that guilty, triumphant cry. In this poem and several others, Dickey seems to share Norman Mailer's sentiment that sex would be meaningless if divorced from "guilt." What role does the woman play in this male scenario? She is evidently real enough, since she is driven to tears by the impossibility of the adulterous situation; but in a more important sense she does not really exist, for she is one of those "poor mortal perishable women" temporarily illuminated by the man's anima-projection, and she is "as dust" compared to the fantasy that arises from the depths of the lover's being. Descartes' *I doubt, hence I think; I think, hence I am* has become, for those who despair of the Cartesian logic of salvation, *I love, hence I exist; I am loved, hence I must exist.* . . .

With Dickey this fear is closely related to the fundamental helplessness he feels as a man trapped in a puzzling technological civilization he cannot totally comprehend. Even the passionate love of women and the guilt of adultery will not be sufficient, ultimately, to convince the poet that he will continue to exist. He identifies with the wolverine, that "small, filthy, unwinged" creature whose species is in danger of extinction, in the poem "For the Last Wolverine." The wolverine is an animal capable of "mindless rage," enslaved by the "glutton's internal fire," but Dickey recognizes a kinship with it in the creature's hopeless desire to "eat/The world. . . ."

Yet, for all its bloodthirsty frenzy, the wolverine is in danger of dying out. It is a "nonsurvivor" after all. The poet's mystical identification with this beast is, paradoxically, an identification with death, and death driven, indeed, is the impulse behind his musing: "How much the timid poem needs/The mindless explosion of your rage. . . ." Like Sylvia Plath and innumerable others, the poet imagines a division between himself as a human being and the rest of the world—the universe itself—symbolized by the fact that his consciousness allows him to see and to judge his position, while the rest of nature is more or less mute. It is doubtful, incidentally, that nature is really so mute, so unintelligent, as alienated personalities seem to think; it is certainly doubtful that the human ego, the "I," is in any significant way isolated from the vast, living totality of which it is a part. However, granted for the moment that the poet is "timid" when he compares himself to the most vicious of animals, it is still questionable whether such viciousness, such "mindless explosion" of rage, is superior to the poem, to the human activity of creating and organizing language in a coherent, original structure. The prayer of the poem is very moving, but it is not the wolverine's consciousness that is speaking to us: "Lord, let me die   but not die/ Out."

Dickey has dramatized from the inside the terrors of the personality that fears it may not be immortal after all; its control of itself and of other people and of the environment seems to be more and more illusory, fading, failing. "Entropy"—a much-used and misused term—refers to the phenomenon of energy loss and increasing disorder as a system begins to falter, and is always a threat, a terror, to those who assume that the system to which they belong or which they have themselves organized was meant to be infinite. There is no space here to consider the psychological reasons for the shift from man's assumption of immortality as an abstraction (the "immortal" soul was expected to survive, but not the "mortal" man—the personality or ego) to his frantic and futile hope for immortality in the flesh. There are cultural, political, economic reasons, certainly, but they cannot entirely account for the naïveté of the wish: *I want to live forever.* Because this wish is so extraordinarily naïve, even childish, it is never allowed in that form into the consciousness of most intelligent people. When it emerges, it is always disguised. It sometimes takes the form of a vague, disappointed despair; or rage without any appropriate object; or a hopeless and even sentimental envy of those human beings (or animals) who strike the despairing one as too stupid to know how unhappy they should be. The excessive admiration of animals and birds and other manifestations of "unconscious" nature is, in some people, a screen for their own self-loathing. They are in "hell" because the activity of their consciousness is mainly self-concerned, self-questioning, self-doubting. The rest of the world, however, seems quite content. As entropy is irrationally feared by some, it is as irrationally welcomed by others. Disorganization—chaos—the "mindless explosion" of repressed rage: all are welcomed, mistaken for a liberating of the deepest soul.

Mysticism: Evolution, Dissolution

Mysticism is generally considered in the light of its highest religious and spiritual achievements. Most literature on the subject deals exclusively with saintly human beings, some of whom have experienced not only a powerful emotional enlightenment but an intellectual enlightenment as well. These mystics are the ones who have, in a sense, created our world: it is unnecessary to mention their names, since in a way those of us who live now have always lived, unconsciously, involuntarily, within the scope of their imaginations—as a writer lives, when he is writing, within the vast but finite universe of his language. There is an existence beyond that, surely; but he cannot quite imagine it. That I exist at this moment— that I am a writer, a woman, a surviving human being—has very little to do with accident, but is a direct, though remote, consequence of someone's thinking: *Let us value life. Let us enhance life. Let us imagine a New World, a democracy.* . . . It is not true, as Auden so famously stated, that poetry makes nothing happen. On the contrary, poetry, or the poetic imagination, has made everything happen.

Yet "mysticism" can swing in other directions. Essentially, it is a loss of "ego," but it may result in a loss of "ego control" as well. A mysterious, unfathomable revolution seems to be taking place in our civilization, and like all upheavals in history it is neither knowable nor governable; like inexplicable branchings in the flow of life, in evolution, it goes its way quite apart from the wishes of entire species, let alone individuals. However, it seems to be characterized by loss of ego, by experiences of transcendence among more and more people, especially younger people. Yet one brings to that other world of mysticism only the equipment, the conscious moral intelligence, that one has developed through the activities of the ego: the experience of oneness with the divine, the knowledge of *That Art Thou*, gives us in its benevolent expression Jesus Christ, Gautama Buddha, and other founders of great religions, and in its malignant and grotesque expression a Hitler, a Stalin, a Charles Manson. The most important study of this subject still remains William James's *Varieties of Religious Experience*, since it was written by a man who did experience a sense of his ego's dissolution but who had not a ready-made religious structure into which he might leap. The mystic breaks free of human codes of morality, of all restraints, of "civilization," of normality itself. Useless to argue with him, for he *knows*. When D. H. Lawrence declares that he is allied with the sun and not with men, he is speaking out of the certainty of his religious knowledge that he *is* a form of energy and derives his finite being only from a higher, external form of energy. Literary critics may concern themselves with metaphors, symbols, and allusion, but most writers are writing out of their deepest experience; the playful organization of words into structures, the aesthetic impulse, is always a secondary activity. And so is social action. And so is that social being, the "ego."

But when the conscious ego has despaired of discovering values in the social world or in the world of spirit, the dissolution of that ego will probably not result in a higher wisdom, in an elevation of the moral sense so passionately required for survival. Instead, the mystic may plunge into his own ancestral past, into his own "animal" nature. This is especially tempting in an era characterized by superficiality, bad thinking, and outright inhumanity, for these abnormalities are considered "normal" and therefore "human."

Something must be valued—some god must be worshiped. Where is he? Where is it? *Who has experienced him?*

So it is not surprising that many people value the "animal" over the "human," as if animals were not extraordinarily intelligent in their own contexts. In any case animals are not valued for what they are, but for their evidently uncivilized qualities; perhaps even for their cunning and savagery, their "innocence." Should it be argued that animals live and die within strict codes of behavior (which in our species is "morality"), the romantic will not listen; he is certain that *his* animals are free, wild, even immortal in their own way. They always do all the things he has wished to do, but has not dared. They are not so obviously and embarrassingly his own creation as a cartoonist's animals are his, but they share, often with the female sex, that special numinous grace of being the image bearers of men. If it is a question of mere survival, the ideal will be a predator who cannot not survive, because he demands so little of his environment. Ted Hughes's *Crow* poems, for instance, are concerned with a minimal consciousness that is always human, though reduced to beak and claws and uncanny keenness of vision. But the poems are, upon examination, oddly abstract, even rhetorical and argumentative; they have very little of the slashing emotional immediacy of Dickey's best poems. What to Ted Hughes is an allegorical possibility is for Dickey an existential fact.

As the poet wakes from his dream of "stone," enters the turbulent contests of "flesh," he will no longer be able, even, to "sail artistically over" the wars of his civilization. He must participate in them as a man; if they will not come to him, he must seek them out.

The horror of Dickey's novel *Deliverance* grows out of its ordinary, suburban framework, the assimilation of brutal events by ordinary men; not near-Biblical figures like Crow, or men trapped in a distant and hostile world, but four middle-aged, middle-class men who want to canoe along a dangerous but attractive river not far from their homes. The novel is about our deep, instinctive needs to get back to nature, to establish some kind of rapport with primitive energies, but it is also about the need of some men to do violence, to be delivered out of their banal lives by a violence so irreparable that it can never be confessed. It is a fantasy of a highly civilized and

affluent society, which imagines physical violence to be transforming in a mystical—and therefore permanent—sense, a society
in which rites of initiation no longer exist. This society asks its men:
How do you know you are men? But there is no answer except in
terms of an earlier society, where the male is distinguished from the
female, so far as behavior is concerned, by his physical strength and
his willingnes to risk life. But killing other men can be made into a
ritual, a proof of one's manhood; *Deliverance* is about this ritual. It
is like Mailer's short novel *Why Are We in Vietnam?* in its consideration of homosexuality, though for Mailer homosexuality
evokes terror and for Dickey it evokes loathing. The boys in the
Mailer novel tremble on the verge of becoming lovers in their Arctic
camp, but they draw back from each other, terrified, and are then
given tremendous energies as "killer brothers" now united to go
fight the war in Vietnam. Both novels demonstrate not any extraordinary fear of homosexuality but, what is more disturbing, a fear of
affection. Dickey has so created his backwoods degenerates as to be
beyond all human sympathy, so that most readers are compelled to
become "killers" along with the narrator. The murder of the
homosexual threat, whether an exterior force or an inner impulse,
results in an apparent increase in animal spirits and appetite, and the
narrator is able to return to civilization and to his wife, a man with a
profound secret, in touch with an illicit, demonic mystery, delivered. Violence has been his salvation—his deliverance from ordinary life.

*The Eye-Beaters, Blood, Victory, Madness, Buckhead and
Mercy* is as crammed and various as its title suggests. A few poems
are bluntly confessional, the "Apollo" poem is linked to a historic
event, and all are in the same tone of musing, sometimes cynical,
sometimes tender contemplation. The volume ends with "Turning
Away: Variations on Estrangement," a complex, abstract work of
philosophical inquiry; but most of its poems are linked firmly to
domestic things, and even the difficult subjects of disease and death
are made "livable," in Dickey's words.

The book is disturbing because it asks so many questions but
refuses to answer them. It is filled with questions: *What did I say?
Or do? Am I still drunk? Who is this woman? Where? Can you see
me? Can the five fingers/Of the hand still show against/anything?*

Have they come for us? It is also disturbing because of its attitude toward certain subjects: men suffering from diabetes and cancer are not treated solemnly, and in Dickey's fantasy of dying from a heart attack (or love) he and the nurse/prostitute flicker downward together "Like television   like Arthur Godfrey's face/Coming on   huge   happy." The book's seventeen poems are of widely varying length and seem to make up a dialogue or combat among their various themes, as if the poet were entering into a battle with aspects of his soul—the word "battle" used deliberately here, because Dickey declares in "Turning Away" how it is necessary to turn "From an old peaceful love/To a helmet of silent war/Against the universe."

Many of the poems are about diseased emotions or diseased forms of hope, such as the futility of seeking out one's youth by "going home" decades later; but several deal with specific disorders—"Diabetes," "The Cancer Match," "Madness," and "The Eye-Beaters" (which is about both blindness and insanity). "Diabetes" is a brutally frank, sardonic confessional poem in two parts which begins with the poet's gigantic thirst: "One night I thirsted like a prince/Then like a king/Then like an empire   like a world/On fire." But the thirst is not a thirst for life, it is not a metaphor; it is clinically real. After the illness is diagnosed, the poet sees sugar as "gangrene in white," and his routine of exercise is attended by an ironic counting, a parody of his earlier poetic themes:

> Each time the barbell
> Rose   each time a foot fell
> Jogging, it counted itself
> One death   two death   three death and resurrection
> For a little while. Not bad! . . .

He will endure a "livable death," scaled down and presided over by a nice young physician. The second half of the poem, "Under Buzzards," has Dickey imagining in heavy summer the "birds of death" attracted by the "rotten, nervous sweetness" of his blood, the "city sugar" of his life. In a final, defiant gesture, the poet deliberately summons the birds of death, but he does it in a curiously unheroic way, by taking a forbidden drink of beer:

> Red sugar of my eyeballs
> Feels them [the buzzards] turn blindly

       In the fire   rising   turning   turning
         Back to Hogback Ridge, and it is all
    Delicious, brother: my body is turning   is flashing unbalanced
    Sweetness everywhere, and I am calling my birds.

Characteristic of this volume is a repeated use of terms to link the
reader with the poet: "my friend," "brother," "companion," "my
son," "you." The whole of "Venom" is a kind of prayer, the poet
and his listener joined as brothers who must "turn the poison/
Round," back on itself, the venom that comes "from the head" of
man and corrupts his life blood. "Madness" is about a domestic dog
that contracts rabies and must be killed, but it is also a call for
"Help   help   madness   help."
    Balancing the poems of disease are several about Dickey's sons
and the *Life*-commissioned double poem, "Apollo," placed near the
physical center of the magazine and divided by a black page—a
symbol of the black featureless depths of space in which our planet,
"the blue planet steeped in its dream," has a minute existence. The
poems to or about Dickey's sons are all excellent, though there is an
air of sorrow about them. "The Lord in the Air" is prefaced by a
quotation from Blake: ". . . If the spectator could . . . make a friend
& companion of one of these Images of wonder . . . then would he
meet the Lord in the air & . . . be happy." Dickey seems to be re-
imagining an earlier role of his own as he describes a son's performance with a crow whistle, so deceiving the crows that they come to
him from miles away, "meeting the Lord/Of their stolen voice in the
air." The crows have but one word, a syllable that means everything
to them, and in gaining control of it the boy becomes a kind of poet.
A "new/Power over birds and beasts" has been achieved by man,
but "not for betrayal, or to call/Up death or desire, but only to give"
a unique tone "never struck in the egg." *O Chris come in, drop off
now* is the language Dickey allots to himself; magic has become the
property of his boy.
    "Messages" deals with images of life (butterflies with "ragged,
brave wings")—and death (a cow's skeleton), and matches the
father's protectiveness with his wisdom, which his sleeping son
cannot yet be told: that life is a gamble, a play "in bones and in wings
and in light." The poem is also about the necessity of a father's
surrendering his son to life—"to the sea"—with the reminder that

human love exists in its own world, unchallenged by the nihilistic depths of the ocean or the speechless primitive world. The love evident in the "message" poems is totally lacking in the disease poems, as if the speakers were angrily fighting self-pity; "The Cancer Match" imagines cancer and whiskey fighting together, in the drunken mind of a dying man who has "cancer and whiskey/In a lovely relation": "I watch them struggle/All around the room, inside and out/Of the house, as they battle/Near the mailbox. . . ." No dignity here, even in dying; the poem refuses to mourn the body's decay.

Addressing himself to the Apollo moon shot, Dickey synthe-sizes the diverse emotions of awe, suspicion, cynicism, and acquies-cence; like Mailer in *Of a Fire on the Moon*, he cannot help but wonder if some catastrophe will be unleashed ("Will the moon-plague kill our children . . .?"), and just as Mailer contemplated photographs of the moon's surface and thought of Cézanne, Dickey, in the imagined consciousness of one of the moon explorers, hears lines from Gray's Elegy "helplessly coming/From my heart. . . ." A triumph of technology is seen in terms of aesthetic triumphs of the past. Both men express doubt about the future, but both accept its inevitable direction, though Dickey is characteris-tically more emotionally involved:

> My eyes blind
> With unreachable tears   my breath goes all over
> Me and cannot escape. . . .
> Our clothes embrace we cannot touch we cannot
> Kneel. We stare into the moon
> dust, the earth-blazing ground. We laugh, with the beautiful craze
> Of static. We bend, we pick up stones.

The future is explorable, however, only through one's imagi-native identification with other men. The most powerful poems in *The Eye-Beaters* are those that refuse to deal with the future at all and explore old obsessions with the past. The pathetic double poem "Going Home" takes the poet ("the Keeper") back to his own lost childhood, where he encounters his Old Self like a "younger brother, like a son," in a confusion of homes, times, places, rooms that live "only/In my head." His childhood is distant from the adulthood he now inhabits, in which he is a Keeper of rooms "growing intolerable," through which he walks like a stranger, "as though I belonged there." The riddle of *Identities! Identities!* the younger Dickey puzzled over (in the poem "Mangham" of *Buckdancer's Choice*) still taunts him, as past and present contend, and the Keeper fears he will go mad with his questions:

> And tell me for the Lord God
> 's sake, where are all our old
> Dogs?
>   Home?
>   Which way is that?
> Is it this vacant lot? . . .

In a final admission of defeat, the "mad, weeping Keeper" realizes that he cannot keep anything alive: none of his rooms, his people, his past, his youth, himself. Yet he cannot let them die either, and he will call them "for a little while, sons." In "Looking for the Buckhead Boys," a poem on the verge of turning into a short story, the futile search for one's youth in the past is given a specific location, and the poet returns to his home town to look for his old friends; if he can find one of them, just one, he believes his youth will once again "walk/Inside me like a king." But his friends are gone, or changed, or paralyzed or, like Charlie Gates at the filling station, not really the person for whom the poet has a secret "that has to be put in code." The poem ends with a flat anticlimactic imperative: "Fill 'er up, Charlie." Encountering one's past, in the form of an old friend, underscores the impossibility of "keeping" the past.

"The Eye-Beaters" is an extravagant, curious fantasy, supposedly set in a home for children in Indiana. In this home some children have gone blind, evidently since admission; not just blind, but mad, so that their arms must be tied at their sides to prevent their beating their eyeballs in order to stimulate the optic nerves. By no naturalistic set of facts can one determine how this "home" can be real, and so the reader concludes that the entire poem is an explorative fantasy, like "The Owl King," which dealt with a child's blindness. The blindness of the children and their pathetic response to it is so distressing that the Visitor must create a fiction in order to save himself from madness. He tries to imagine what they see:

> Lord, when they slug
> Their blue cheeks blacker, can it be that they do not see the wings
> And green of insects   or the therapist suffering kindly   but
>   a tribal light old
> Enough to be seen without sight?

The vision he imagines for them is prehistoric; a caveman artist, "Bestial, working like God," is drawing beasts on a cave wall: deer, antelope, elk, ibex, quagga, rhinoceros of wool-gathering smoke, cave bear, mammoth, "beings that appear/Only in the memory of caves." The niches of the children's middle brain, "where the race is young," are filled not with images of the Virgin but with squat shapes of the Mother or with the bloody hand print on the stone "where God gropes like a man" and where the artist "hunts and slashes" his wounded game. Then the Visitor's rational, skeptical nature argues with him, addressing him as "Stranger"; perhaps the children want to smash their eyes in order to see nothing, and the Visitor's invention of the cave-man artist is an expression of his own blindness, his hope for magic that might "re-invent the vision of the race." He admits his desire to believe that the world calls out for art, for the magical life-renewal of art, and not for the blankness of nothing save physical pain. Otherwise it is possible that he will go mad. Otherwise what can he value in his own poetry? The artist must be a therapist to the race, and not simply to himself; but Dickey concludes this complex poem by acquiescing to his own self-defined "fiction," a kind of lie that enables him to identify himself with the cave-man artist and to escape the deadening truths of his Reason by choosing "madness,/Perversity." He projects himself back into a dim racial memory, a hideous vision that excludes history. No salvation, except by way of a total surrender to the irrational and uninventive:

>   Beast, get in
> My way. Your body opens onto the plain. Deer, take me into your life-
> lined form. I merge, I pass beyond in secret   in perversity and the sheer
> Despair of invention   my double-clear bifocals off   my reason gone
> Like eyes. Therapist, farewell at the living end. Give me my spear.

The prayer, addressed to a "Beast," necessarily involves the poet in a transformation downward, into a kind of human beast whose "despair of invention" forces him to inarticulate, violent action. It is possible that the conclusion is an ambiguous one—the artist denying his art through a self-conscious work of art—or, as Raymond Smith has seen it, in an essay called "The Poetic Faith of James Dickey,"[8] the poet rejecting any art-for-art's-sake aesthetic. However, the final words of the poem seem the expression of a suicidal loss of faith in anything but action, and that action primitive and bloody.

Dickey had diagnosed this action as "Perversity," and the poem has a passionate, religious feel about it, the testament of a loss of faith in one religion (Art) and the tentative commitment to another (the "Beast"). This is the mystical leap that Dickey's imagination has yearned for, the defiance of his higher, artistic, moral self, experienced in middle age as a banality from which he must—somehow—be delivered.

The forms of Dickey's "heroism" are anachronistic, perhaps, but his despair may be prophetic.

In these later poems, the poems of "flesh," there is a dramatic ferocity that goes beyond even the shimmering walls of words he created for "Falling" and "May Day Sermon." Dickey is there, inside the poem; reading it, we are inside his head. He is willing to tell everything, anything; he is willing to become transparent, in war now against his own exquisite sensibility. *Help   help   madness   help:* the book's shameless cry.

Society did not always shy away from the self-expression of its most sensitive and eccentric members. Much has been written about the relationship of so-called primitive people with their priests and shamans: these societies benefited from their leaders' ecstasies and bizarre revelations and did not destroy them as heretics or castrate them by interpreting their visions as "only poetry." What value can the visionary give to his own experience if, returning to the world with it, he is at the very most congratulated for having invented some fascinating, original metaphors? Dickey, so disturbing to many of us, must be seen in a larger context, as a kind of "shaman," a man necessarily at war with his civilization because that civilization will not, cannot, understand what he is saying. Mircea Eliade defines the shaman as a "specialist in ecstasy": traditionally, he excites himself into a frenzy, enters a trancelike state, and receives the power of understanding and imitating the language of birds and animals. He is not a "normal" personality, at least in these times. He participates in what is believed to be divine.

If the shaman, or the man with similar magical powers, has no social structure in which to interpret himself, and if he is obviously not normal in the restrictive sense of that word, his instincts will lead him into a rebellion against that world; at his most serene, he can manage a cynical compromise with it. Irony can be a genteel form of savagery, no less savage than physical brutality. In some intellectuals, irony is the expression of disappointed hopes; in others, it is a substitute for violence. It *is* violent. If the release offered by words no longer satisfies the intense need of the sufferer, he will certainly fall into despair, estrangement. Hence a preoccupation, in Dickey, with physical risk, a courting of the primitive in art and in life (in carefully restricted areas, of course), and a frantic, even masochistic need to continually test and "prove" himself.[9] The ritual of hunting cannot ultimately work, because it is so obviously a "ritual"—a game—and bears no relationship at all to what hunting was, and is, to people who must hunt for their food. It is just another organized adventure, another "timid poem." Consciousness is split on a number of levels: the sensual keenness inspired by adultery and guilt, the excitement inspired by near death, the mindless rage of the beast who fears extinction, the plight of the overweight suburban homeowner, the husband, the father, the poet . . . and yet the truest self seems somehow detached, uninvolved. "Turning Away," the last poem in *The Eye-Beaters*, deals with aspects of estrangement not simply in terms of marriage but in terms of the self, which hopes to see "Later, much later on" how it may make sense—perhaps as a fictional creation, in a book.

If regression cannot be justified by calling it "ritual"—hunting, fighting, excessively brutal sports—it must be abandoned. If the poet can no longer evoke the "primitive," since his body cannot keep pace with the demands of his imagination, the primitive ideal must be abandoned. Physical prowess—extraordinary keenness of eyesight—can be undermined by that baffling human problem, mortality and disease. Death awaits. Yet one is not always prepared for it. If it is seen as an embarrassment, another obscure defeat, it will never be accepted at all; better to pray for the Apocalypse, so that everyone can die at once, with no one left to think about it afterward. The stasis celebrated in much of contemporary literature, the erecting of gigantic paranoid-delusion systems that are self-enclosed and self-destructing, argues for a simple failure of reasoning: the human ego has too long imagined itself the supreme form of consciousness in the universe. When that delusion is taken from it, it suffers. Suffering, it projects its emotions outward onto everything, everyone, into the universe itself. Our imaginative literature has largely refused to integrate ever-increasing subtleties of intuitive experience with those of intellectual experience; it will not acknowledge the fact that the dynamism of our species has become largely a dynamism of the brain, not the body. Old loves die slowly. But they die.

The concluding poem in *The Eye-Beaters* differs from the rest in many ways. It is primarily a meditation. It is almost entirely speculative, an abstract seventeen-stanza work dealing with the mystery of the soul. The familiar theme of battle and certain specific images involved (helmets, meadows of "intensified grass") are used in a way new to Dickey; its tone of hard, impassive detachment contrasts with the despairing ferocity of "The Eye-Beaters" and the poems of disease.

The immediate occasion for the poem is evidently dissatisfaction with an "old peaceful love." Another person, nearby, is "suddenly/Also free . . . weeping her body away." But the confessional quality of the poem is not very important; the poet's detachment approaches that of Eliot's in "Four Quartets." Dickey could very well be writing about himself—his relationship with his "soul" (which in mystical literature is usually identified with the feminine, though that interpretation is probably not necessary). The poet's problem is how, as a "normal" man, to relate his predicament with the human condition generally. As in "Reincarnation (II)," the poet discovers himself released from one life and projected into another where he feels himself "Like a king starting out on a journey/Away from all things that he knows." Outside the "simple-minded window" is a world of ordinary sights from which one may take his face; yet this world is one of danger and "iron-masked silence." In utter stillness the poet stands with his palm on the window sill (as he once stood with his palm on the fence wire) and feels the "secret passivity" and "unquestionable Silence" of existence: man wears the

reason for his own existence as he stands and, in such a confrontation, the "tongue grows solid also."

Imagined then as a kind of Caesar (Dickey would like to "see
with/the eyes of a very great general," here as elsewhere), he realizes
he has nothing to do in his own life with his military yearnings and
his hope for himself to be utterly free of any finite time or place, an
omni-potent life force released from identity to "breed/With the
farthest women/And the farthest also in time: breed/Through bees,
like flowers and bushes:/Breed Greeks, Egyptians and Romans
hoplites/Peasants caged kings clairvoyant bastards. . . ." His
desire is so vast as to exclude the personal entirely; he must turn
away, at least in imagination, from the domesticity of his life, so that
his soul can achieve the release it demands. It is nothing less than the
wide universe that is the object of its desire; like the wolverine, the
poet's soul hungers to "eat the world." This desire is in itself a kind
of miracle or reincarnation:

> Turning away, seeing fearful
> Ordinary ground, boys' eyes manlike go,
> The middle-aged man's like a desperate
> Boy's, the old man's like a new angel's. . . .

Dreaming, the poet sees horses, a "cloud/That is their oversoul,"
and armed men who may spring from his teeth. He must speak of
battles that do not stain the meadow with blood but release "inner
lives"—as if through a pure concentration of will, of artistic creation, the poet realizes:

> So many things stand wide
> Open!   Distance is helplessly deep
> On all sides   and you can enter, alone,
> Anything   anything can go
> On wherever it wishes   anywhere in the world or in time
> But here and now.

What must be resisted is the "alien sobbing" nearby; the poet's
attachment to a finite self, a domestic existence, must be overcome,
as if he were a guard on his duty to prevent the desertion of the
higher yearnings of his soul. The most abstract charge of all is his
sense that he might be, even, a hero in a book—his life might be "a

thing/That can be learned,/As those earnest young heroes learned theirs,/Later, much later on."

"Turning Away" is a tentative reply to the despairing vision of "The Eye-Beaters," and it concludes a collection of widely varying poems with a statement about the need to transcend the physical life by an identification with the timeless, "physical life" having been examined frankly and unsparingly and found to be generally diseased. The poem's immediate occasion is marital discord, but Dickey's imagery of battle is a very generalized one—"So many battles/Fought in cow pastures   fought back/And forth over anybody's farm/With men or only/With wounded eyes—" Dickey's most inclusive metaphor for life is life-as-battle; for man, man-as-combatant.

The emphasis Dickey places in his later poems upon decay, disease, regression, and estrangement suggests that they may constitute a terminal group of poems: terminal in the sense that the poet may be about to take on newer challenges. Having developed from the mysticism of Stone into and through the mysticism of Flesh, having explored variations on unity and variations on dissolution, he seems suspended—between the formal abstractions of "Turning Away" and the jagged primitive-heroic music of "The Eye-Beaters," perhaps still seeking what Blake calls the "Image of wonder" that allows man to "meet the Lord in the Air & . . . be happy."

In any case, Dickey's work is significant in its expression of the savagery that always threatens to become an ideal, when faith in human values is difficult to come by—or when a culture cannot accommodate man's most basic instincts, forcing them backward, downward, away from the conscious imagination and back into the body as if into the body of an ancient ancestor: into the past, that is, forbidding intelligent entry into the future.

NOTES

1. *The Suspect in Poetry* (Madison, Minnesota: The Sixties Press, 1964), p. 47.
2. Lewis Thomas, M.D., "Information," in the *New England Journal of Medicine*, December 14, 1972, pp. 1238–39.

3. Dickey either literally or figuratively puts on masks in any number of poems—notably "Armor," "Drinking from a Helmet," and "Approaching Prayer" (in which he puts on a "hollow hog's head").

4. Dickey's perfect vision singled him out for training in night fighters in the Army Air Corps. Throughout his poetry there is a concern, not just imagistic or metaphorical, with vision—eyesight—that makes doubly poignant his conclusion in "False Youth: Two Seasons" (from *Falling*) that his youth was "a lifetime search/For the Blind." Also, the conclusion of "The Eye-Beaters" shows us the poet "in perversity and the sheer/Despair of invention" taking his "Double-clear bifocals off"— then succumbing to a fantasy of regressive madness.

5. *The Suspect in Poetry*, p. 77. The word "helplessness" is repeated several times in connection with Jarrell, and in an essay on Howard Nemerov (a review of Nemerov's *Selected Poems*, 1960), Dickey praises Nemerov for what seem to me the wrong reasons: ". . . the enveloping emotion that arises from his writing is helplessness: the helplessness we all feel in the face of the events of our time, and of life itself: the helplessness one feels as one's legitimate but chronically unfair portion of all the things that can't be assuaged or explained" (p. 67). Throughout *Self-Interviews*, which seems the work of a different James Dickey, one who cannot do justice to the excellence of the essential Dickey, there is a reliance upon an inner, moral helplessness, as if certain emotional prejudices were *there*, in human nature, and one might as well acquiesce to them; though elsewhere does Dickey take on as rigorously combative a tone as Nietzsche in feeling that the true artist would not tolerate the world as it is even for one instant.

6. From Dickey's account of his growth as a poet, in *Poets on Poetry*, edited by Howard Nemerov (New York, 1966), pp. 225–38. It is ironic that Dickey should so distrust and mock his own reflective, intellectual nature, since he knows himself a poet of the "Second Birth"—one who has worked hard at his craft. Yet his finest poems give the impression of having been written very quickly; one feels the strange compulsion to read them quickly, as if to keep pace with the language. Dickey's poems are structures that barely contain the energies they deal with. That "agent" in the poem known as the "I" is unpredictable, at times frightening, for he may lead us anywhere. Dickey might have written extraordinary short stories had he not chosen to develop himself as a poet almost exclusively. In an excellent essay, "The Self as Agent," from *Sorties*, Dickey says that the chief glory and excitement of writing poetry is the chance it gives the poet to "confront and dramatize parts of himself that otherwise would not have surfaced. The poem is a window opening not on truth but on possibility . . ." (p. 161).

7. Dickey's reviews of *Howl* and *Kaddish* are both negative. He says that Ginsberg's principal state of mind is "hallucination" and that the poetry is really "strewn, mishmash prose." Yet Dickey allows that, somewhere, in the Babel of undisciplined contemporary poets, "there might one day appear a writer to supply the in-touch-with-living authenticity which current American poetry so badly needs, grown as it has genteel and almost suffocatingly proper." From *The Suspect in Poetry*, pp. 16–19. When a poet-critic speaks in these terms, one may always assume he is talking about himself, whether he knows it or not.

8. Raymond Smith, "The Poetic Faith of James Dickey," *Modern Poetry Studies*, Vol. 2, No. 6, pp. 259–72. Masculine response to Dickey's poetry probably differs inevitably from a woman's response.

9. Dickey has granted a number of interviews, all of them characterized by an extraordinary frankness. In a recent one, the poet William Heyen asks him to discuss the violent "morality" of *Deliverance*, and Dickey states that there is a kind of "absolutism" about country people in his part of the world: "Life and death . . . are very basic gut-type things, and if somebody does something that violates your code, you *kill* him, and you don't think twice about it. . . . the foremost fear of our time, especially with the growing crime rate, crime in the cities and so on, . . . the thing that we're most terrified of is being set upon by malicious strangers. . . ." He therefore agrees with the decisions his characters make in the novel, and it is clear from his discussion of Ed Gentry's decision to kill and Gentry's growing realization that he is a "born killer" (Dickey's words) that the novel, like much of the poetry, is an attempt to deal with an essentially mystical experience. That it is also brutal and dehumanizing is not Dickey's concern. Murder is "a quietly transfiguring influence" on the novel's hero. "A Conversation with James Dickey," ed. by William Heyen, *The Southern Review* (Winter, 1973) IX, 1, pp. 135–56.

LAWRENCE LIEBERMAN

James Dickey:
The Deepening of Being

THE POETIC VISION IN James Dickey's fifth volume of
poems, *Falling*, contains so much joy that it is incapable of self-
pity or self-defeat. There is a profound inwardness in the poems,
the inner self always celebrating its strange joy in solitude, or
pouring outward, overflowing into the world. No matter how
much suffering the poet envisions, the sensibility that informs and
animates him is joy in the sheer pleasure of being.

The condition of joy works remarkable transformations, in
literature as in life, often converting the tragic condition into a
saving buoyancy. This power to transform is typical of the best
poems in the Romantic tradition. It derives from a special conjunction of the intelligence with the poetic imagination. The transforming joy in Yeats's poetry works its way into the antithetical
spheres of private and public life. One measure of the greatness of
Yeats's achievement is the expansion in the scope of his vision to
include, with equal rigor and authority, personal disasters of the
self and global catastrophes such as the Irish Revolution and World
War I. The joyful vision of Theodore Roethke, the American poet
for whom Dickey feels the strongest spiritual affinity, rarely extends into the political arena; instead, it journeys forever inward,
probing darker and more perilous recesses of the interior self. The
more tragic emotion—suffering, bitterness, despair—art can absorb and transmute into joyousness of being, the healthier it is.
Dickey's vision aspires, above all, to that kind of supernal health-
iness, but it moves uneasily into larger sociopolitical issues of war

and race. His joyousness is generous to a fault, uncontrollable—thus working to disadvantage in a few of his most ambitious poems. In "The Firebombing" and "Slave Quarters," for example, the moments of ecstasy threaten to overbalance the moments of agony.

In the four volumes prior to *Falling*, Dickey seems to vacillate, as did Yeats, between two spiritual poles: stoicism and romantic passion. The problem of facing death without fear elicits by turns, now one, now the other, as in "The Ice Skin":

> Not knowing whether
> I will break before I can feel,
>
> Before I can give up my powers,
> Or whether the ice light
>
> In my eyes will ever snap off
> Before I die.

The ice light, a heroic "masterly shining," is a dispassionate state, a calm radiance of the spirit learned through a series of existential encounters with "the dying" and the "just born." The prevailing spirit of the poem is the power to endure suffering and meet death quietly, with steadiness and poise—a stoical transcendence over death by intellect.

However, Dickey's vision is far more sustaining when he achieves transcendence over death by passion, intensity of self, deepening of being, as in "The Performance," an early war poem that, with "The Jewel," initiates a sequence of war poetry culminating in a poem of the first importance, "The Firebombing."

In making an assessment of Dickey's war poetry we must ask, Does the sum total of the author's writings on the subject of war move us to respond humanely to the massive political crisis of our generation—that is, to respond with the human, or superhuman, compassion and commitment necessary to redress the wrongs, first, in our individual souls, and last, in the soul of our age?

In "The Performance," the Japanese executioner will have to carry the scars of Donald Armstrong's death in his soul, since, miraculously, Armstrong's ritual performance has converted the mechanical, inhuman relation between executioner and victim into a personal and inescapably spiritual—an existential—encounter:

> . . . the headsman broke down
> In a blaze of tears, in that light
> Of the thin, long human frame
> Upside down in its own strange joy,
> And, if some other one had not told him,
> Would have cut off the feet
> Instead of the head. . .

The fatally impersonal relation between man and man is a central dilemma of our time, occurring in its ultimate form in war. In "The Firebombing," Dickey conceives the dilemma of impersonality as being insoluble. The protagonist, however hard he tries, cannot connect spiritually with his victims below. Conversely, in "The Performance," the ritual acrobatic stunts create personal being, restore the I-thou, so that even the headsman, though powerless to disobey his superiors and follow his impulse to spare Armstrong's life, finds a kind of spiritual absolution during the killing. Armstrong's acrobatics transform the killing relation between them into a saving relation, a forgiving relation. Both souls are saved.

If many veterans are content to claim the depersonalization of their acts and the beings from which they sprang—in wartime—as grounds for absolving themselves of personal responsibility for their crimes, James Dickey is not. Witness his mercilessly uncompromising self-judgment in "The Jewel." Recalling his years as a fighter pilot, not only does he impute personal involvement to his flying missions, but he remembers feeling the sort of joyful fascination for his life in the cockpit that men ordinarily feel for precious gems. He is a passive lover—mated to his plane—who allows himself to be abducted by the overpowering beauty of the machinery, "being the first to give in/To the matched priceless glow of the engines." He sees himself lovingly enclosed in the jewel-cockpit, as in the warmth of a womb. Now, years later, in the warmth of the family tent during a holiday, he recalls the pleasure he received from the enclosure of the plane. The old joy floods into the present, mocking his present security, leaving him feeling, once again, more than ever alone in his soul's late night.

"The Jewel" is one of Dickey's earliest attempts to identify and cope with the residue of guilt left by his role in the war. In the poem, the poet seems himself more as a paroled or pardoned criminal than as a survivor. But can he pardon himself? Does he qualify as a spiritual parolee? "The Jewel" is a predecessor of "The Firebombing" in a way the other war poems are not. In "The Performance" and "Drinking from a Helmet," he allows himself to feel the innocence and compassion of the detached bystander, a stance that conveniently removes the persona from his guilt, so the horror of war may be treated as a subject in itself, apart from whatever moral responsibility he may himself feel for perpetrating evil of his own making or perpetuating evil set in motion by the state.

In "Drinking from a Helmet," a new form—employing short, self-contained numbered sections in place of the usual stanza units—facilitates a rapid, to and fro fluctuation between inner experience and external action. It moves almost effortlessly between controlled hallucination and stark realism, a remarkably apt strategy for a poem that sets out to present extraordinary spiritual events in a setting of extreme dehumanization. Written in a tradition of war poetry, running from Wilfred Owen to Randall Jarrell, in which spiritual uplift in the midst of carnage of battle would be unthinkable, Dickey's poem provides uplift as much because of the soul's depravity as in spite of it.

In the opening sections of "Drinking from a Helmet," the level of awareness of the speaker keeps shifting, refocusing. He is possessed by two beings recognizably separate early in the poem. Who is speaking, I or ultra-I?

> In the middle of combat, a graveyard
> Was advancing after the troops . . .
> A green water-truck stalled out.
> I moved up on it, behind
> The hill that cut off the firing. . . .
>
> I swayed, as if kissed in the brain.

One being perceives everything with a casual directness, a down-to-earthness necessary to mental self-preservation ("A green water-truck stalled out"); the other registers profound ultra-events ("I swayed, as if kissed in the brain"). The two zigzag, at irregular intervals, through the voice of the speaker, without any noticeable jarring of tone. The voice provides a continuum that can contain both irreducible beings, and gradually the two converge and inter-penetrate in the vision of the poem's action:

> I threw my old helmet down
> And put the wet one on.
> Warmed water ran over my face.
> My last thought changed, and I knew
> I inherited one of the dead.

The speaker has imbibed and mystically reincarnated the spirit of the dead soldier in his own living spirit by drinking water from the man's helmet.

In the closing sections, as he envisions a plan to transport the dead man's spirit to his brother's home in California, incredible life bursts into the poem:

> I would survive and go there,
> Stepping off the train in a helmet
> That held a man's last thought . . .
> I would ride through all
> California upon two wheels . . .
> Hoping to meet his blond brother,
> And to walk with him into the wood
> Until we were lost,
> Then take off the helmet
> And tell him where I had stood,
> What poured, what spilled, what swallowed:

> And tell him I was the man.

The poem creates the illusion, finally, of being a prayer girding the speaker for a move back into life. The poem is like a launching pad to an actual experience; simultaneously, it contains within itself that future experience and opens into the event-to-be. The barrier between poem and lived act is swept away, just as the threshold between the living and dead soldiers was dissolved earlier in the poem.

In "The Firebombing," also, two beings function simulta-neously but separately. In "Helmet," the two beings are coincident in time but move on different psychic levels. In "The Firebomb-ing," present being collides with past being. Both seem to be hope-lessly blocked, ineligible for entry into the full import of the expe-rience—one lost in time, the other in moral stupor. Will the collision between the two lost selves, in the dream-dance of flight, result in a clarity of mind within which the unified self may seek absolution through a true confrontation with its crimes? This question comprises the central strategy of "The Firebombing."

At the finish, Dickey explicitly admits his failure to achieve his intended end: to assuage the moral guilt for past crimes by experiencing again the events of the imagination. He tried, through the medium—and mediation—of the poem, to feel some of the human horror and shame that his moral conscience tells him he should have felt twenty years before, and thereby to achieve moral expiation through art—the fire in the peom would cleanse the author's soul, purify it, burn away the sense of sin. But he finds, in the most piercingly honest revelation the peom affords, that art itself is an unclean instrument in his hands. The feelings of guilt and horror stirred by the experience of the poem cannot effect catharsis because they are hampered by the remembered sense of beauty and joy felt during the act of murder, "this detachment,/ The honored aesthetic evil,/The greatest sense of power in one's life."

Early in the poem, it becomes evident to the reader that the moral jeopardy of the present is just as insuperable as that of the past. Self-purification must occur in the world of the suburban present, but the handicap of present prosperity and excess spreads across the poem in a Whitmanesque catalog of luxuries that quickly accumulate into an insurmountable obstacle to the self's redemption. There are many self-scalding images that take the speaker partway through the complex initiation ceremonies his redemption requires:

> It [the blazing napalm] consumes them in a hot
> Body-flash, old age or menopause
> Of children, clings and burns . . .

If such images don't contain seeds of expiation, how can ideas or slogans, or even direct prayer, redeem him?

Dickey finds himself in much the same position as Claudius, who fails in the sincere attempt to repent of the murder of the elder Hamlet because he still possesses the spoils of the crime, queen and kingdom, and knows he is too weak to give them up. Likewise, not only is Dickey still blessed, or cursed, with the luxuries of the

American suburban middle class, but he persists in being as "American as I am, and proud of it." Further, Dickey's incapacity "to get down there or see/What really happened" can be attributed to other factors. First, the only way you can know exactly what it feels like to see your own child (or your neighbor's) walk through a door "With its ears crackling off/Like powdery leaves" is to see it actually happen. Second, in writing the poem, Dickey places himself once again in the "blue light" of the "glass treasure-hole," deep in the same "aesthetic contemplation" he felt as he flew over "The *heart* of the fire." His spirit is perplexed by his joy in the act of writing, trapped in the tools of his art.

The poet senses that the experience of the actual firebombing gave birth in his soul to his deepest aesthetic instincts and talents, which he has never before more directly exploited than in the writing of "The Firebombing." Ironically, the poem seems better even for his having interrupted its flow of experience at the finish to comment on its inevitable failure to achieve its main goal:

> Absolution? Sentence? No matter;
> The thing itself is in that.

Perhaps this is a sort of ironic punishment: the poem gets better as the author backs away from it, refuses to exult over its beauties, insists that the purely human act of salvation from this massive sin is too great a burden for this poem, or indeed any poem, to carry.

How, then, do we account for the success of the poem, not only as art, but as a human (politically human, even) document? How account for the success of a major poem which unconditionally fails to achieve what the author explicitly intended it to achieve? Simply by acknowledging that whatever is not contained in "the thing itself"—the dramatic confrontation between self and its guilt, its crimes, in the action of the poem—cannot be stated parenthetically at the end as an afterthought, a dissipated message. To state it so would be to falsify the poem's central concern and mode of delivery. The writer has attempted the impossible, and he admits it. He is not ready for self-forgiveness yet, because he is not yet able to feel a guilt commensurate with his crimes. Perhaps he never will be ready. These are grave truths, but they are fully realized truths nonetheless, however lacking they may be in the kind of heroism fashionable at peace rallies in the sixties.

Moreover, if the poem admits its own failure to feel what must be felt, it carries the reader a step closer to having the feelings necessary to spiritual survival, and carries the instrument of language a step closer to meeting the ultimate life-challenge art faces in our time. If we read this poem—and, indeed, all Dickey's best work—with the brain in our eyes, with the intelligence to see that we call a *vision,* we find it to be poetry that constantly sends *us* back from the printed page to the gravest life-challenges.

As a survivor of two wars, Dickey feels spiritually hunted by disinherited beings (pursued by the "downed dead," as in "Pursuit from Under"), who silently accuse him of usurping their birthright to existence, leaving him with intimations of spiritual illegitimacy:

> Out of grief, I was myself
> Conceived, and brought to life
> To replace the incredible child . . .
> *Dead before I was born.*

("The String")

In a number of war poems—"The Firebombing" particularly—Dickey feels like a cosmic criminal who, by luck or trickery, has miraculously escaped punishment and walks in freedom while innocent souls rot in purgatorial confinement, serving an eternal sentence for another's, his, crimes. He finds most harrowing the thought that he has been personally responsible for the death of many Japanese women and children, and in some poems he tries desperately to make his peace with the phantoms from death's dream kingdom.

Another source of these psychic misgivings is the stories he was often told by his parents about the brother who was "dead before I was born," stories antedating his war years by long enough to have been buried deeply in his memory, ready to be disinterred years later. The stories became indelibly, if invisibly, stamped on his impressionable young mind, and they haunted his early childhood, when he often felt as if he were possessed by a disembodied alter-self, living "within another's life." This long-forgotten obsession revisits him in his early poems, and he shapes it into a unique personal myth or legend. It is the first in a chain of mystiques that embody Dickey's developing logos of being.

To assuage his inexplicable guilt, the poet seeks devices for the revival of dead beings. In "The String," the dying brother's string tricks, such as "foot of a crow," are conceived of as the ritual magic that can guarantee his eternal return in living beings. The performance can be imitated by the living and used as a way of entering the dead child's being or of taking his being into oneself. The ritual performance with the string converted the brother's dying into an act of love. But it was purely self-love. There was no hint of the child's reaching out to others—parents or friends—through the string game. Contrarily, the speaker's performance with the string is a love act that engages the other being deeply. It connects him with the dead brother, and he aspires to use it to connect the living parents to the brother, but fails: "I believe in my father and mother/ Finding no hope in these lines."

A comparison between "The String" and the later "Power and Light" can be used to illustrate the remarkable distance Dickey's art has traveled between his first book and *Falling*. In "The String" he connects his own being to the Other, the spirits of the dead, but cannot, or will not, mediate between others as a neutral, but fiercely charged, spiritual conductor, as in "Power and Light":

        and I feel the wires running
Like the life-force along the limed rafters and all connections
With poles   with the tarred naked belly-buckled black
Trees I hook to my heels   with the shrill phone calls leaping
Long distance   long distances through my hands   all connections

Even the one
With my wife, turn good . . . Never think I don't know my profession
Will lift me: why, all over hell the lights burn in your eyes,
People are calling each other weeping   with a hundred thousand
Volts   making deals   pleading   laughing like fate,
Far off, invulnerable   or with the right word pierced

To the heart
By wires I held, shooting off their ghostly mouths,
In my gloves.

The power lines of this poem exceed the string by the same vast margin as "Power and Light" surpasses "The String" in spiritual intensity.

In "The String," as in most poems in *Into the Stone,* ritual hangs back from the reader in an ephemeral landscape of dream-memory. The reader is enticed by the strangeness of images, and if he feels somehow left outside the speaker's experience—a charmed, but displaced, onlooker—he is persuaded mentally by the ingenuity of the poem's argument:

> My eyes go from me, and down
> Through my bound, spread hands
> To the dead, from the kin of the dead . . .

In a number of the earlier poems, however, the gap between the reader's life experience and the poem's drama is too large. In an attempt to bridge the gap, the mind's activity, in the form of willed images or willed ideas, dominates the poem. The reader recoils from the tone of intellectual stridency as the poem's ever-extended machinery quavers like a house of cards.

In contrast, in many lines of "In the Tree House at Night," a later poem that revives the dead brother's spirit, there *is* something of the lightness of air—one can almost hear inbreathing sounds, a wind-sucking voice:

> The floor and walls wave me slowly . . .
> In the arm-slender forks of our dwelling
>
> I breathe my live brother's light hair.

It is perhaps no accident that in the early poems we find the inexplicable beginnings of a vision of genesis in air that eventually develops into the fulfilled air-birth of Dickey's most achieved vision, in "Falling." Unlike the play dwellings of "The String," the hypnotic lyricism of "Tree House" creates a castle in air that takes the reader's heaviness away and converts him into a being afloat, a just-lighter-than-air self. The poem's drama instills the sense of flying, of a soul set free in its body:

> When may I fall strangely to earth,
>
> Who am nailed to this branch by a spirit?

In "Tree House," atmospheric elements of scene, setting, time of day—all become dynamically enmeshed in the poem's drama. As in a movie, these elements create the illusion of action taking place *now.* The ritual magic of the poem's movement pulls the reader, irresistibly, into its happenings. He is himself one of the actors, sharing the tree house of the poem's ritual flight with "My brothers and I, one dead,/The other asleep from much living,/In mid-air huddled beside me."

In "Tree House," as in the other best poems of the second volume, *Drowning with Others,* Dickey evolves a mode of experiencing a double vision that seems ideally suited to his poetic imagination, thereby anticipating the more complex dualism of later poems like "Drinking from a Helmet" and "Firebombing." Two separate, but interdependent, dramas occur simultaneously in "Tree House." A familiar scene or event is presented directly, and an equally clear and sharp experience of the spirit is envisioned through it. Usually, in the best poems, the two dramas, outer and inner, are nearly evenly balanced. Neither dominates the poem. The poem can be read with equal interest at either level, but it is experienced, ideally, at both.

A lifeguard trying to forgive himself for letting a child drown, two brothers striving to oppose the real world with the fantasy world of their tree house—both are familiar experiences and hence create immediate and intensified human interest, but they become unfamiliar, beautiful, and strange as a unique spiritual experience is filtered through them. The familiar story seems, of necessity, to call up from the inner depths a strangely new spiritual history to explain it. At the same time, the spirit half-creates the illusion of being the reflection or mirror image of the story half—the familiar leading effortlessly into the unfamiliar, and back again. If the spirit half dominates many of the best early poems, the story half dominates Dickey's best later poems—"Shark's Parlor," "The Sheep Child," "Falling"—in which the poet is bent on exploring novel, rather than ordinary, experience, to stir up strangely new spiritual overtones, and to extend the resources of his art.

In "Tree House" and "The Lifeguard," a familiar experience is turned inside out. As the poems proceed, the focus of the drama shifts from the outer world of story to the inner world of magic. What begins as a tale of two boys playing house in a tree changes into a mystical vision in which the speaker experiences a transmigration of three beings—his own, his dead brother's, and his sleeping brother's—through the medium of the tree. The state of spirits in flux is expertly dramatized by lines that enter the inexplicable thresholds between brother and brother, alive and dead, asleep and awake:

> I stir
> Within another's life. Whose life?
> Who is dead? Whose presence is living? . . .
> Can two bodies make up a third?

The lifeguard returns to the scene of his defeat and recounts his failed attempt to save the drowned child's life in details that suggest the pain of self-mutilation:

> And my fingertips turned into stone
> From clutching immovable blackness.

His ritual suffering, in memory, summons the dead child's spirit to his aid. Though he is still "thinking of how I may be/The savior of one/Who has already died in my care," paradoxically, the relation between saver and saved is reversed through the medium of water as the dead child's spirit rises to free the living, helpless man from his guilt.

Both poems awaken the reader to the unexpected realization that a profound spiritual life lies hidden just below the surface of most routine experiences, and that perhaps this inner life of being is inherent in all experience, waiting to be released by the healthy imagination. This inner life erupts with the intensity of hallucination and pervades our being with the strangeness of the supernatural, yet it is, at all times, available to the normal mind. It is a richer totality of being than we are accustomed to enjoying in our daily lives. It seems to be delivered to the conscious self as from an inexhaustible source. At a moment's notice, it can transform grief into boundless joy. It is a state in which each one's being is both alone in a self-contained peace and indissolubly connected, in love, to other beings, living and dead, as in the beautiful closing lines of "Tree House":

> To sing, must I feel the world's light?
> My green, graceful bones fill the air

> With sleeping birds. Alone, alone
> And with them I move gently.
> I move at the heart of the world.

Never again in his poems about children does Dickey achieve such a full expression of the way he perceives the strange beauty—the otherness—of children's fantasy vision as he does in "The Lifeguard" and "Tree House." Yet in neither of these poems do we find purely a child's vision; rather, they offer a vision inaccessible to children, possible only to a man childlike in his freedom from incapacitating rigidities of mind and in his absolute faith in the saving power of imagination. The lifeguard's vision contains, in addition, the belief that a powerful healing forgiveness dwells in the souls of small children: a forgiveness strong enough to balance a man's guilt for taking the place of the brother "dead before I was born," and a healing power soothing enough to close temporarily the wound sustained by his spirit when he poured fire-death on the children of Japan. The evidence of thematic development strongly suggests that the guilt that is partly assuaged through the persona of the lifeguard is only temporarily forestalled, while the poet gradually fortifies his craft to deal with the larger challenge of a direct encounter, in art, with the events of the war which planted in his heart seeds of guilt that can never be entirely purged or expunged. The searing, insurmountable guilt is presented in raw form in many lines and images in "The Firebombing," and, again, in the final passage of "Slave Quarters," in which the southern white father meditates on the face of his choice possession, an illegitimate mulatto son:

> . . . There is no hatred
> Like love in the eyes
> Of a wholly owned face? When you think of what
> It would be like   what it has been
> What it is to look once a day
> Into an only
> Son's brown, waiting, wholly possessed
> Amazing eyes, and not
> Acknowledge, but own?

Dickey's imagination is obsessed with a man's responsibility—human and mystical—for the lives of children, especially those entrusted to his care. It is one of the very few themes that have engaged him deeply at each stage of his development, the problem having its own self-defined limits, peculiarity, and obsessive strangeness. Dickey is always at his best when he tackles a subject that entirely engrosses and excites his imagination, such as the most basic challenges to his manhood—befriending, fathering, husbanding.

One of Dickey's most sustaining and pervasive faiths is his absolute belief that the human imagination can save us from anything. No human disaster or tragedy is too large for the imagination to encompass or too crushing for imagination to convert it into life-savingness. This credo reaches its culmination, and its apotheosis, in the poem "Falling." Who would have guessed that a woman's falling to her death from a plane could be converted by Dickey's imagination into a symbol of fantastic affirmation of life? The thought of his being responsible for the death of a child fills Dickey's heart with extreme terror, a terror that arouses an instantaneous sympathy and recognition in most readers. Every parent harbors a secret voice in his soul repeating over and over—consciously or unconsciously— that if harm or injury comes to his child through his neglect, he'll never forgive himself. That *never* is a powerful and terrifying idea, and Dickey's imagination obstinately refuses to submit to never. Some of his best poems, such as "The Lifeguard" and "The Firebombing," are desperate attempts to forgive himself, spiritually, for what he recognizes to be humanly unforgivable.

The development of Dickey's treatment of the theme of human/animal relations is central to his art. Moreover, since this theme is unhampered by the overwhelming moral guilt of much of the war poetry and the poems about children, it can be used to demonstrate an evolving logos of being.

Dickey's engagement with the animal world was never cultivated simply as equipment for his poetry. He is intent on exploring the animal's dimensions of being. His experience of hunting, like that of soldiering, antedates his career in poetry by many years. As in the war poetry, the passion he feels for hunted animals is so intense that it enables him to put out of his mind the tradition of nature poetry in English—D. H. Lawrence's excepted—and induce a literary amnesia, allowing him the latitude of imagination necessary to do justice to a series of strangely unique human/animal encounters.

The stages of relationship he depicts closely resemble those of a love affair between man and woman, especially in the way the poet's mind explores possibilities—limits—of relationship in search of a truer sense of identity. Dickey's realization of personal identity is always sought through a deep conjunction with the Other, whether the Other happens to take the form of animals, children, man, or woman. Consider, for example, "The Heaven of Animals":

Here they are. The soft eyes open.
If they have lived in a wood
It is a wood.
If they have lived on plains
It is grass rolling
Under their feet forever.

Having no souls, they have come,
Anyway; beyond their knowing.
Their instincts wholly bloom
And they rise.
The soft eyes open.

To match them, the landscape flowers,
Outdoing, desperately
Outdoing what is required:
The richest wood,
The deepest field.

For some of these,
It could not be the place
It is, without blood.
These hunt, as they have done,
But with claws and teeth grown perfect,

More deadly than they can believe.
They stalk more silently,
And crouch on the limbs of trees,
And their descent
Upon the bright backs of their prey

May take years
In a sovereign floating of joy.
And those that are hunted

Know this as their life,
Their reward: to walk

Under such trees in full knowledge
Of what is in glory above them,
And to feel no fear,
But acceptance, compliance.
Fulfilling themselves without pain

At the cycle's center,
They tremble, they walk
Under the tree,
They fall, they are torn,
They rise, they walk again.

"The Heaven of Animals" is a classically pure statement. It pictures the animals in an utterly unpeopled landscape that recalls D. H. Lawrence's wistful misanthropic vision in *Women in Love* of a world "all grass and a hare standing up." Dickey conceives of the animals as being ideally beautiful and innocent, incapable of evil. All violence, or bloodshed, is performed with "claws and teeth grown perfect." The spilling of blood is a necessary condition of this idyllic state that "could not be the place/It is, without blood." If the animals' "soft eyes open," they are capable of ferocity, as well as of gentleness, "More deadly than they can believe." But the victims are spared both fear and pain since hunter and hunted alike flourish in a "sovereign floating of joy." "At the cycle's center," killing and being killed comprise a total love-relation, a fulfillment of animal life, since all beings are instantly reincarnated and reborn: "They fall, they are torn,/They rise, they walk again."

At times, Dickey's unqualified adulation for animals, like his glorification of the healthy-mindedness of children, verges on absurd romanticism. The vision in "The Heaven of Animals," however, as in most of Dickey's poems, works two ways. It suggests that man is the only corrupt animal. If he were removed from earth, beatitude would automatically transpire, just as it must have prevailed before his coming. The vision also anticipates later poems, beginning with "Fog Envelops the Animals," in which man the hunter tries to qualify for re-entry into the animal heaven from which he has been excluded. To do so, he must purify himself, divest himself of all those aspects of humanness that unfit him for animal beatitude. The fog is the medium of purification: "Sound-lessly whiteness is eating/ My visible self alive./ I shall enter this world like the dead." As the visible self is eaten away, the fear and guilt of man the hunter are dissolved. Despite the fact that he kills, he can feel innocent.

In the earlier poems, the action is symbolic ritual; in "Springer Mountain," the action is realistic narrative interrupted by the advent of miracle—a plunge into the mystical beyond. If the earlier poems offered symbolic justification of the master-slave relation between hunter and hunted, "Springer Mountain" converts that relation into an erotic encounter between two equal, but qualitatively distinct, beings. The man spontaneously strips off his clothes and runs joyously in the woods with the deer. The hunter expresses his love for the animal-being in a more direct intimacy than ever before. He approaches the deer on a strictly human level, expressing the ardor and laughter of exuberant human affection. In contrast, in "Fog Envelops the Animals," he entered the animal's life-sphere by giv-ing up his human qualities entirely to the transforming symbolic fog. The gains for entry into the foreign element were balanced, or canceled, by losses of realism and human identity. There is a kind of emotional dishonesty in glorifying the animal's otherness and integr-ity of being while debasing one's own human otherness, as though it can be taken off and put back on with one's clothes. Thus in "Springer Mountain" a deeper honesty is exhibited than in earlier poems. Though the hunter has become farcical in his excessive attempt to assume the identity of the deer-beloved, he has retained his human personality, and even though he ludicrously overshoots his human limitations in trying to identify with the deer, he salvages a sizable reward:

> For a few steps deep in the dance
> Of what I most am and should be
> And can be only once in this life.

The ultimate lesson Dickey brings back from his poems would seem to be wisdom of being. The poems teach him how to be, and we may suppose he learns as much from blundered tries for impossible being as from the successes.

As a poem, "Springer Mountain" is less successful than "The Heaven of Animals," because it is less compact and less technically achieved. As the poem searches for a new experience, a further reach of vision, the rhythms fall into a decadent sing-song and the experience is diffused, not intensified. Also, the laughter in the poem occurs at the extremity, rather than at the center, of its experience. It does not become a controlling point of view, as does the comic spirit in later poems like "Power and Light" and "Encounter in the Cage Country," but the poem winds up a chapter in Dickey's art. Once he has loved a deer with personal intimacy, he can never return to the master-slave relation again. He has hunted "Deer for the first and last time." He is a man who has learned, irrecoverably, that a deep give-and-take exchange is possible between man and animal, an exchange that maintains the identity in separateness of each being. He is now ready to bring to the final and fulfilled meetings of "The Sheep Child" and "Encounter in the Cage Country" a full quotient of human personality.

But first, it remains for the speaker of the poems to stretch beyond human limits in another extreme direction. In "Reincarnation (II)," man literally becomes a bird, not merely evolving certain birdlike characteristics as in earlier poems. Kafka has captured the horror of man's turning into an animal in "Metamorphosis"; Dickey evokes the beatitude of man reborn as animal. Gradually, in Dickey's vision, man has qualified for complete entry into animal heaven. In "Reincarnation (II)," entry, following elaborate ritual initiation, is irreversible. Man reborn as a bird can never change back into man again, as he can in myths and fairy stories of human/animal interchange. Early in the poem, the man senses that he has been transformed into a bird, and that he must learn to live with it. He still has human feelings and ideas, so they must either become annexed to the new bird-instincts, bird-senses, and bird-spirit, or give place to them. On one level, the man gradually divests himself of all aspects of humanness as he learns his new life, wears his new bird-identity. On another, the entire experience is perceived through the human awareness of the author. So man-spirit and bird-spirit are wedded in the bird's body, much as owl-spirit and blind child's spirit had become wedded in the father's dream song in "The Owl King."

Somehow, the conception of "Reincarnation (II)" seems too settled in advance, and the experience seems contrived. In "The Sheep Child," terror and sexual mystery achieve the focus and compression of experience the other poem lacks. Too much of "Reincarnation (II)" is diffused in the bloodless void of philosophical abstraction, but one really believes the sheep child's vision because its identity is so palpable, so uniquely realized in language of passionate intensity:

> *I am here, in my father's house.*
> *I who am half of your world, came deeply*
> *To my mother in the long grass*
> *Of the west pasture, where she stood like moonlight*
> *Listening for foxes. It was something like love*
> *From another world that seized her*
> *From behind, and she gave, not lifting her head*
> *Out of dew, without ever looking, her best*
> *Self to that great need. Turned loose, she dipped her face*
> *Farther into the chill of the earth, and in a sound*
> *Of sobbing   of something stumbling*
> *Away, began, as she must do,*
> *To carry me.*

"The Sheep Child" develops in two movements spoken by two separate personae, the narrator and the sheep child, a method that recalls the method of "The Owl King," in which each of three speakers views an experience from a different angle of vision. The sheep child is a vastly better poet than the narrator, exceeding him as the superhuman exceeds the human. The narrator's introductory remarks are delivered with the maundering stammer of a southern yokel spinning a ghostly yarn. In his soliloquy (above), the sheep child maintains that the farm boy regarded his sheep-mate as a thing without being, selfless, defenseless, caught unawares. To couple with the sheep would be a mere extension of the act of masturbation, like coupling "with soft-wooded trees/ With mounds of earth." Shrewdly, the sheep complies with this falsification of her role to trap the boy into completing the act of bestiality. The boy mistakes the female sheep's absorbed passiveness for indifference, for *"she gave, not lifting her head/ Out of dew, without ever looking, her best/ Self to that great need."* The ewe experiences a perfect fulfillment of being; the farm boy, "stumbling away," is sobbing, haunted, driven wildly afraid by the profundity of her experience. His fear is mixed with guilt for having committed the forbidden act.

The ewe takes her place alongside "Crazy Jane" in the gallery of mindless sexual heroines in modern poetry in English. The farm boy's amazement and terror at her unexpected passion dramatize, in an original and unpredictable way, the mystery and depth of female sexuality. Yeats provided religious-erotic motifs that anticipate this poem in "Leda and the Swan" and "The Second Coming." But while Yeats molds the poem around myths taken from Bible, folklore, or literary tradition, Dickey draws on legends concocted by nonliterate, superstitious people to curb the wildness of the young. The poem combines the supernatural otherness of nightmare with Ripleyesque shock effects, but the vision is so powerfully conceived that it escapes sensationalism.

If "The Sheep Child" opens up new possibilities for deepening man's sexual identity, "Encounter in the Cage Country" explores opportunities for deepening his spiritual identity in a worldly setting (in this poem, the zoo). "Encounter" succeeds because the fabulous experience occurs unexpectedly, in a completely mundane context. The astonishing recognition and exchange between the narrator and the leopard unmistakably carries the ring of truth. Mystical events very likely do seem to invade the author's worldly life, leaping into his experience where he least expects to find them. They strike him, and those witnesses who happen to be present and looking on, with crushing reality:

> Among the crowd, he found me
> Out   and dropped his bloody snack
> And came to the perilous edge
> Of the cage, where the great bars tremble
> Like wire. All Sunday ambling stopped,
>
> The curved cells tightened around
> Us all   as we saw he was watching only
> Me.

"Encounter" is a celebration of individual uniqueness. As in "Snakebite," the protagonist pictures himself as the *one chosen*, chosen by some mysterious intelligent agent in the universe who

> was given a life-
> mission to say to me hungrily over
>
> And over and over   *your moves are exactly right*
> *For a few things in this world: we know you*
> *When you come, Green Eyes, Green Eyes.*

Most of the poems that employ the theme of human/animal relations try to maintain a balance between emotional extremes of joy and terror. In "The Heaven of Animals" and "Springer Mountain," the terror is felt to be too easily contained, or counterbalanced, by the joy. An irrepressible terror is unleashed in "The Sheep Child." Finally, a truer balance between deepened emotions is achieved in the vision of "Encounter in the Cage Country," in which the comic spirit becomes a center of focus:

> . . . at one brilliant move
>
> I made as though drawing a gun from my hip-
> bone, the bite-sized children broke
> Up   changing their concept of laughter,
>
> But none of this changed his eyes, or changed
> My green glasses. Alert, attentive,
> He waited for what I could give him:
>
> My moves   my throat   my wildest love,
> The eyes behind my eyes.

While the humor enhances the seriousness of the exchange between man and beast, it also balances the terror as the poem rises to a peak of spiritual transcendence.

In the earlier poems, Dickey supposed he could give up his human self to the animal realm. The human/animal encounter in the last poem of the series, "Encounter in the Cage Country," has become a medium through which his human limitations can be transcended, but in going beyond his human condition, he no longer transforms into a new, wholly other being; instead, he intensifies and deepens the human self by adding animal powers to it. He becomes more truly human by realizing and releasing animistic powers recognized to have been inherent in him all along but not available until the fulfilled vision of the later poems. It is a vision which places the living man before us, a man whose daily experience may, at any moment, speak to him in the profound otherworldly language of dreams, a man who is instantly recognized by his spiritual kin among the animal kingdom, a man whose days are lit with wonders that never cease to amaze both himself and witnesses standing by, when they occur: "the crowd/Quailed from me   I was inside and out/ Of myself."

HERBERT LEIBOWITZ

The Moiling of Secret Forces:
The Eye-Beaters, Blood, Victory, Madness, Buckhead and Mercy

IN OUR AGE OF SELF-CONSCIOUS POETRY, when most poets double as schoolmen, the encounter with nature is usually mythic or literary, as if from a visit to a Museum of Natural History, owing much to Freud, Jung, and Frazer and almost nothing to elemental contact. In its most common form, landscape, nature is as conventional as iambic pentameter. It is a source of metaphors, not powers, a traditional shorthand that is useful in analyzing emotions or cultural breakdown. This attitude costs heavily, forcing the poet to sell a large part of his imaginative birthright, that Orphic immediacy Melville, for example, gained by direct experience of the sea's wonders and terrors.

To this tradition, canonized and fossilized in "The Waste Land," James Dickey stands off center. Behind his pose of North Georgia suburban backwoodsman lies a shrewd and troubled knowledge of the "primal powers" of rivers, woods, snakes—and a dramatic skill in presenting the endless beauty of instinct, the feel of icy undertows and warm shallows, the bloodlettings which are a regular part of nature's law. When, in the early poem "Kudzu," the hogs are let loose to root out the snakes nesting in this Japanese vine, the noises of rage, fear, and excitement are purposeful instances of the "moiling of secret forces" in the animal world from which man cuts himself off at great peril.

In the best poems of *Helmets* and *Buckdancer's Choice*, and in his recent novel *Deliverance*, Dickey initiates a contest with nature

129

to discover his proper relation to its "uncomprehending conse-quence." Not that he fails to worship the household gods of order. Rather, he believes that the shark must be made at home in the parlor, not as a souvenir or atavistic gesture, but as the retention of a necessary primeval wildness.

Poems 1957–1967 summed up this long quest for the grail. A poet of process, a celebrator of the miracles of motion, by an ecstacy of pure act (and risking death) he had reached the heart of nature's dark energy, and been rewarded with the bestowal of a private wisdom that lived on in the body as an "utter, unseasonable glory." This was magic without primitivism, spiritual grace with-out mysticism. The poems, finely modeled, spare, lucid, and calm at the center, avoided irony and the language of romantic intoxica-tion.

The balance of pure abandon and meticulous observation breaks apart in Dickey's latest volume, *The Eye-Beaters, Blood, Victory, Madness, Buckhead and Mercy.* (The inflated title is a clue that something is awry.) As the material thins out, the voice be-comes more public, forensic, even maudlin, as in "Looking for the Buckhead Boys," "Living There," and "Mercy," perhaps because the poet needs to conceal from himself his worry about where next to turn and how to avoid repeating himself. Having matched him-self against his own limits, leaped the rapids in *Deliverance,* he has landed in a poetic backwater.

A stagy, unpleasant hysteria enters the poems, a spirit of re-ligiosity, as though they were infected by the diseases and blind-ness that afflict the poet and the people in his poems. The "wail of mortality" as he reads in the Book of the Dead, pursuing the ghosts of memory and wishing the reincarnation of the "Old Self, like a younger brother, like a son," comes very close to childish petulance and nervous chatter: an embarrassing ploy to cheat and defeat time. The gambling with unbalance which before seemed an austere, heroic effort now seems sheer bravado; "everything is how much glory is in it" is bad as poetry and as a rule of conduct.

The poems yield few answers to the cause of this self-mistrust and backsliding. A way out of this destructive externality is, how-ever, suggested by "The Eye-Beaters." As this brilliant, harrowing poem recreates the "pure killing fury pure   triumph pure accept-ance" of the blind children as they burst the bonds that tie their hands and beat at their eyes for sight, it also debates the future course of Dickey's art. He argues against reason that the desperate beating of the eyes can induce vision, that the children are artists inscribing on the cave walls of their darkness "the original images of mankind."

At first his faith in his poetic inventions appears only a "makeshift salvation," but it grows into conviction. He can live now with the fact of mortality. Nature had, after all, prepared him for his visionary contest with the "art-crazed beasts" for survival as poet and man. The will of the imagination is godlike, and this "Lord of the Air" can confer the ultimate glory, a "wholly human art":

> Power over birds and beasts:
>   something that has come in
> From all over   come out but
>   not for betrayal, or to call
> Up death or desire, but only
>   to give   give what was
>   never.

LINDA MIZEJEWSKI

Shamanism toward
Confessionalism:
James Dickey, Poet

SINCE THE MID-SIXTIES OR SO, one or two people at almost any English Department cocktail party have had a James Dickey story. Perhaps even more amazing than the stories themselves has been Dickey's mercurial quality that renders an anecdote from nearly every college reading and from so many personal encounters. After 1972, the stories became Jim Dickey-Burt Reynolds stories, and after January, 1977, there were tales from Carter's inaugural, but by then they were appearing in popular news magazines. Developing as a celebrity-poet, Dickey has broken from the university circuits of rumors and readings, and materialized in middle-class living rooms—in glossy coffeetable books and on the television screen, where he is likely to be reciting from his Biblical prose-poetry on a talk show.

President Carter certainly blessed an unusual inaugural poet. Unlike E. A. Robinson or Robert Frost, who had been nationally honored by Theodore Roosevelt and Kennedy, Dickey does not write an easily accessible "popular" poetry. His poems are certainly not academic, but the average reader who believes he can understand the somewhat deceptive simplicity of Frost or the small-town characters of Robinson might be confused by Dickey's elaborate sentence structures that snake like the Coosawattee and make breathtaking turns around tricky prepositional phrases. He might be disturbed by a poetry that, far from making Frost's humanizing inquiries into nature, sees man as an animal coded to hunt and survive by blood in the natural world, so that war, too, is a natural human activity. He might be disturbed by a poetry in which a middle-class, middle-aged man tries to reckon with how he had firebombed the Japanese by understanding his own sense of personal power as godlike destroyer and suburban builder—all this in semi-Biblical, Southern rhetoric.

This fine, complex poetry, in which the imagination is often the subject as well as the creator, is probably not the work of Dickey's that most Americans know. Far more have probably read his novel, *Deliverance,* and the fiction in *Esquire.* Even more than that identify him with the movie version of the novel, or know him as the publicized poet of inauguration week when Dickey, identified by the media as "the voice of the South," interpreted the election of a Southern administration as no less than a Biblical event. Dickey has promoted not just a Southern mystique, but a Dickey mystique, and has become not just a nationally known poet like Frost, but a personality as self-mythologizing as the President's own brother.

The showmanship of the yarn-spinning and rhetoric during inauguration week is a trademark of the poet whose best work has always been charged with the presence of the master performer. The best of his *Poems 1957–1967* work like an ideal, reversed ending of the Oz story: the curtain might be pulled aside for a glimpse of the professor working the levers to produce the sound effects and smoke, but the wizardry—contrived as it may be—continues anyway, and with a great deal of success. There is no demand for a return to the farm in Kansas—or Georgia—where real life is without magic and masks altogether. Instead, all sorts of bizarre and unlikely conjurings go on: a traffic jam becomes the Apocalypse, a military execution turns into an acrobatic stunt, a man's legs fall asleep and pick up the dream of the hunting dog sleeping on his feet. The artifices of showmanship and magic *save* us in poems such as "The Hospital Window," "The Celebration," "Slave Quarters," "Power and Light." They save us from sentimentality, pain, or self-pity. "Guilt is magical," says the speaker at the end of "Adultery," because guilt has been *performed* in the poem, exorcised by a shaman-narrator who has dissolved the walls of a motel room and extended the risks of a love affair into all the open frontiers of American history.

The presence of the poet-performer in those poems is as intense as the personal presence by which Dickey has become nationally known in the media over the past year. However, the public personality—of shaman, storyteller, good ole boy—is always that of a man who knows he is onstage and who keeps an actor's distance between himself and his audience. In the earlier poems, Dickey did likewise, always avoiding the "confessional" sort of personality found in Lowell, Snodgrass, Berryman, or Sexton. Dickey was especially critical of Sexton's work, which he found indulgent and uncontrolled. But while the public Dickey was developing as a showman, the poet Dickey was experimenting with how loosely personal his act could become. *Eyebeaters* showed some of this experimentation, but his most recent poetry, the book-length poem *The Zodiac* shows an actor-poet who has gone as far as he can, almost on a dare, into a painful, public exploration of trauma. While Snodgrass or Lowell would have written unabashedly personal accounts of the loneliness, fear of failure, terror of mortality, and struggle with language that haunt *Zodiac*, Dickey opts for the shaman's mask again—this time, the mask of an historical person far removed in location and time.

In this case, though, the mask is too flimsy and the role too superficial, so that not even Dickey can play it right. Juggling with materials that he does not want to play confessionally, Dickey slips in his act and is finally unable to achieve the distance of the public, acting figure. *Zodiac*, which awed and puzzled most of its critics, demonstrates enough of the old Dickey eloquence and power to make it worthwhile to ask what went wrong. More than that, it asks us to examine what is perhaps the real difference between confessional and non-confessional poetry: the extent to which the speaker is onstage consciously enjoying his own performance as shaman, wizard, showman.

Zodiac has all the material for shamanistic transformations. The main character, Hendrick Marsman, is a hallucinating, half-mad poet-sailor who wants to "relate himself, by means of stars, to the universe," as Dickey explains in the introduction. The scene is Europe in the late thirties or early forties, just before Marsman's death. Like an epic poet-hero sailing into the stars, Marsman knows he is a man in the hands of patterns and monsters created by someone or something else in the sky, and he is trying to construct a fantastic sort of metaphysics of the constellations.

But this time Dickey's conjurings fail. The power behind the poetic machinery blinks off, and the transformations never occur. Because there is often very little distance between Dickey and his subject, Marsman never becomes as dramatic as the self-performing speakers of the earlier poems. Often the metaphors are not imaginative juxtapositions but attempts by a drunken narrator to relate himself to *anything*. And even though Marsman is attempting to recreate a zodiac, the zodiac never becomes a real structure for his personality or imagination. The twelve sections take different scenes in a four-day span, alluding randomly to some of the constellations and signs, giving brief vignettes, and always returning to Marsman's terror of and fascination with the night sky. But there is no sense of closure to this loose history except for Marsman's impending death. When last seen, Marsman is writing and/or being firebombed, and the final affirmation of the transcendence of his art seems tacked-on in relation to Marsman's miserable, drunken wanderings throughout the other sections. Nothing in those other scenes justifies a triumph of either Marsman or the universal artist suggested throughout. In general, without the transformative magic of drama and distance, there is a sad exposure of the poet stepping out to admit it's all been just levers and smoke, and willing to give us now an "honest" account of the impossible attempt to transcend pain through language.

The transformations that do go on in *Zodiac* are mostly those between drunkenness, sleep, and brief periods of sobriety. Using alcoholic spiels as frames for monologues, like using dreams, allows for repetition, illogical apposition, random imagery, and quick shifts of scene. But unlike the dreamer, the drunk is also subject to misinterpretation and misperception of what is really there. Like Lowry in *Under the Volcano*, Dickey is relying on a belief in moments of drunken clarity and even brilliance, the ability of the drunk to come to realizations he could not have made sober. In a novel the length and scope of Lowry's, it is possible to develop a character who is a lucid and magnificent drunk. But in Dickey's poem of less than sixty pages, no character equalling the magnificence of the Consul is developed, although Dickey clearly intends to suggest an experience much wider than the historical Marsman's. As critics have pointed out, this is Dickey's most ambitious work, the epic that summarizes the themes of all his early work: the poet as part of history, man as an alien to nature and able to enter it only through the moment of the imagination, and language as the shaman's power against mortality.

Marsman, then, is romanticized as the poet-sailor to the extent that his "craft"—poetry and ship—becomes in the end the death-ship similar to the Anglo-Saxon burial ships for kings. In the last stanzas, Marsman identifies his personal struggle and extinction with the tragedy of all mortal poets attempting immortal tasks. His dramatic directives—". . . put me in a solar boat. . ./ That I can steer this strange craft to morning"—suggest the epic adventurer, too. But when Marsman hopes to "steer" to morning, he also simply wants to make it through another drunken night. So the question is whether Marsman's experience as presented by Dickey is, in fact, raised to such heroic stature—that is, if there is justification for such intimate and painful exploration of this speaker's psyche.

Facing the dilemma of how to give this kind of serious, even tragic stature to a character who is a personal and professional failure, Dickey attempts, like Lowry, to identify the "fall" of his character with the decline of western culture during the rise of Fascism and Nazism. But Dickey's background scenes, the European war setting, are only vaguely described. In most of the scenes, Marsman could actually be in any city in any historical period. We're told several times that Europe is itself at the edge of disaster, but in each instance this seems to be a momentary judgment made by Marsman in his own disastrous condition. At one point the comparison generalizes, "He goes on without anywhere to go. This is what you call Europe./ Right?" Marsman is wandering the city drunk, and we know *he* has no place to go, but there are no details given to suggest that all of Europe, too, is about to collapse. The observations about the historical situation seem oddly out of place, as in Part II when after telling us "His life is shot   my life is shot," the narrating voice concludes that "The gods are in pieces/ All over Europe," even though all we have seen up to that point is one of Marsman's hallucinations from the DT's. Marsman, we're told, has "been there/ Among the columns:/ among Europe. He can't tell Europe/ From his own death."

However, except that we know the general time period, the idea of European decline is never fully developed. We never get the impact of a landscape like Lowry's, which is made real *outside* of the Consul's perceptions of it through the reports of the Battle of the Ebro, the Day of the Dead, the oppressive heat and dust, the overpowering presence of the ravine or *barranca*. Dickey uses a ravine, too, in two different places, but we can't be certain either is real like the real ditches all over Lowry's Quauhnahuac. Once Marsman imagines the sky as full of "gullies" with the moon itself fallen into one. But the hallucination is not very convincing, since the image dissolves into undescribed "Realities." Marsman decides that "the key *image/* Tonight *tonight/* is the gully gullies:/ Clouds make them, and other Realities/ Are revealed in Heaven,/ as clouds drift across." The problem is that the metaphor seems appended rather than conjured, especially since it is self-consciously labeled by the poet Marsman as "the key image."

As a poet, Marsman worries aloud frequently about this problem of his own perspective and "universality." He comes across the other ravine image when he wanders the city one morning, either drunk or very hungover, and finds "some kind of/ Lit-up ravine" which he can't cross and which seems to "move across" him. He asks quickly, "But is it universal?", using the word half-mockingly as he does on two previous occasions when he addresses God in poet-*vs.*-the-cosmos challenges. He taunts God in those earlier scenes as a "universal son of a bitch," the creator to whom the critics can't object, the poet who is *always* universal. But in the third reference at the ravine hallucination, the term actually raises a serious problem in Dickey's book. It begins a long description of the zodiac, explaining how the ravine—that is, Marsman's spiritual abyss and ruin—has "been lifted from the beginning/ Into this night-black—/ Into the Zodiac." Marsman's question here is significant: are his perceptions of himself in the gullies of the world and sky the hallucinations of one drunken artist, or are they symbols of a sustained tragic vision? Is Marsman's failure to "relate himself, through stars, to the universe" the failure of one mad poet or a symbol of what all artists attempt and fail to achieve?

This question is complicated by the dual nature of Marsman's crisis. His struggle for a metaphysical zodiac is therapeutic as well as artistic; he is seeking not just a spiritual framework, but a way to deal with his loneliness, alcoholism, sense of failure, and sense of his approaching death. One way to do this is to see an animistic universe which is dying *with* the personal self and which is full of symbols, signs, and some degree of empathy.

The constellations are the most obvious "signs," and Marsman is especially obsessed with how they are full of "beasts," animals and monsters that make a "scrambled zoo" similar to his personal zoo of hallucinations. Ironically, the only effective shamanistic move in the book occurs when Marsman decides to create a new constellation to fight Cancer or death: the Lobster, which sadly and comically turns into one of his creatures from the DT's and which turns on him and attacks him. The difference between this move and the metaphoric transformations in earlier Dickey poems is its self-consciousness. "Imagination and dissipation both fire at me," Marsman says, thereby stepping out of the role of shaman and pointing to what he's doing, identifying it as *just* metaphor, which can't help him personally. "I didn't mean it," he apologizes, at the mercy of his own hallucination. Unfortunately, the metaphors in *Zodiac* often really do control the poet rather than vice versa.

Essentially, they are personifications, attempts to identify with and humanize the world rather than transform it. The confessional poetry of Sexton uses this technique again and again as a desperate kind of therapy. In *Zodiac*, these metaphors are sometimes forced or heavyhanded in the struggle to appropriate the external world into the psyche of the speaker. Describing his rooms, Marsman asserts that "A flower couldn't make it in this place./ It couldn't live, or couldn't get here at all./ No flower could get up these steps,/ It'd wither at the hollowness/ Of these foot-stomping/ failed creative-man's boards." This is an explanation that the "boards" of the artist—perhaps in the sense of the stage as well as of "drawing boards"—have failed, but the metaphor itself fails by getting out of control, switching contexts from creative survival to the more far-fetched concept of the plant walking upstairs. Stranger things have happened in earlier Dickey poems—a man is hooked up to his own house wiring, or a shark gets loose in a living room—but only in a context that prepares us for the imaginative leap gradually through tone and narrative detail. That context is missing here, and we're left only with the desperate need to personify.

This happens several times in *Zodiac* when the appropriateness of the metaphor is clear only in relation to Marsman's undependable perception. We must take the word of the speaker that "The fish, too,/ Are afraid of the sun," or that the "Innocence" of water is an "ultimate marigold horror." At one point a painting "squeezes art's blood out of the wallpaper," a bridge is a "slain canal," and the "gully of clouds" in the sky is "a shameless place" where "the rest of nature is." All these are equations of Marsman's misery with a more universal misery, but they are also flat assertions rather than conjurations of a credible animism. This kind of exaggerated, bombastic metaphor led Stanley Plumly to ask in a review if Dickey has perhaps gone beyond hyperbole into "superbole."

Wayne Shumaker suggests in *Literature and the Irrational* that all metaphor is essentially a belief in or hope for animism. But the personification used in *Zodiac* shows a shift in Dickey from magic to a kind of psychotherapy, or from lyric celebration to a thinly disguised confessional poetry. Part of this is the fault of the failed distancing device, which is an intermittent third-person narrator whose tone is never clear and who is rather extraneous to what is really Hendrik Marsman's poem. While Dickey at times seems to identify with Marsman wholly, at other times this third-person voice seems straining for objectivity, judgment, even reproach.

Zodiac opens with this narrator who is clearly outside the mind and situation of Marsman, "The man I'm telling you about," as he says in the first line. Sometimes the shift from this objective narrator to an interior monologue is obvious, as when the narrator is used to introduce a thought of Marsman's. But often the point of view is ambiguous enough to be either interior monologue or objective description, and this creates a problem in tone. We're sometimes not sure if the perceptions are the results of Marsman's limited vision or alcoholic fantasies, or are descriptions of a setting from a more removed and dependable narrator. This is actually the problem with some of the personification metaphors which might come from a paranoid Marsman, or, more problematically, from the narrator who is in charge of Marsman's story.

Part of the problem is that the narrator sometimes uses the diction of Marsman, even the drunken diction, and this is a real shift from the historical voice of the opening. Before we get to the first interior monologue by Marsman, the third-person voice has already dropped such lines as "Hot damn, here they come!" to describe the DT's, and "You talk about *looking:* would you look at *that*/Electric page." In general, though there are first-person and third-person technical points of view, the voices are identical, and it is difficult to account for the presence of the outside narrator at all. Not only are they identical, but they are not very different in diction and sociology from the speakers in some of Dickey's earlier work. Drunk or sober, Marsman more often comes across as an out-of-shape Southern ex-football player than a Dutch sailor. He addresses Pythagoras as his "old lyre-picking buddy," and he later laments, "O flesh, that takes on any dirt/ At all/ I can't get you back in shape." Even some of the images are the same as those Dickey has used to describe other personas. When Marsman "polar-bears through the room," it's difficult not to remember the middle-aged teacher at the end of "False Youth: Two Seasons" who "skates like an out-of-shape bear" to his car.

In spite of this strained characterization of Marsman, the more important question in the end is whether the poem's form resolves the problems of the speaker. Although the twelve-part division suggests, like Lowry, a "twelfth hour" or end of a cycle, the structure of the poem is actually not a pattern of hours, months, or zodiac signs. It works instead as a looser pattern of drunkenness, ambition, self-reproach, and finally hope. While Marsman is obsessed with the zodiac, it is never actually materialized and never used as a means to structure his imagination. So the kind of resolution in the last section tries to be a closure to a structure and heroic pattern that is never really there. For the last lines of the book make a case for the triumph of Marsman, if not as an individual, then as symbol of a universal artist who might find the "instrument   the tuning fork" that can create a music of the spheres which is possible "So long as the hand can hold its island/ Of blazing paper, and bleed for its images."

Without the integrity of a justifiable character and a clear structure behind it, the entire last section seems somewhat overwritten. Poetry, or at least the nobility of the poet's struggle, is affirmed in a sort of revelation like a thunderbolt: "A day like that. But afterwards the fire/ Comes straight down through the roof, white-lightning nightfall,/ A face-up flash. Poetry." This also suggests a night bombing or even Marsman's death by torpedo which had been mentioned in the introduction. Throughout, Marsman asserts that poetry for him is a way of reading and writing in the night sky among the constellations. So having the sky literally fall on him can be either tragic or sadly and almost comically ironic. The problem is that the lines themselves become inflated at this point: "Poetry. Triangular eyesight. It draws his/ fingers together at the edge/ Around a pencil. He crouches bestially,/ The darkness stretched out on the waters/ Pulls back, humming Genesis." This carries mixed connotations of a football quarterback and an epic Biblical movie. Unfortunately, Marsman has done nothing to make himself godlike enough for Genesis. In fact, one of the better passages in the book shows Marsman as poet opposing God as creator, setting up a nice contrast between creation of the universe by God and trans-formation of the universe through the imagination of man. "I say right now," Marsman challenges at that point, ". . . like a man/ Bartending for God,/ What'll it be? . . . my old man/ Was an astronomer, of sorts, and didn't he say the whole night sky's/ *invented?*" But the invention never materializes in the poem itself, neither in any poem by Marsman nor in Dickey's romanticization of Marsman.

It is sad that the poet who criticized Sexton for her lack of control should write a long work that Harold Bloom hesitantly calls "obsessive and perhaps even hysterical." Yet *Zodiac* illustrates all the hazards of confessionalism, despite its removed character and setting: the problem of justifying interest in the detailed personal problems of the speaker, the risks of using metaphor as a means of humanizing and appropriating a hostile world, and most of all, the problem of how to make the imagination transcend intense subjec-tivity so that there is a resolution in the art, if not in the troubled mind, of the poet.

Finally, it is ironic that the poem about poetry for which Dickey may be best remembered is in his very first volume of poetry—his elegy for Donald Armstrong, "The Performance." Here we find many of the themes later developed in *Zodiac*. It is about how the poet, the man who died, and all men who know they are playing temporary roles can use the imagination to make the final surprising gesture which is the only recourse we have against death, uncertainty, and "the great untrustworthy air" in which Donald Armstrong flies as a pilot in the war. Armstrong's real, faulty acrobatic act is finished and perfected in the poet's memory and in his acrobatics of the imagination. And like the acrobatics, the stanzas and syntax are orchestrated "under pressure" in long, dazzling sentences and in a breathtaking handstand that turns reality upside down and gives us the vision that is suddenly clear and perfect, the vision of a man whose blood has rushed to his head. The background and character are entirely credible—and entirely credible, too, is the sudden back-flip from the actual experience into the poetic fantasy. This is the Dickey most of us love and remember, the man who loves to dazzle his readers, "Doing all his lean tricks to amaze them," like Armstrong's imaginary stunts. And this is the Dickey we hope to see again in his future work—for though Dickey is not a young poet anymore, he demonstrates the enormous amount of energy of the master performer who can avoid the confessional poet's trap of becoming too entangled in experience to use the magic and artifice of Prospero and Oz.

JANE BOWERS-MARTIN

Jericho and *God's Images:*
The Old Dickey Theme

In 1970 JAMES DICKEY PUBLISHED three books, *The Eye-Beaters, Blood, Victory, Madness, Buckhead and Mercy,* a volume of poems; *Deliverance,* his best-selling novel; and *Self-Interviews,* a book based on a series of tapes on which Dickey served as his own interviewer. These were followed in 1971 by *Sorties,* composed of Dickey's journals and several essays. This burst of activity has been mirrored in the two final years of the decade. *The Enemy from Eden* (Lord Jon Press), *The Owl King* (Red Angel Press), *In Pursuit of the Grey Soul* (Bruccoli-Clark Press), *Head Deep in Strange Sounds* (Palaemon Press, Ltd.), and *Tucky the Hunter,* Dickey's children's book, all appeared in 1978 or 1979. The difference in the books published ten years ago and those published in the last eighteen months is in the kind of publisher Dickey used and the kind of market he aimed at. *The Eye-Beaters* volume, published by Doubleday, and *Deliverance,* published by Houghton Mifflin, are generally considered part of Dickey's major body of work and both are the subject of varous critical articles. *Self-Interviews* and *Sorties,* both from Doubleday, have significant comments on Dickey's own work and the modern literary scene. These are books for scholars and readers of serious literature. By the end of the seventies, ten years away from his *Collected Poems* in 1968, a dozen away from the 1966 National Book Award, Dickey's books, with the exception of Crown's *Tucky the Hunter,* come exclusively from small, private publishing concerns which have produced luxury-edition books, available to a much smaller, less scholarly-inclined audience. The artistic reasons for this abrupt turnaround in the career of a major poet can best be traced through an examination of the three books published between these two distinct groups of books.

Of the three books published in the mid-seventies, *The Zodiac* (from Doubleday), Dickey's 1976 book-length poem, is the one that belongs with and, in fact, culminates the exploration of transcendence through the idiom of the creative lie which dominates Dickey's poetry. *The Zodiac*'s exaggerated horizontal shape is a miniature version of the books that preceded and followed it, the large coffee-table volumes *Jericho: The South Beheld* (1974) and *God's Images* (1977). And like *The Zodiac*, based on a poem of the same name by the Dutch poet Hendrick Marsman, both *Jericho* and *God's Images* are inspired by other sources, *Jericho* by the traditional Southern mythos and *God's Images* by the Bible. *The Zodiac* also provided the first evidence of Dickey's interest in the luxury, collector's-edition market. The working manuscript for the poem was divided into several scores of sections, each of which was bound into a special-edition volume; these Bruccoli-Clark collector's editions were then sold by private subscription at a cost of $400 per book. But *The Zodiac* should logically be grouped with Dickey's serious poetry because of its close thematic ties to the other poems and because it seems to be the ultimate exploration of Dickey's creative lie.

Jericho and *God's Images,* on the other hand, belong in the group of books published by and for different people than the people who read Dickey's poems. Both books come from Oxmoor House, Inc., the book division of The Progressive Farmer Company; both are oversized volumes which combine Dickey's writing with illustrations, Hubert Shuptrine's paintings in *Jericho* and the etchings of Marvin Hayes in *God's Images*. Both books seem aimed at the scholar's mother, even his grandmother, more than at the scholar himself. But neither volume denies the theme that is the center of Dickey's poetry, that of transcendence, or what Dickey calls "the fusion of inner and outer states."[1] It is in the examination of this theme, the one Dickey himself calls "the old Dickey theme," in his notes for "Madness,"[2] and the way that Dickey uses it in these two books, books different from his award-winning poetry and his best-selling novel, that we can see why Dickey's publishing history makes its drastic turn in the seventies. *Jericho* and *God's Images*, and all the luxury editions from relatively obscure presses that follow them, are books written by a man unable to find new subjects and themes around which to build new poems. And more importantly, since *The Zodiac* brought Dickey to the inevitable conclusion of the poetic idiom he had been exploring throughout his career, he has been unable to develop a new idiom through which to present his central theme. Thus, *Jericho* and *God's Images* are attempts to get extra mileage from what has worked before.

This recycling of his successful themes and techniques might have worked—and does to some extent. But *Jericho* and *God's Images* fall far short of the poems they echo because Dickey either shuts himself off from or rejects the main sources of his power. The first typical Dickey technique to fall is his own artistic control of the transcendent experience he hopes to present. It falls in the introduction to *Jericho* when Dickey asks the reader to become a "beholder." A beholder is someone who "is able to enter into objects and people and places with the sense of these things entering into him. What starts out as a deliberate act of attention ends as though he were not so much performing a rendition of Reality, but that a living action were being perpetrated on him."[3] In his poem called "The Beholders" (*Falling*, 1967), Dickey gives the reader the experience of beholding through the successful fusion of the poem's personae and their environment, but the implication of the approach he takes in *Jericho* by asking the reader to become a beholder at the outset is that Dickey cannot give his reader that energy, that transcendence, himself. Rather, the reader must provide a significant part of the energy for fusion; he must make himself transcendent: "You, reader, must open up until you reach the point . . . of sensing your locality pour into you simultaneously through every sense . . ." (*Jericho*, 16–17).

In addition to relinquishing part of his power to manipulate the reader, Dickey also eliminates the need for the creative lie. In *Self-Interviews* he says: "But I think I really began to develop as a poet . . . when I saw the creative possibilities of the lie."[4] And it is, indeed, his creative lying that makes him successful at giving his reader a transcendent experience. He gives us a sheep child, two young lovers forever living in the mist that envelopes the trail of their wrecked motorcycle, a stewardess who begins to live only as she falls to her death, a mad dog's head that blazes with consequence, blind children who tear loose their bound fists to pound vision into their eyes, and in all of these cases, even those in which the lie that gives us the transcendent experience is as self-conscious and overt as it is in "The Eye-Beaters," even then, we believe. We have been *given* those experiences through the poet's skilled use of his idiom, the lie. It does not matter that there are no sheep children; Dickey gives us one. In *Jericho* and *God's Images* Dickey uses traditions and stories that he expects his reader to be familiar with, asks the reader to look at them in a heightened way—to behold them, and hopes those who do will come away feeling more a part of the stories that are already a part of them. This premise cuts Dickey off from what he is best at. He cannot give us a new experience; he cannot lie to us. So he must be content to serve as a sort of tour guide, taking us to places we have been before, hoping we will see them differently, better, for his presence.

The persona Dickey adopts to carry the reader on his tour of the South as Jericho, the Promised Land, is that of a seabird, hovering, swooping, changing forms, becoming whatever best suits a particular experience, but always the one bird, a consistent narrator, who accompanies the reader through a series of "flickers," as Dickey calls the experiences in *Jericho*. The perspective gained by beholding through the eyes of the bird combines with the necessity for contact with the ground, the real world, established in *Jericho's* epigraph from Joshua—"Loose thy shoe from off thy foot; for the place whereon thou standest is holy"—to set up a framework of fusion of two worlds. And the series of images called flickers fits into that framework.

Beginning the flickers in St. Augustine, the South's oldest city, Dickey immediately establishes an important aspect of the fusion he is exploring. The bird's eye is caught by an oyster shell, one whose condition symbolizes one of *Jericho's* major concerns: "It is not lying on a beach, half-embedded in sand, but is jutting from a wall at an angle it never had in the sea" (*Jericho*, 21). This conjunction of the natural world and the man-made world is echoed when the bird flickers to the gardens of Mobile: "No matter how close to them we are, no matter whether we help them grow or kill them, they are forever beyond us, these flowers" (*Jericho*, 24). Mississippi riverboats self-consciously seek the natural center of the river, "looking for a way back in" (*Jericho*, 24). In the Texas panhandle wild antelopes pick up radio signals in their antlers; West Virginia offers the bird her industry-scarred face. The southern people also embody this fusion of the natural and the man-made in the strange dichotomy of their lives, partly grounded in the past with its dependence on nature, the land, and partly rooted in the increasingly industrial future. The flickers take the reader into the lives of a quarry worker being hoisted past layers of earth, measurements of time, a buck-dancing auto worker, a cowboy killing alligators for their skins, a worker in a public garden replacing the worn-out gnomon on a sundial. The fusion of the two worlds is most clear in the face of a mill-team softball player: "One of the ways we rose from the ashes was into the mill. The faces belong to the land, the fingers to the thread" (*Jericho*, 68).

Jericho ends with a word of warning about the fragility of this fusion on which the Promised Land, the new South, is built. In Birmingham, Vulcan, the god of steel, upon whose shoulders the fusion rests, says to the bird and to the reader: "All this hardware I make: well, don't tell those new high-rising buildings of Jericho I told you; men used to call me Mulciber. You know what that means? The softener. They might get jittery. I might fall off this hill" (*Jericho*, 119). And so Dickey gives us in this final flicker that moment with the elements of danger, repose, and joy that he hopes to incarnate in his poems.[5] But after the series of flickers, he must again draw back and leave the reader to unify the experience for himself, as he enjoins him to "Come down, reader, and be whole here" (*Jericho*, 157).

Dickey doesn't use the label "flicker" for the scenes in *God's Images*, but it fits them as well as it does the scenes in *Jericho*. And again Dickey's randomly presented material eliminates the need for the creative lie. He depends on each reader's having his own personal interpretations for the Biblical stories presented: "We all have our images of God, given to us by the Bible, which is the word of God. These images are ours, and in calling them up in our minds we are living witnesses of the fact that the kingdom of God is within you."[6] Dickey hopes to use each reader's personal images from the Bible in combination with his own interpretations to lead the reader to a higher recognition of each story's oneness with both the reader's inner self and the outside world, the kingdom of God. He depends not upon his abilities as creative liar but upon the reader's pre-established, long-standing connection to the Biblical episodes to produce the desired fusion of inner and outer states, thus requiring the reader of *God's Images* to provide his own transcendent energy in the same way the reader of *Jericho* had to.

But *God's Images* forfeits another of Dickey's strengths, one retained in *Jericho*, and because of the additional departure from his usual approach toward his subject, the episodes, or "flickers," in *God's Images* are more fragmented, less unified, less successful as a complete work, than those in *Jericho*. In this second coffee-table book, Dickey fails to provide the strong narrative voice, the often unique narrative voice, that makes the best of his poems work. We believe the lies that give us the sheep child, the "May Day Sermon" lovers, the stewardess, and the blind children largely because we believe the voice that tells us about them. We become sure of the sheep child when he speaks for himself. The lady preacher convinces us of the truth of the lovers' experience as surely as they ever could, probably more surely; our feeling for the blind children is more vivid because we receive it through the visitor desperate to give them sight. And in "Falling" we believe that the perceptions we are given are those of the stewardess and that they are accurate perceptions because of a narrative technique Dickey describes in his notes for "Madness," another poem with a strong narrative voice. He says he wrote that poem wanting to "imply the first person without ever *using* it."[7] Thus, he gives us the immediacy of first person and the objectivity of third person narration to create the feeling of "heightened reportage" that Laurence Lieberman has seen in his work.[8]

While this sense of heightened reportage, or in *God's Images* heightened retelling, is exactly what Dickey, in the book's introduction, says he wants to achieve, he completely abandons the idea of a single narrative voice, resorting to whatever voice strikes him for each episode. Most often the voice that strikes him is that of an omniscient third person, a voice that has no trace of the feeling of first person he achieves in poems like "Falling" and "Madness." Of the fifty-two episodes in *God's Images*, twenty-two have the omniscient narrator. In a breakdown of the two sections, sixteen of twenty-nine Old Testament scenes resort to an omniscient narrator, as do six of twenty-three in the New Testament section. So part of the weakness of *God's Images* can be attributed to Dickey's own inability to fuse with the characters and incidents he presents.

The proportionally greater reliance on the omniscient narrator in the Old Testament section indicates that it is the weaker of the book's two sections, the one in which Dickey less frequently provides his believable fusion of inner and outer states. There are flickers of the old theme. In the account of Jacob wrestling with an angel, for instance, Jacob says: " . . . the strength of a great antagonist flows into me. . . . Neither one of us can win. Neither of us can lose." The exchange, the fusion of two separate states of being, is more important than an outcome; the same is true in the case of Joseph and the coat of many colors, where the coat serves as the connecting link between father and son. The omniscient narrator says, "He will die remembering how those colors fell and felt upon him." And again, in the image of the baby Moses floating peacefully in his basket, in harmony with the river, the land, the fish, and the woman who finds him, Dickey employs his theme of fusion. But there is little to connect these flickers; each is a discrete moment, frozen in its own boundaries, like Dickey's image of Lot's wife: "Lost woman fixed in shimmer, departing forever into immobility and indifference." This immobility negates the motion, the energy, that allows Dickey's best ideas to work. Most of this section suffers from a paralysis of narrative energy; the lasting impression is of a writer who did not know which voice to use, who, like Dickey's Abraham, heard more than one and was torn between them. Unlike Abraham, Dickey receives no sign that tells him which voice to use, and thus, the Old Testament section of *God's Images* remains a gathering of fragmented thoughts, loosely based on Dickey's standard theme of transcendence.

It is not surprising that the New Testament section less frequently displays the failure to fuse with the subject matter, because the New Testament stories are ones that allow Dickey to more naturally use his familiar theme of the merging of two forces, of the creation of the fusion he seeks. Christ, the embodiment of the fusion of God and man, is the speaker in five scenes in this section, and he also serves to connect the voices of other speakers in the section when he is their subject, as he is in almost every case. The presentation of Christ is much like that of the sheep child, whom we know through his own report and through the report of the farm boy, in that we come to know him both through other voices which report his significance to them and through his own report of his experience. Mary says of her son at his birth: "He is mine, or at least half of him is mine. . . . I cannot understand any of this, but I do know I hold in my lap a child who comes from me. . . . God needs a human mate to bring forth a human child." This same feeling of both knowing and not knowing Christ runs through most of the section. Christ himself speaks of his connection to and separation from the real world: "Men speak of me as a man of pain and sorrow, but they have not reached the other side of God, and while I was here among you, the pain and terror were balanced by a good deal of teasing that nobody believed but God; by a great grin into nothingness, which justified everything. . . ." Like the sheep child, Christ has dual vision, the ability to see the world from both sides, which allows him a kind of repose that single-sighted men lack. For the last supper scene, Dickey uses an omniscient narrator who summarizes Christ's role for the disciples and for the various speakers of the New Testament section. He says: "Jesus is like them, and they can understand Him deeply on the basis of His manhood. But He is also profoundly different, giving them an inkling of what men through God may *become*."

It is this idea of what man might become that dominates Dickey's essay "The Energized Man." In it he says that the energized man, his idea of the kind of man needed to save us from our modern tendency to ignore our potential and drift apathetically through life, stands "not like a creature from another planet, giving off strange rays of solar energy, but as a human creature, like you, like me—like you *could* be, like I like to think *I* could be."⁹ This energized man, this almost Christ-like saviour, who reminds us of both what we are and what we could be, is still what Dickey *could* be. His retreat from his real poetry into the luxury-edition, coffee-table book market, his work over the past decade, has been the kind of drifting through a life with "Comfort" as its ideal that he warns against in "The Energized Man."¹⁰ It has been easy, lazy work. In his *Paris Review* interview, conducted as he was completing work on *The Zodiac*, Dickey speaks of what the poet's real task is: "The main thing in poetry is the discovery of an idiom and the exploitation of it over an area of thought for a long time."¹¹ Dickey has succeeded here; the creative lie has served him well throughout his career, especially as the idiom through which he has explored transcendence. But in the *Paris Review* he goes on to say: "Listen, a poet's pages are filled up with what he's done, that he can live on and trade on; but he has *got* to find some way to love that white empty page, those words he hasn't said yet."[12] And it is here that *Jericho*, *God's Images*, and Dickey's more recent work fall short of Dickey's own goals, his own hopes as a poet. They are his old pages repackaged, and the process diminishes their quality. He has lived and traded on the old work for ten years; with Doubleday's forthcoming publication of a new book of poems, *The Strength of Fields*, Dickey will perhaps finally give us those words he hasn't said yet. The return to the empty white page, to his real work, should be welcomed by those who view Dickey as a serious poet. And their grandmothers will still have two nice books for their coffee tables.

NOTES

1. James Dickey, "The Poet Turns on Himself," in *Babel to Byzantium: Poets and Poetry Now* (New York: Farrar, Straus, and Giroux, 1968), p. 287.
2. Notes from "Madness," James Dickey Papers, 1954–1970, Box 8, Folder 111, Washington University Libraries, St. Louis, Miss.
3. James Dickey, *Jericho: The South Beheld.* Hubert Shuptrine, illus. (Birmingham, Ala.: Oxmoor House, 1974), p. 15.
4. James Dickey, *Self-Interviews*, ed. by Barbara and James Reiss (Garden City, N.Y.: Doubleday, 1970), p. 32.
5. Dickey, *Babel to Byzantium*, p. 292.
6. James Dickey, *God's Images.* Marvin Hayes, illus. (Birmingham, Ala.: Oxmoor House, 1977), n. p.
7. Notes for "Madness," Dickey Papers, Box 8, Folder 111.
8. Laurence Lieberman, "Notes on James Dickey's Style," in *James Dickey: The Expansive Imagination*, ed. by Richard J. Calhoun (DeLand, Fl.: Everett/Edwards, 1973), p. 201.
9. James Dickey, "The Energized Man," in *Billy Goat*, ed. by Robert W. Hill (Clemson, S.C.: Billy Goat Press, 1979), p. 3. Reprinted in this book, pp. 163–65.
10. Dickey, "The Energized Man," p. 1.
11. "James Dickey, the Art of Poetry XX," *The Paris Review*, 65 (Spring 1976), 81–82.
12. "James Dickey, the Art of Poetry XX," 76.

DAVE SMITH

The Strength of James Dickey

JAMES DICKEY, AS A SELF-DEFINED POET of "The Second
Birth," has always been committed to discovering and exploring
"his own uniquely human segment of the common consciousness"
and to developing "a characteristic style suited to express his dis-
coveries." *(The Suspect In Poetry)*. To an unusual degree Dickey's
critical prose illuminates his poetry and while he has attained to a
style that is, as Pound says, "uncounterfeitable," Dickey's description of Robinson Jeffers speaks volumes about the poetry Dickey
has published in the decade of the 1970's:

> Surely he provides us with plenty to carp about: his oracular
> moralizing, his cruel and repellant sexuality, his dreadful lapses of
> taste when he seems simply to throw back his head and howl, his
> slovenly diction, the eternal sameness of his themes, the amor-
> phous sprawl of his poems on the page. The sheer power and drama
> of some of his writing, however, still carries the day despite every-
> thing, and this is not so much because of the presence of the Truth
> Jeffers believes he has got hold of but because of what might be
> called his embodiment of that Truth: Jeffers's gorgeous panorama of
> *big* imagery, his galaxies, suns, seas, cliffs, continents, mountains,
> rivers, flocks of birds, gigantic schools of fish, and so on.
>
> *Babel to Byzantium*

In subject and style and appetite, Jeffers fathers Dickey. Perhaps the single and profound difference is that Dickey has also and
always lived in the social house, not totally uncomfortably, and his
poetry has consistently described a man's oscillating journey from
that house to the fieldlife of Nature. Behind this imaginative travel
has been the conviction that man is everywhere the powerless
stranger, a spectre of himself, and the further conviction that

through moments of electric, or energized, union with the world a man might become a heroic messenger to his kind. His problem has been to contact the power circuit of the universe and turn headlong for joy where "all things connect   and   stream toward light and speech." Before visions of exhaustion and language gone static, opaque, or habitual, many poets turned quiet minimalists. Dickey chose not merely grandeur, but the grandeur of failure always exhibited by the monomythical Hero: his best poems imply comedic and courageous resolution but end before the tragic dominance of the indifferent universe. His style has progressively altered to demand a full fronting of poem and reader within the context of the failed power-search whose aesthetic kinship is Romantic, revolutionary, and especially American.

Dickey's *Poems 1957–1967*, often as good as American poetry has gotten, shows the slow and steady development of the dense, drummingly cadenced poem that was intensely personal and privately imagistic in statemental lines alternately composed of kinetic verbals and mystic assertions with the present tense. There was throughout this selection a reliance on narrative, or linear progression, though narrative is often sacrificed for poems of contemplation and there are few poems not marked by a tenuous balance of story and meditation. Typically, there is movement from early poems overwhelmed by the lushness of sound to poems in which narrative and hypnotically gorgeous texture marry to produce poems of hallucinatory clarity and amazing power, for example "The Heaven of Animals," "Pursuit from Under," and "Encounter in the Cage Country." Within the framework of narrative the poet is a Chosen Man whose mission was always two-dimensional: to operate as the monomythical warrior for vitality and fertility and to personally transform a man's ennervated selves to cohesive unity by engaging the infinite through finite actions and moments. H. L. Weatherby has clearly shown Dickey's attempts to exchange the spirit of humanness with recipients in the not-me Natural world.

The emphasis on Dickey's story-telling and beast-vision has, I think, masked an equally powerful and characteristic side of his poetry, his attempt to dramatize the social house, or contemplative states of being. Because the wandering hero is always engaged in motorcycling, hunting, flying, climbing mountains or making love, we perhaps fail to observe that he is inevitably a prisoner. His act of the mind is to know "Identities! Identities!" ("Mangham") as a kind of horizon he will never reach. Or, if reached, leaves a man not energized but once more a prisoner of illusion. Experiential reality it seems is no more fixed in the memory of combat than in mathematics contemplated as language, but James Dickey's poetry has been as much sorties in epistemology and ontology as in the spoors of the dark woods. Because the search for the energizing Truth was always doomed, as Dickey's poems know, he has been a poet for whom "the embodiment of that Truth," or style, was very nearly all there could be.

If journey's end is foreclosed, the form of the poem need not be. The history of contemporary American poetry will record massive movement toward conventionally open style. Ginsberg, Warren, Wright, Lowell, Roethke, Dickey and others have been accused of abandoning something like an ideal music for an inferior form. This argument is not resolvable because it masks political, economic, and cultural arguments metastisized to aesthetics. All we can really ask, must ask, of a poet is that his poem in part and in whole give pleasure, be durable, and lead us to know better what we dimly intuit as the reality of life. For Dickey, this meant the form of "The Fiend," "Falling," or what he called a "shimmering wall of words." It was a form identified by long lines and sweeping periodic sentences in which the single poetic line carried truncated and whole his earliest 2, 3, and 4 stress statement-lines. Lines are printed for opportune enjambments and include complete actions within the gap-punctuated sentence. Dickey understood graphics as well as Olson. With "May Day Sermon to the Women of Gilmer County, Georgia, by a Woman Preacher Leaving the Baptist Church," Dickey had taken this variation of his song to its extreme and every subsequent poem has shown a gradual return to more conventional lineation.

Oddly enough, Dickey's formal evolution was away from narrative's temporal progression and resolution and toward spatial experience, which consists in spite of talky rhetoric in image and symbol density. Poetry is mind-flow and intrinsically spatial; it seeks circularity and simultaneity. Dickey's hero-journey linearly tries to organize what is spatially presented, the Truth of emotional complexity and psychological depth. At his extreme in

"May Day Sermon" Dickey had moved as close to cinematic poetry as possible, seeking dimension and action through what remained an oral and intensely stressed convention, the rhetorical poetry of the sermon. Dickey's formal oscillation parallels that earlier myth of oscillation between field and house and, without being at all judgemental, we can see the analogues of the energized man and of the power of poetry from Beowulf to Jekyl and Hyde to The Hulk. Dickey's progression as a poet, that is to say, has been Faustian: from lyric toward epic, to novel and film, with the final choice of mindless explosion or retrenchment to controlled art. That is precisely what *The Zodiac* (1976) enacts, its dying poet exclaiming:

> But I want to come back with the secret
> with the poem
> That links up my balls and the strange, silent words
> Of God   his scrambled zoo   and my own words
> and includes the earth
> Among the symbols.

The Zodiac is a poem about fear and estrangement and what poetry can do to make felt "The star-beasts of intellect and madness." Dickey's preface tells us this is:

> . . . the story of a drunken and perhaps dying Dutch poet who returns to his home in Amsterdam after years of travel and tries desperately to relate himself, by means of stars, to the universe.

Organized in twelve zodical and seasonal panels, occurring within a brief period, and being an approximation of the dying poet's mind-flow mediated through Dickey, with intrusive commentary by Dickey, *The Zodiac* is not a narrative progression except as the poet's hero's madness implies the eternal story of "connecting and joining things that lay their meanings/Over billions of light years," or the madness of failure and fear. Nature, in *The Zodiac,* is either the meaning of stars or their deadness. Dickey's oscillating journey, in the poet's "story," is now between the failure of everything on earth (history, time, love, home—all betrayals) and whatever, if anything, stars are saying. In this sense, *The Zodiac* is entirely self-referential and everything to which the poet responds leaves him aware he is only a prisoner of illusion. Darkness reigns.

The Zodiac seems to me important as an impressive failure and as a transitional poem for Dickey. Its failure is partially caused by the absence of narrative and hence an absence of event which might generate the storm of emotional rhetoric and partly caused by the artificial organization of zodical panels which remain static and shed little if any of the Pythagorean aura of divine immanence. Drunk not only on *aquavit* but on cosmological abstractions, Dickey's poet is harassed by images of Time in both the world-city and in the "Peaceful-sea-beast-blue" of universal space but his life in time is a failure and an imprisonment. He has no life in or out of the world and his homecoming is the occasion to ruminate, while attempting to write, on all the great unknowns. But why this apparently diseased and world-bruised symbolic man should particularly constitute a window into some universal reality, or how, is never quite clear. For all the poem's tortured anguish and virtually hacked-out-alive language, it has the feel of ideas sketched hugely but not dramatically. There is no sense the emotional progression comes to rest except that the poet sits writing a prayer for "the music/That poetry has never really found." Lacking necessity and motion, failing to coalesce around the secret it wanted, *The Zodiac* turns Dickey's spatial organization into spatial occupation. On the other hand there is so much plainly good and true writing in the poem I am tempted to feel it is impertinent to cavil. Ignoring the poet who writes "He polar-bears through the room. . . ," is sometimes all you can do before ghostly luminosity, the sheer screaming silence, the gentle wonder of vision when:

> He looks sideways, out and up   and there it is:
>   The perpetual Eden of space
>   there where you want it.

If *The Zodiac* suffers from Faustian explosion, Dickey's newest collection does not, or not on the whole. This is perhaps because ten of the poems in "The Strength of Fields" section were published by 1973 and are, in character, continuous with the style appearing late in *Poems 1957–1967* and in *The Eye-Beaters, Blood, Victory, Madness, Buckhead and Mercy* (1970). The poems in this section are not walls of words but they avoid such conventions as a continuous left-hand margin, stanzas, repetitive line-lengths, and consistent punctuation. Ordinarily such matters have little to do with what poetry is but Dickey calls our attention to them to insist he is working less with narrative than with spatial suspensions of states of being. In fact, there is little new in these fourteen poems, nor does that compromise their general excellence. In all of them we find Dickey's obsessive and linking image patterns of water, flight, evasion, ascent, descent, the ghosts of the dead, and mythopoeic animals, though Dickey's metaphoric transformation with the beast-world is remarkably absent. Dickey seems, since *The Eyebeaters,* to locate his poems more firmly in the social and public house of human society and the genesis of the energized man finds its most dramatic moments in sexual epiphanies and the dangers of war. At age 58, Dickey's vision of heroic glory remains intact but the Melville-like dark abysm against which the powerless man contends has come, like the military drums of Fort Jackson, closer to the living place. Still, Dickey's problem in "The Strength of Fields" (1977) is:

how

    To withdraw   how to penetrate and find the source
      Of the power you always had

especially when all one's best strengths and efforts have revealed that icily indifferent universe of *The Zodiac.* It is possible now, I think, to argue that that pattern of oscillation in Dickey's poetry was also between a tragic anguish and a comedic joy. Where earlier Dickey's vision of connection and resolution seemed dominant, perhaps the product of a war survivor's faith in the future, his poems now stand in the present of "death-mud shaking" and look backward in tragic despair.

Dickey's title poem, "The Strength of Fields," believes however that "We can all be saved/ By a secret blooming." In it, as he has before, Dickey skates the thin ice of fear and trembling, courageously and believably assuming the role of the Chosen Man doomed to bring back from the psychic underworld the secret of life's fertility and renewal. There is no dramatic occasion or plot save the presiding ghost of the monomyth's rite of passage but the poem has the force of the private man's public declaration of faith in the earth and the dead who speak to us through "the renewing green" and "the homes of men." Straight through Dickey speaks with the power of a man who has seen beyond the surfaces of things and, as hard as it is to say it, he redeems us.

Each of the thirteen other poems in Dickey's first section aspire in one way or another to acts of redemption. "Root-Light, or the Lawyer's Daughter," the tightest of them all, is an epiphany of passion's beginning, a kind of folk religion's "Image/ Of Woman to last/ All your life" as she was once seen diving into and rising up from the St. Mary's River. Its reverent excitement matches the sexual aura and jittery magic of "The Voyage of the Needle," in which a man taking a bath remembers himself as a child who learned from his mother the "scientific trickery" that lets a sewing needle float. "Remnant Water" alone returns Dickey to the animal world and, here, to the death of a pond. As if an extension of the last, dying carp, Dickey is the shamanistic genius of the place whose words alone can redeem "my people gone my fish rolling" and whose mission is "Suffering its consequences, dying,/ Living up to it." There are five poems of war experience (Dickey had once called this collection *War Embrace*) and each is a kind of latter day redemption of those lost not to war deaths but to war's betrayals of ordinary human responsibility. None of the poems glorify combat but in the context of "O why/ In Hell are we doing this?" each seeks to celebrate those who passed through the valley of death with human distinction, which is to say committed acts of fearful evasion and bright courage. "Camden Town," which may be the best of all of Dickey's war poems, shows a cadet pilot's training flight, the fear which causes him to hide under his instruments so that his ship becomes a Flying Dutchman until he gathers himself and swings the ship "East, and the deaths and nightmares/ And training of many." It is not too much to say that with these poems Dickey reminds us that all war survivors may be psychological and emotional flying dutchmen. We live in a time once again of rattling sabers and one has only to read these poems to comprehend the huge psychic wound of war, a debt really and one whose amortization is endless.

The best of these poems, however, are "False Youth: Autumn: Clothes of the Age" and "Exchanges." This latter takes the form of an interlineated dialogue with the dead poet Joseph Trumball Stickney. Here exchanges are not the transformations Dickey used to make but a juxtaposition of what we give and are given of value in our lives. In *Sorties* (1971) Dickey said of the poem:

I have got in some of the current preoccupation with the environment, as well as a good deal about Los Angeles, nature, space exploration, and damn near everything else except Vietnam.

We cannot say, of Dickey, he is too modest. Dickey and a lover sit atop a Pacific cliff at Zuma Point where, he recalls, "we sang and prayed for purity" while surrounded by smog and oil-slick. In changes of time that shift like his guitar Dickey reveals that his lover has died, who with him had gone to watch the Apollo moonshot. Where now, the poem appears to ask, is the dead place—that far shining rock or this "deadest world of all"? Orchestrating "ballad/ After ballad" of what he calls "Appalachian love" with Stickney's vision of *"The last of earthly things/ Carelessly blooming in immensity,"* Dickey creates a vision of death grinding against the life necessarily celebrated by "all those/ *Of the line of wizards and saviors.*" Dickey imagines that the Apollo moon-exploration may very well signal "the quality of life/ And death changed forever" as some kind of new dimension of being beyond Cartesian reality may have happened. But, he says, "Nothing for me/ Was solved." All we have ever asked of poets is to insist on life and often enough that is what they redeem from the chaos of experience and words. In "Exchanges" Dickey has done that and more.

In spite of the general and significant accomplishment of *The Strength of Fields*, the book has some pronounced disasters. "For the Running of the New York Marathon" reminds me of Dickey's early and uncollected poem "The Sprinter's Mother." It is a bathetic and sentimental grabbing of the cosmic hand-mike to proclaim they also win who only show up and trot. A similar failure, with better moments, is "For the Death of Lombardi," a poem which demonstrates by implication Dickey's formidable power and a singular weakness. Ostensibly Dickey hovers near the cancer-dying legendary football coach, one hero paying homage to another's manly courage, pride, passion, and sacrifice. Lombardi, we remember, said "Fatigue makes cowards of us all." But he also said "Winning isn't everything. It's the only thing." Was Lombardi a tragic hero? There is every opportunity for a great elegy of interrogation, drama, and grand resolution and Dickey seems to have had this in mind but there is no dramatic occasion out of which oracular moralizing *must* arise, so that Dickey is just gratuitous when he says "Did you make of us, indeed,/ Figments   over-specialized ghosts/ Who could have been real/ Men in a better sense?" Such writing smacks of superior postseason banquet bouquets.

Dickey must know this as well as anyone, for his splendid poem "The Bee" *(Poems 1957–1967)* does right what "For the Death of Lombardi" does wrong: it dramatizes human weakness and the necessity of manly virtues. There a middle-aged father has to summon emotional and physical powers, taught to him by Coach Shag Norton, to redeem a son frightened into traffic by a bee. He knows he will, and does, hurt the child to save him, and maybe won't. When Dickey writes "God damn/ You, Dickey, *dig*" all the force of education, love, and art demand those words, while the "Drive, *Drive*" of the Lombardi poem is habitual rhetoric. Dickey's powerful vision of the Viking death and life of every man is tragically real in "The Bee" but undercut by the sententious conclusion of "For the Death of Lombardi" which is "We're with you all the way/ You're going forever, Vince." Lombardi's death is naturalistic, man turned meat with tubes, not tragic. Dickey has given no occasion to make *felt* the idea that the hero's importance is not merely death but his lifelong defeat of spirit-sickness in each act of courage. Lombardi forced fatigue to strength and fear to energizing vision. On his best days Dickey has been Lombardi's equal and would have cut this poem.

Fourteen poems comprise the second half of Dickey's book, "Head-Deep In Strange Sounds: Free-Flight Improvisations From the UnEnglish," and are, apparently, what he called in *Sorties* "misreadings." Each carries an acknowledger such as *from, after, near* and most hail poets like Montale, Aleixandre, Paz. "Three Poems With Yevtushekno" are near-translations, though what precisely the others are I do not know, and therefore treat them as new poems. All continue Dickey's theme of the heroic Energized Man but all are, in style, radically discontinuous with Dickey's characteristic work. They are short, terse, and intensely imagistic of body though written mostly in long, gap-punctuated and spatially dispersed lines. There was always a surreal quality to Dickey's poetry and it is strong here. If there is a precursor in his poems, it is *The Zodiac* and its heightened dream of vitality surrounded by disease, death, and doom. Each poem feels like a parable but is not, being essentially a kind of nakedly psychic speech, studded with image clusters, that blurs both dramatic occasion and public clarity. "Low

Voice, Out Loud" is a familiar plea for sexual intensity: "Let us go back into the immense and soft-handed double/ Fire-bringing ignorance." "Nameless" is a statement about evil, good, and beauty. "Math" continues Dickey's fascination with pre-Socratic philosophy and the mysticality of language. "Small Song" and "Poem," "When" and "A Saying Of Farewell" are rages against the imprisonment of death. Several more seem to me virtually impenetrable. The best of them all is perhaps "Purgation," which is addressed to the 9th century Chinese master-poet Po Chu-yi. It describes the emotional "season for wildfire" and renewal. It is a stunning and wonderfully gentle piece, as a few lines will show:

> My ancient friend, you are dead, as we both know.
>
> But I remember, and I feel the grass and the fire
> Get together in April   with you and me, and that
> Is where I want to be
>   both sighing like grass and fire.

I cannot help feeling that these poems from the UnEnglish and *The Strength of Fields* "carries the day despite everything," as Dickey said of Jeffers, but not merely because of his embodiment of *his* Truth. No, it is because he returns us to our most deeply longed-for lives, and shows us those lives, as few are gifted to do. There are changes in James Dickey's poetry, a deepened sense of mortality and fragility, a less frenetic impatience with the constraints of form, and a joy less the result of making literature than of setting the large visionary personality against fear and tembling. No one was ever a greater lover of poetry, of the sheerness of sound and the honesty of feel that poetry makes our first and last way of knowing the labor that life is. No one has demanded more of art as the ungulled and absolute measure of the individual existence. Dickey's strength, the strength of this book, is that he is not a poet of argument but one who turns the world "tall/ In the April wind." Here, reader, is a splendid poem:

FALSE YOUTH: AUTUMN: CLOTHES OF THE AGE

—For Susan Tuckerman Dickey

> Three red foxes on my head, come down
> There last Christmas from Brooks Brothers
> As a joke, I wander down Harden Street

DAVE SMITH

In Columbia, South Carolina, fur-haired and bald,
Looking for impulse in camera stores and redneck greeting cards.
A pole is spinning
Colors I have little use for, but I go in
Anyway, and take off my fox hat and jacket
They have not seen from behind yet. The barber does what he can
With what I have left, and I hear the end man say, as my own
Hair-cutter turns my face
To the floor, Jesus, if there's anything I hate
It's a middle-aged hippie. Well, so do I, I swallow
Back: so do I   so do I
And to hell. I get up, and somebody else says
When're you gonna put on that hat,
Buddy? Right now. Another says softly,
Goodbye, Fox. I arm my denim jacket
On and walk to the door, stopping for the murmur of chairs,
and there it is   hand-stitched by the needles of the mother
Of my grandson   eagle riding on his claws with a banner
Outstretched as the wings of my shoulders,
Coming after me with his flag
Disintegrating, his one eye raveling
Out, filthy strings flying
From the white feathers, one wing nearly gone:
Blind eagle but flying
Where I walk, where I stop with my fox
Head at the glass to let the row of chairs spell it out
And get a lifetime look at my bird's
One word, raggedly blazing with extinction and soaring loose
In red threads burning up white until I am shot in the back
Through my wings   or ripped apart
For rags:

Poetry.

JAMES DICKEY

The Energized Man

I MUST BEGIN BY SAYING THAT *I* am not the energized man, but I may be different from most people in that I believe in his existence. But to define the energized man I first must make a few remarks on what he is not.

The main feeling I have as I live longer and longer is a sense of purposelessness, of drift, of just getting along from day to day, of using only those faculties which we must use in order to earn a living, or in order to experience a few of the well-known physical pleasures so dear to the American heart. One gets the impression of moving among a vast number of well-meaning zombies; one moves among them, also, as a kind of well-meaning zombie with regrets. The enormous discomfort that settles on Americans as they grow older: the enormous discomfort that settles on them in the midst of all their Comforts, and we can spell that word with a capital, is that their lives—their real lives—seem somehow to have eluded them: to have been taken away from under their very noses. They feel—they *know* their real life, a life of vital concerns, of vivid interest in things, and above all, of *consequence,* was there, someplace: I just laid it down a minute ago . . . and so on. We somehow lead ourselves to believe that the moments of youth—ah, youth, indeed!—were those times when our faculties responded and we loved and hated violently, spent sleepless nights, conceived great projects, and lived in a world of purpose which could not have existed without us. We pursuade ourselves that, yes, it was nice, but it was a long time ago, and we should turn to other things: things like . . . well, comfort.

With drift, habit, and the general sense of the purposelessness of life sets in a genuine malaise: the malaise that lends a gigantic helping hand to filling the alcoholic wards of hospitals, to filling the insane asylums and the divorce courts. There has never been, I expect, an unhappier people. And at the very center of this unhappiness, I am convinced, is the feeling, not only that we are not using our energies properly, as we have been meant to use them, but that we are hardly using them at all, in any significant way.

But it is within this kind of neon-lighted dark night of the soul that poetry happens, functions, can function. For poetry believes: believes like a child or an angel, in the energized man: the man with vivid senses, the man alert to the nuances and meanings of his own experience, the man able to appreciate and evaluate the relation between words in the right order—and the rightest order for words is in poems—the relation between words in the right order and his perceptions and his mental faculties in *their* right order: not used simply to sell neckties or industrial machines or to make cocktail conversation, but to serve as the vital center of a moving and changing, perceiving and evaluating world which, as long as it lasts—as long as *he* lasts—is that world of delivery from drift and inconsequence: the world where things are seen and known and felt not for the sake of use or profit, but simply for their *own* everlasting sake, for *his* sake, the man's sake, the energized man's sake.

For, as Auden says, *poetry makes nothing happen.* It makes nothing happen because it *is* a happening, but a happening at a far deeper level than most others, or perhaps than any others. It is a happening in depth, rather than at the surface: a happening at that level of the personality where things really matter, not because they are supposed to matter—the whole public world of publicity and advertising and promotion is always glad to tell you what things are *supposed* to matter—No; poetry happens at the level, not where things are supposed to matter, but where they *do* matter: they matter because of what they are, and because of what *you* are. There is an essential connection—a *possible* essential connection—between the world and you, and it is as divine intermediary between you and the world that poetry functions, bringing with it an enormous increase in perceptiveness—who can see water flowing as well as Gerard Manley Hopkins: who can understand the empty sky better than Mallarmé—an enormous increase in perceptiveness, an increased ability to understand and interpret the order of one's experience—all this, and one has yet said nothing of the sheer *pleasure* of good poetry, the gift of being able to enter the sound patterns, to ride on the rhythms, to get as far into a great good place—the poem itself—as one can, bringing only the best of oneself: one's sharpest perceptions, one's best mind, one's most hilarious and delighted and tragic senses. Well—all these things. They are all the property of the energized man, the man who functions with not, say, fifteen per cent of his faculties, as advertisers and psychologists say the average or statistical man does, but ideally, with a hundred percent, a veritable walking A-bomb among the animated or half-animated spectres of the modern world. The only trouble the energized man has is in containing himself, for there is a great, constantly surprising joy in him, a joy that changes from moment to moment as the world offers unexpected encounters and observations: his other trouble is that he wants to shake the amiable and intent business men and housewives by the shoulders and shout at them in French, in the French of Paul Valéry. If his subject is interested, instead of frightened out of his wits, the energized man will always translate thusly: "Why are men content to go through life with so little recompense? Why will they not make just a *small* effort? Why must they be content to have, really, so little of themselves?"

That is the ultimate horror, I think: to pass on without having had more than a fraction of one's own life—own interests, own perceptions, own sense of consequence. It is against all this that the poet—who at his best approximates the energized or fully awake man—it is against this sense of inconsequence and fruitless drift that the poet stands: that the energized man stands. Let me leave you with that image: the energized man standing against the forces, the vast, sluggish forces of habit, mechanization and mental torpor: let us see him for a moment standing there against those forces we all know so well: he is standing, not like a creature from another planet, giving off strange rays of solar energy, but as a human creature, like you, like me—like you *could* be, like I like to think *I* could be: that is our image for this evening. Remember it, for we must support the energized man against the forces of comfort and the deadly sense of drift that threaten more and more each day. If he falls, everything goes.

JAMES DICKEY

The Imagination as Glory

Let those who hear this voice become aware
The sun has set. O night-time listeners,
You sit in lighted rooms marooned by darkness,
And a voice is speaking to bid you
All reminded that the night surrounds you.

ONCE I WAS SITTING IN A LONDON PUB listening to the
wireless—or the radio, as we call it—and I heard that: it is the
beginning of a radio play by David Gascoyne. It made an odd
impression on me to be sitting, minding my own business in a pub,
and hearing such words come over the radio, in a lull of my conversation with the pub-keeper. I could not, in the first place, imagine hearing such a thing on the radio, telling me about darkness
rather than about the merits of Dial soap or telling me to stop using
that greasy kid stuff. The feeling I had was undecidely unusual,
and I thought, as nearly as I can remember: "Yes, that's so. We *are*
all alone, in our lighted rooms, pathetically hoping for some certainty, hearing time tick on, and on, and on. The night is so tremendous, and I, too, like Pascal looking up at the stars, 'fear the
silence of the infinite spaces.' " Then, and later, I remembered the
voice coming out of nothingness, coming out of the night, when I
read this:

> In the dark wood the man of thirty-five
> Knows as he wakes in the rare light of dawn
> How privileged he is to be alive.
>
> Each sun that brings renewal comes to warn
> That every privilege is transient
> And may at any moment be withdrawn.

As shadows lengthen on the steep descent
He learns, with luck, before it is too late,
That he may cure his gnawing discontent

If he will school himself to meditate,
To be alone in one room and sit still,
To suffer uncomplainingly and wait,

Because there is so little time to kill.

As in this poem—by John Press—it isn't just at night that we get the desperate feeling of terror, or being metaphysically trapped in an existence which by its own nature destroys us: it is also when we wake up, and when consciousness returns. I used to think of this often during the war—both at night and at morning—and think that if I survived I would do something wonderful with my life: I would . . . I would . . . what? Life seemed such a precious thing then, as it always does when you may lose it. But when we're safe, we don't feel quite the same way: habit comes in, and the vast destructive powers of "the things that have to be done": the little things that kill by inches, and leave behind nothing but the body of one who kept neat ledger sheets, or another who never allowed rust to form on her kitchen appliances.

I am not suggesting for a moment that the thing I am pleased to call imagination is a way out of all these dilemmas, or of any of them. I would only suggest that a fully alive mind—an aliveness which includes and may *be* imagination—is better than a dull one: that if you have a great many ideas, comparisons, metaphors, memories you love and learn from and cherish, a great many words and pictures and things closely observed in your mind, the possibility of some of them—of *more* of them—being of value to you is greater if you didn't. And in this respect the imagination *can* guarantee you one thing: it can guarantee that you will have armor, at the end of your life, against the worst feeling that the human mind can conceive, and that so many die with: the feeling that you have not really *lived* your life: that you have died before you ever began to live.

The imagination—the individual method of perceptiveness and relation and the assignment of meaning to the data of experience, as random or as calculated as they may be—is each person's method of imposing an order on the general chaos: it is the power that enables him to perceive *his* kind of normalcy within the abnormal, within the otherwise senseless flux of events. The instantaneous disclosures of living are actually disclosures of the normal, however wondrous they may also be. They depend on you, the observer and the imaginer, and would not exist—and would not be disclosed—if it weren't for you, and if you weren't what you are. The problems of any man are the problems of the normal—of a kind of personal *rightness* that he injects into the world as he perceives it, and in order to solve these problems, he needs all that imagination can give. Each of us is continually re-creating the world in keeping with our own point of view and our own personality. What we want, really, is for the world to be like we think it ought to be. If we see the ripples on a lake as knife-like, we want them to *be* knife-like, more knife-like than they are. For us, though we know they are made of water, they are knives, or almost knives: certainly more like knives than they are for some other person, who sees them as feathers.

My point here is that the imaginative conceiving and perceiving of a thing alters its reality for the observer: it is his way of possessing it, of installing it in a private Heaven which he reserves for all his sacred objects: cat-eyes, girls' backs, silk, fence-wire, the steam-look of one's own breath in the cold, the first rise of whiskey into the brain, while looking at something *big*, like mountains, the time he stole something and it made him happy: all sorts of things. Here, in that Heaven, that place of Glory in his mind, the things are not what they were in the world. Though they keep pretty much distinct from each other, in the mind's eye, they also tend to get mixed up: above all, they somehow or other, in a lot of cases, take on metaphorical associations. I like water, for example, and look at it a lot. And clouds are good, too. I've been in lots of them in airplanes, as I suppose you have too, and have always been disappointed to be there. But I know quite well, as an earth-dweller, that they are not really made of rather low-grade and dirty fog, they are . . . they are, as I said in a poem once: they are enormous groups of weathered statuary: they are rounded masses of imperceptibly dissolving time: they are like a kind of phantom triumph, delayed but still just moving. These are things I thought of, during the fact but mostly after the fact, remembering and wanting to possess the clouds, wanting to put them in a Heaven other than the one they are in. Or water: what about it? The wonderful thing about water is its incessant movement: it will fill your mind with pleasantness for hours at a time and lead your thoughts into endless variation: this is the oldest kind of happiness, the only enduring one. Let's think, for a moment, of water, and put some sun on it. Let's make it the sea, just for the immensity of it, and the sun on the sea. There it is, a vast, unlimited expanse of blue—is it blue?—and calm, with light coming down on it and stopping, and—doing what? Well, it's sparkling: that is just ordinary. It *is* doing that, of course, but it could sparkle for anyone: we don't need a stock response furnished from Woolworth's at practically no expense, to enable us to watch the ocean. Let's look a little closer. Now there are a lot of little winks or blinks on the water. The odd thing about them is that they never come in the same place, and they never come from quite where you expect them to, but they are going on all over the place. It is something like the lights blinking on the face of one of those immense computers—ah! you see how the age modifies the metaphors of its poets! Shakespeare wouldn't have thought of that!—Well now: like a computer, is it?: that doesn't seem exactly it, does it? Something too mechanical about the comparison—that is only half a joke—but these little blinks of light seem to be doing something *actively*, energetically . . . and yes, purposefully. There's one . . . there's another flash, right under me, another over there—can I count them? One, two, no, *that* wasn't one—oh, I can't count them, there are too many: only the sea knows how many there are! uh huh! By George, that's it! Now let's try that one out: The sea, a blaze that is counting itself. By Heaven, that's what it's doing! It's *counting* itself! Or so it seems to be doing, endlessly. That is our observation, that is our metaphor, by God, that's our ocean!

I don't mean to regale you with the account of how a line in a poem that someone, myself, may have used—did use—in a poem, came to be written. And I also don't want to give you the impression that you have to *verbalize* everything—turn it into words, in order to possess it imaginatively. You don't, though I have always suspected that hidden in everyone there *is* a poet, one equipped with the most vivid, profound, and satisfying imagination imaginable, and all the words to make it live for others, too—a poet that is almost always stillborn in the ordinary body he lives in, all his life, as a small, protesting voice, and in which he dies the same way, instead of as the joyous giant that he was intended to be, could have been. I believe in this buried poet as I do in no others that have ever actually written: I believe in him more than I do in Shakespeare. And it is also my belief that, with every person I meet, he—this buried poet—may step out of a garage mechanic or the checking girl at the grocery store and say something that will be part of my personal Heaven forever, because it was so much a part of another person's. That won't happen, I guess, but it may yet. But, regardless of whether or not these images, convictions, and comparisons are put into words, the process is essentially poetic, just the same, the process of the imagination: of possessing the things of this world in the ways in which only you can possess them, because of the unique perspective that your life and your own personality give you. Just to throw this down the drain, or to turn and say to it, like to a child or a dog, "*Will* you shut up and quit following me around?" is the greatest cruelty we can inflict on ourselves: this deliberate cutting off of our own wellsprings of life and meaning in favor of the vastly inferior article that the world—the public world—tells us we must accept, and that the "facts"—those measurable things that exist only by virture of the calibrations of instruments, themselves essentially abstractions—are said to back up. For it is not by the world of propaganda that we really live, and not by the world of fact—scientific fact—that we really live. In order to illustrate this, I went in search of a Fact—capital F. I found it—it was easy to find in a copy of an old textbook I had in college: Lamb's *Hydrodynamics*. I wanted to stick with water, you see! The Fact is this: "The equations 12 and 13 of the preceding Article enable us to examine a related question of some interest: the generation and formation of waves, and their maintenance against viscosity, by suitable forces applied on the surface. If the external forces $P'_{yy} P_{xy}$ be given multiples of $e^{ikx + n\tau}$, where k and n are prescribed, the equations in question determine A and C, and thence the value of η. Thus we find

$$\frac{P'_{yy}}{g\rho\eta} \quad \frac{(n^2 + 2vk^2n)A - i(\sigma^2 + 2vkmn)C}{gk(A - ic)}$$

where σ^2 has been written for $gk + T'k^3$ as before."

And so on for two pages. (I didn't make this up: that really *is* one of the formulae for wave-generation!) At the end, it's made clear that a wind of less half a mile an hour will leave the surface unruffled. At a mile an hour the surface is covered with minute corrugations due to capillary waves which decay immediately when the disturbing cause ceases. At two miles an hour the gravity waves appear. As the author modestly concludes, "Our theoretical investigations give considerable insight into the incipient stages of wave formation."

Well, they do, they do! But these figures—impressive as they are—are not the way we live with waves and *experience* them, or, really, the way we know them. Here are some *big* waves, and some fishermen in a boat going back toward land through them.

> We haul the last
> Net home and the last tether off the gathering
> Run of the started sea. And then was the first
> Hand at last lifted getting us swung against
> Into the homing quarter, running that white grace
> That sails me surely ever away from home.
> And we hold into it as it moves down on
> Us running white on the hull heeled to light.
> Our bow heads home
> Into the running blackbacks soaring us loud
> High up in open arms of the towering sea,
> The steep bow heaves, hung on these words, towards
> What words your lonely breath blows out to meet it.
> It is the skilled keel itself knowing its own
> Fathoms it further moves through, with us there
> Kept in its common timbers, yet each of us
> Unwound upon
>
> By a lonely behavior of all the common ocean.
> I cried headlong from my dead. The long rollers,
> Quick on the crests and shirred with fine foam,
> Surge down then sledge their green tons weighing dead
> Down on the shuddered deck-boards. And shook off
> All that white arrival upon us back to falter
> Into the waking spoil and to be lost in
> The mingling world.

A difference, surely. The waves were acting, no doubt, in keeping with the figures in the formula, but the formula was not required just then, and the sea was not presented to the men in the boat by means of the formula. I don't mean, here, to get into the difference and similarities between science and poetry, or science and the arts generally, but only to reiterate the difference between what is on the one hand scientific fact, verifiable and unchanging, and the emotional, half-animal, intuitive way in which we actually experience the world. It is in this recognition—and in the delight, the animal and human delight that is in such recognition—that the imagination dwells and revels, making its Heaven of sacred objects, of scenes and memories and comparisons that only it could make, and introducing order into them, and so making of them a quite different *kind* of fact: a fact whose truth comes, not from figures of measurement, but from truth to feeling: what really *is* felt about what really *was* lived. In this truth to feeling, in this imaginative and eager play of the mind, is all the freedom there is in this life: in this, above all, receptivity to things, this perpetually virgin and disinterested awareness. It is the individual's truth, and it perishes with him, but while he lives, it is, nonetheless, the Truth. Jesus said, "Ye shall know the Truth, and the Truth shall make you free." This is not the kind of truth he was talking about, but it is truth just the same, and should, in its certainty, always be set against Pontius Pilate's desperate words, "But what is Truth?" In the imagination, all things are true, and need no further verification than they *feel* true. It is good to have a full, glowing Heaven, with infinite possibilities and an eagerness about more and more additions, an eagerness about every new day of life, than a poor, starved, skinny Heaven, full of guilt and hopelessness about the utter uselessness of its own existence. "Exuberance is beauty," Blake said, and it is. And if there are others to whom your imagination is available, give to them without stint, as much as you can, and if possible, marry one. A young mountain-climber dying of tuberculosis was asked why he climbed mountains, and he said this:

> I am dead because I lack desire;
> I lack desire because I think I possess;
> I think I possess because I do not try to give.
> I have nothing to give because my mind is so poor,
> and because I do not love things enough.
> In trying to give, you see that you have nothing.
> Seeing you have nothing, you try to give of yourself;
> Trying to give of yourself, you see that you are nothing;

Seeing that you are nothing, you desire to become;
In desiring to become, you begin to live.

It is in this kind of giving, and of having something to give, that the final vindication of the imagination lies: it is capable, finally, of providing something worth living for, not only in our own case, but sometimes in the cases of others. When you live enough in the imagination, your loves get to be very deep and gentle; they seem not be centered in islands of possessions, like most human loves, but to be diffused among people and animals and plants, and the shapes and colors and smells and sounds of things.

I hope you will remember this, when I am gone from these parts, and will remember these talks, which I have called "The Uses of the Imagination." That is not a good title, I see now, for what they really are, I guess, is a kind of vindication of the imagination and the imaginative, responsive life, beside which no other is worth living, or is even conceivable. I can't really do better, I suppose, than to end what I have to say with the end of a poem by Wallace Stevens, written at the end of his life. Stevens is saying that one thing seen well enough, and held in the mind deeply enough, is part of the sum total of the reality that there is, in delicate keeping in every individual who lives. It is, as Stevens says,

part of the colossal sun,

Surrounded by its choral rings,
Still far away. It is like
A new knowledge of reality.

DENNIS VANNATTA

James Dickey: A Checklist
of Secondary Sources

THE FOLLOWING CHECKLIST includes those secondary sources that I feel would be useful and interesting to scholars and students of James Dickey's work. I have omitted citations that contain scant mention of Dickey or his work. I have also omitted most brief reviews published prior to 1975 and too insubstantial to be particularly useful. Such reviews are annotated in James Elledge's painstakingly thorough *James Dickey: A Bibliography, 1947–1974*. I have, however, listed most shorter reviews appearing after the publication of Elledge's bibliography.

Most of my citations were gleaned from the annual *MLA International Bibliography, Book Review Digest, Book Review Index, American Literary Scholarship*, and earlier checklists and bibliographies concerning Dickey.

Bibliographies

1. Ashley, Franklin. *James Dickey: A Checklist*. Introd. by James Dickey. Detroit: Gale Research Co., 1972.
2. Elledge, James. *James Dickey: A Bibliography, 1947–1974*. Metuchen, N.J.: Scarecrow Press, 1979.
3. Glancey, Eileen. *James Dickey, the Critic as Poet: An Annotated Bibliography with an Introductory Essay*. Troy, N.Y.: The Whitson Co., 1971.
4. Hill, Robert W. "James Dickey, a Checklist." *James Dickey: The Expansive Imagination: A Collection of Critical Essays,*

pp. 213–28. Ed. Richard J. Calhoun. Deland, Fl.: Everett-Edwards, 1973.

Books

Note: The following citations do not include most material in reference works since such works are well known and easily accessible to most scholars and students.

5. Atherton, John. Pref. *A Private Brinkmanship: An Address by James Dickey, Poet-in-Residence, San Fernando Valley State College at the First Pitzer College Commencement, June 6, 1965.* Claremont, Cal.: Pitzer College, 1965.
6. Beaton, James J. "Dickey Down the River." *The Modern American Novel and the Movies,* pp. 293–306. Ed. Gerald Peary and Roger Shatzkin. New York: Ungar, 1978.
7. Bruccoli, Matthew J. "James Dickey." *Conversations with Writers,* I: 25–45. Ed. Matthew J. Bruccoli, C. E. Frazer Clark, Jr., Richard Layman, Margaret M. Duggan, Glenda G. Fedricci, and Cara L. White. Detroit: Gale Research Co., 1977.
8. Calhoun, Richard J., ed. *James Dickey: The Expansive Imagination; A Collection of Critical Essays.* Deland, Fl.: Everett-Edwards, 1973. Contains the following:
   a. Carolyn Kizer and James Boatwright, "A Conversation with James Dickey," pp. 1–33.
   b. Peter Davison, " 'The Great Grassy World from Both Sides': The Poetry of Robert Lowell and James Dickey," pp. 35–51.
   c. H. L. Weatherby, "The Way of Exchange in James Dickey's Poetry," pp. 53–64.
   d. Laurence Lieberman, "The Worldly Mystic," pp. 65–76.
   e. Arthur Gregor, "James Dickey, American Romantic: An Appreciation," pp. 77–80.
   f. William J. Martz, "A Note on Meaningless Being in 'Cherrylog Road,' " pp. 81–83.
   g. Thomas O. Sloan, "The Open Poem Is a Now Poem: Dickey's May Day Sermon," pp. 85–104.

h. Daniel B. Marin, "James Dickey's *Deliverance:* Darkness Visible," pp. 105–17.

i. Richard J. Calhoun, "Whatever Happened to the Poet-Critic?" pp. 119–33.

j. Richard Kostelanetz, "Flyswatter and Gadfly," pp. 135–41.

k. Robert W. Hill, "James Dickey, Comic Poet," pp. 143–55.

l. George Lensing, "James Dickey and the Movements of Imagination," pp. 157–75.

m. Paul Ramsey, "James Dickey: Meter and Structure," pp. 174–94.

n. Laurence Lieberman, "Notes on James Dickey's Style," pp. 195–201.

o. Richard J. Calhoun, " 'His Reason Argues with His Invention': James Dickey's *Self-Interviews* and *The Eye-Beaters*," pp. 203–12.

p. Robert W. Hill, "James Dickey: A Checklist," pp. 213–28.

9. Carrol, Paul. *The Poem in Its Skin.* Chicago: Follett Publishing Co., 1968.

10. Clark, Robert. Foreword. *Poems*, by James Dickey, pp. 5–8. Melbourne, Australia: Sun Books, 1968.

11. Cott, Jonathan. "The New American Poetry." *The New American Arts*, passim. Ed. Richard Kostelanetz. London: Collier-Macmillan, 1965.

12. Dodsworth, Martin. "Introduction: The Survival of Poetry." *The Survival of Poetry: A Contemporary Survey*, passim. Ed. Martin Dodsworth. London: Faber and Faber, 1970.

13. Donadio, Stephen. "Some Younger Poets in America." *Modern Occasions*, passim. Ed. Philip Rahv. New York: Farrar, Straus and Giroux, 1966.

14. Ellman, Richard, and Robert O'Clair, eds. "James Dickey." *The Norton Anthology of Modern Poetry*, pp. 1028–30. New York: W. W. Norton and Co., 1973.

15. Finholt, Richard. *American Visionary Fiction: Mad Metaphysics as Salvation Psychology*, passim. Port Washington, N.Y.: Kennikat, 1978.

16. Greiner, Donald J. " 'That Plain-Speaking Guy': A Conversation with James Dickey on Robert Frost." *Frost: Centennial Essays*, pp. 51–59. Ed. Jac L. Thorpe. Oxford, Miss.: University of Mississippi Press, 1974.

17. Hassan, Ihab. *Contemporary American Literature, 1945–1972: An Introduction*, passim. New York: Frederick Ungar Publishing Co., 1973.

18. Hinz, Evelyn J. "Contemporary North American Literary Primitivism: *Deliverance* and *Surfacing*." *Hemispheric Perspectives on the United States: Papers from the New World Conference*, pp. 150–71. Ed. Joseph S. Tulchin. Westport, Conn.: Greenwood, 1968.

19. Howard, Richard. "James Dickey: 'We Never Can Really Tell Whether Nature Condemns Us or Loves Us.' " *Alone with America: Essays on the Art of Poetry in the United States Since 1950*, pp. 75–98. New York: Atheneum, 1969.

20. Jones, Betty Ann. "*Jericho*: The Marketing Story." *Pages: The World of Books, Writers, and Writing*, I: 249–53. Ed. Matthew J. Bruccoli and C. E. Frazer Clark, Jr. Detroit: Gale Research Co., 1976.

21. Kostelanetz, Richard. *The End of Intelligent Writing: Literary Politics in America*, passim. New York: Sheed and Ward, 1974.

22. Lieberman, Laurence. "James Dickey: The Deepening of Being." *The Achievement of James Dickey: A Comprehensive Selection of His Poems with a Critical Introduction*, pp. 1–21. Glenview, Ill.: Scott, Foresman and Co., 1968.

23. Malkoff, Karl. "Dickey, James." *Crowell's Handbook of Contemporary American Poetry*, pp. 100–108. New York: Thomas Y. Crowell Co., 1973.

24. Mesic, Michael. "A Note on James Dickey." *American Poetry Since 1960: Some Critical Perspectives*, pp. 145–53. Ed. Robert B. Shaw. Chester Springs, Pa.: Dufour Editions, 1974.

25. Mills, Ralph. *Creation's Very Self: On the Personal Element in Recent American Poetry*, passim. Fort Worth: Texas Christian University Press, 1969.

26. ———. "James Dickey." *Contemporary Poets of the English Language*, pp. 295–97. Ed. Rosalie Murphy. Chicago: St. James Press, 1970.

27. Nemerov, Howard. "James Dickey." *Reflexions on Poetry Poetics*, pp. 71–6. New Brunswick, N.J.: Rutgers University Press, 1972.

28. Oates, Joyce Carol. "Out of Stone, Into Flesh: The Imagination of James Dickey." *New Heaven, New Earth: The Visionary Experience in Literature*, pp. 205–63. New York: Vanguard Press, 1974.

29. Peary, Gerald, and Roger Shetzkin. *The Modern American Novels and the Movies*, passim. New York: Frederick Ungar, 1978.

30. Reiss, Barbara, and James Reiss. Introd. *Self-Interviews*, by James Dickey, pp. 9–17. New York: Doubleday, 1970.

31. Rodman, Seldon. "American Poetry 1945–1970." *One Hundred American Poems: Masterpieces of Lyric, Epic and Ballad from Pre-Colonial Times to the Present*, 2nd ed., pp. 43–57. Ed. Seldon Rodman. New York: New American Library, 1967.

32. Rosenthal, M. L. "Epilogue: American Continuities and Cross Currents." *The New Poets: American and British Poetry Since World War II*, pp. 310–33 passim. New York: Oxford University Press, 1967.

33. Schorer, Mark. "James Dickey." *The Literature of America: Twentieth Century*, p. 730–31. New York: McGraw-Hill Book Co., 1970.

34. Silverstein, Norman. "James Dickey's Muscular Eschatology." *Contemporary Poetry in America: Essays and Interviews*, pp. 303–13. Ed. Robert Boyers. New York: Schocken Books, 1974.

35. Spears, Monroe K. *Dionysus and the City: Modernism in Twentieth Century Poetry*, passim. New York: Oxford University Press, 1970.

36. Stalker, James C. "Syntactic and Semantic Pattern Matches in James Dickey's 'False Youth: Autumn: Clothes of the Age.'" *Meaning: A Common Ground of Linguistics and Literature; Proceedings of a University of Northern Iowa Conference Held April 27–28, 1973, in Honor of Norman C. Stageberg*, pp. 153–57. Ed. Don L. E. Nilsen. Cedar Falls: University of Northern Iowa, 1973.

37. Stauffer, Donald Barlow. *A Short History of American Poetry*, passim. New York: E. P. Dutton and Co., 1974.

38. Stepanchev, Stephen. "James Dickey." *American Poetry Since 1945: A Critical Survey*, pp. 190–92. New York: Harper and Row, 1965.

39. Waggoner, Hyatt H. *American Poets: From the Puritans to the Present*, passim. Boston: Houghton Mifflin, 1968.

40. Walsh, Chad. "James Dickey." *Today's Poets: American and British Poetry Since the 1930's*, p. 414. New York: Charles Scribner's Sons, 1964.

41. Wheelock, John Hall. "Some Thoughts on Poetry." *Poets of Today*, vol. 7, passim. Ed. John Hall Wheelock. New York: Charles Scribner's Sons, 1960.

42. Westendorp, T. A. "Recent Southern Fiction: Percy, Price, and Dickey." *Handlingen van het XXIXe Vlaams Filologencongres Antwerpen 16–18 april 1973*, pp. 188–98. Ed. J. Van Haver. Available from the secretariaat van de Vlaamse Filologencongressen, Sint-Bavolaan 7, 1730, Zellik, Belgium.

43. Williams, Harry. *"The Edge Is What I Have": Theodore Roethke and After*, passim. Lewisburg, Pa.: Bucknell University Press, 1977.

44. Young, James D. "Ecstacy and Metamorphosis in the Poems of James Dickey." *Americana-Austriaca: Beiträge zur Amerikakund*, Band 3, pp. 139–48. Ed. Klaus Lanzinger. Wein and Stuttgart: Braumüller, 1974.

Periodical Literature

45. Algren, Nelson. "Tricky Dickey." *The Critic*, 28 (May–June 1970), 77–9.

46. Armour, Robert. *"Deliverance:* Four Variations on the American Adam." *Literature/Film Quarterly*, 1 (July 1973), 280–85.

47. Arnett, David L. "An Interview with James Dickey." *Contemporary Literature*, 16 (1975), 286–300.

48. Aronson, James. Rev. of *Self-Interviews. Antioch Review*, 30 (Fall–Winter 1970–71), 463–65.

49. Baker, Donald W. "The Poetry of James Dickey." *Poetry*, 111 (Mar. 1968), 400–401.

50. Barnwell, W. C. "James Dickey on Yeats: An Interview." *Southern Review*, 13 (1977), 311–16.

51. Baro, Gene. "The Sound of Three New Poetic Voices." Rev. of *Into the Stone and Other Poems*. *New York Herald Tribune Book Review*, 30 Oct. 1960, p. 10.

52. Barshay, Robert. "Machismo in *Deliverance*." *Teaching English in the Two-Year College*, 1, no. 3 (1975), 169–73.

53. Baugham, Ronald. "James Dickey's *The Eye-Beaters*: 'An Agonizing New Life.'" *South Carolina Review*, 10, no. 2 (1978), 81–88.

54. "Beat Poetry." *New York Times Book Review*, 24 Sept. 1961, p. 48.

55. Bedient, Calvin. "Gold-Glowing Mote." *Nation*, 210 (6 April 1970), 407–8.

56. Beidler, Peter G. "'The Pride of Thine Heart Hath Deceived Thee': Narrative Distortion in Dickey's *Deliverance*." *South Carolina Review*, 5, no. 1 (1972), 29–40.

57. Bennett, Joseph. "A Man with a Voice." Rev. of *Buckdancer's Choice*. *New York Times Book Review*, 6 Feb. 1966, p. 10.

58. Berry, David C., Jr. "Harmony with the Dead: James Dickey's Descent into the Underworld." *Southern Quarterly*, 12 (Apr. 1974), 233–44.

59. Berry, Wendell. "James Dickey's New Book." Rev. of *Helmets*. *Poetry*, 105 (Nov. 1964), 130–31.

60. "The Best People I Have Ever Known, and Also the Worst, Were Poets." Interview. *Mademoiselle*, 75 (Aug. 1972), 282–83, 417–20.

61. Bledsoe, Jerry. "What Will Save Us from Boredom?" Rev. of the film *Deliverance*. *Esquire*, 80 (Dec. 1973), 227–33.

62. Bleikasten, André. "Anatomie d'un bestseller: A propos de *Deliverance*." *Recherches Anglaises et Americaines*, 4 (1971), 116–29.

63. Bly, Robert. "*Buckdancer's Choice*." *Sixties*, 9 (Spring, 1967), 70–9.

64. ———. "Prose vs. Poetry." Rev. of *Drowning with Others*. *Choice*, 2 (1962), 65–80, passim.

65. ———. "The Works of James Dickey." *Sixties* (Winter 1964), 41–57.

66. Bobbitt, Joan. "Unnatural Order in the Poetry of James Dickey." *Concerning Poetry*, 11, no. 2 (1978), 39–44.

67. Bornhouser, Fred. "Poetry by the Poem." *Virginia Quarterly Review*, 40 (Winter 1965), 146–52, passim.

68. Broyard, Anatole. "Dickey's Likes and Dislikes." Rev. of *Sorties. New York Times*, 17 Dec. 1971, p. 37.

69. Buck, Carol. "The 'Poetry Thing' with James Dickey." *Poetry Australia* (Apr. 1968), pp. 4–6.

70. Burns, Gerald. "Poets and Anthologies." *Southwest Review*, 53 (Summer 1968), 332–36.

71. Calhoun, Richard J. "After a Long Silence: James Dickey as South Carolina Writer." *South Carolina Review*, 9, no. 1 (1976), 12–20.

72. ———. " 'His Reason Argues with His Invention': James Dickey's *Self-Interviews* and *The Eye-Beaters*." *South Carolina Review*, 3, no. 2 (1971), 9–16.

73. ———. "Whatever Happened to the Poet-Critic?" *Southern Literary Journal*, 1 (Autumn 1968), 75–88.

74. Carnes, Bruce. "Deliverance in James Dickey's 'On the Coosawattee' and *Deliverance*." *Notes on Contemporary Literature*, 7, no. 2 (1977), 2–4.

75. Carroll, Paul. "James Dickey as Critic." *Chicago Review*, 20, (Nov. 1968), 82–87.

76. ———. "Twenty-Five Poets in Their Skins." *Choice*, 5 (1967), 82–94, passim.

77. Cassidy, Jerry. "What the Poetry Editor of *Esquire* Is Like: Interview with James Dickey." *Writer's Digest*, 54 (Oct. 1974), 16–20.

78. Cassill, R. V. "The Most Dangerous Game of the Poet James Dickey." *South Carolina Review*, 10, no. 2 (1978), 7–11.

79. Cavell, Marcia. "Visions of Battlements." *Partisan Review*, 38, no. 1 (1971), 117–21, passim.

80. Champlin, Charles. "Men Against River—of Life?—in *Deliverance*." *Los Angeles Times*, 13 Aug. 1972, pp. 1, 16–17.

81. Clark, Robert. "James Dickey: American Poet." *Australian Book Review* (Mar. 1968), p. 83.

82. Clausen, Christopher. "Grecian Thoughts in Home Fields: Reflections on Southern Poetry." *Georgia Review*, 32 (1978), 283–305.

83. Clemons, Walter. "James Dickey, Novelist." *New York Times Book Review*, 22 March 1970, p. 22.

84. Core, George. Rev. of *Spinning the Crystal Ball*. *Georgia Review*, 23 (Summer 1969), 250–51.

85. Corrington, John William. "James Dickey's *Poems 1957–1967*: A Personal Appraisal." *Georgia Review*, 22 (Spring 1968), 12–23.

86. Coulthard, Ron. "From Manuscript to Movie Script: James Dickey's *Deliverance*." *Notes on Contemporary Literature*, 3 (Nov. 1973), 11–12.

87. ———. "Reflections Upon a Golden Eye: A Note on James Dickey's *Deliverance*." *Notes on Contemporary Literature*, 3 (Sept. 1973), 13–15.

88. Cromie, Robert. "Meet James Dickey, A King-Sized Poet." *Chicago Tribune*, 15 Mar. 1966, sec. 2, p. 2.

89. Cross. Leslie. "Wisconsin and America's Poet of the Year, James Dickey, Talks of His Life and Craft." *Milwaukee Journal*, 20 Mar. 1966, part 5, p. 4.

90. Davis, Charles E. "The Wilderness Revisited: Irony in James Dickey's *Deliverance*." *Studies in American Fiction*, 4 (1976), 223–30.

91. Davison, Peter. "The Difficulties of Being Major: The Poetry of Robert Lowell and James Dickey." *Atlantic*, 220 (Oct. 1967), 116–21.

92. De Candido, G. A. Rev. of *God's Images*. *Library Journal*, 103 (15 Jan. 1978), 154.

93. DeMott, Benjamin. "The 'More Life' School and James Dickey." *Saturday Review*, 53 (28 Mar. 1970), 25–6, 38.

94. Dempsy, Michael. "*Deliverance*/Boorman: Dickey in the Woods." *Cinema*, 8 (Spring 1973), 10–17.

95. Dickey, William. "Talking About What's Real." *Hudson Review*, 18 (Winter 1965–66), 613–17.

96. ———. "The Thing Itself." Rev. of *Buckdancer's Choice*. *Hudson Review*, 19 (Spring 1966), 145–55.

97. Donald, David Herbert. "Promised Land or Paradise Lost: The South Beheld." *Georgia Review*, 29 (1975), 184–87.

98. Doughtie, Edward. "Art and Nature in *Deliverance*." *Southwest Review*, 64 (1979), 167–80.

99. Duncan, Robert. " 'Oriented by Instinct by Stars.' " *Poetry*, 105 (Nov. 1964), 131–33.

100. Eagleton, Terry. "New Poetry." Rev. of *The Eye-Beaters*. *Stand*, 12, no. 3 (1971), 68–70.

101. Edwards, C. Hines, Jr. "Dickey's *Deliverance*: The Owl and the Eye." *Critique: Studies in Modern Fiction*, 15, no. 2 (1973), 95–101.

102. ———. "A Foggy Scene in *Deliverance*." *Notes on Contemporary Literature*, 2 (Nov. 1972), 7–9.

103. Ely, Robert. "Rising and Overcoming: James Dickey's 'The Diver.' " *Notes on Modern American Literature*, 2 (1978), Item 12.

104. Evans, E. N. Rev. of *Jericho*. *New York Times Book Review*, 9 Feb. 1975, p. 4.

105. Evans, Oliver. "University Influence on Poetry." *Prairie Schooner*, 35 (Summer 1961), 179–80.

106. Eyster, Warren. "The Regional Novels." *Sewanee Review*, 79 (1971), 469–74.

107. Farber, Steven. "*Deliverance*: How It Delivers." *New York Times*, 20 Aug. 1972, sec 2, pp. 9, 16.

108. Flagep, Bunky. "River Holds Death for Many Who Run It." *Los Angeles Times*, 28 Oct. 1973, part 5, pp. 10–12.

109. Flanders, Jane. Rev. of *The Strength of Fields*. *New Republic*, 182 (5–12 Jan. 1980), 38.

110. Flint, R. W. "Poetry Chronicle." Rev. of *Drowning with Others*. *Partisan Review*, 29 (Spring 1962), 290–94.

111. ———. "Three American Poets." *New York Review of Books*, 2 (25 June 1964), 13–14.

112. Fraser, G. S. "The Magicians." Rev. of *The Eye-Beaters*. *Partisan Review*, 38 (Winter 1971–72), 469–78.

113. Friedman, Norman. "The Wesleyan Poets, II: The Formal Poets, 2." *Chicago Review*, 19 (Jan. 1966), 55–67, 72.

114. Fukuda, Rikutaro. "James Dickey no Shi to Shiron." *Eigo Seinen*, 114 (1968), 576–77.

115. Galler, David. "Versions of Accident." *Kenyon Review*, 26 (Summer 1964), 581–84.

116. Garrigue, Jean. "James Dickey Airborne and Eastbound." *New Leader*, 50 (22 May 1967), 21–23.

117. Goldman, Michael. "Inventing the American Heart." *Nation*, 204 (24 Apr. 1967), 529–30.

118. Goldstein, Laurence, " 'The End of All Our Explorating': The Moon Landing and Modern Poetry." *Michigan Quarterly Review*, 18 (1979), 192–217.

119. Gray, Paul Edward. "New Fiction in Review." Rev. of *Deliverance*. *Yale Review*, 60 (Oct. 1970), 101–8.

120. Greiner, Donald J. "The Harmony of Bestiality in James Dickey's *Deliverance*." *South Carolina Review*, 5, no. 1 (1972), 43–49.

121. Grossman, Allen. "Dream World of James Dickey." Rev. of *Poems 1957–1967*. *Boston Sunday Globe*, 2 Apr. 1967. sec. B., p. 33.

122. Guillory, Daniel L. "Myth and Meaning in James Dickey's *Deliverance*." *College Literature*, 3 (1976), 56–62.

123. ———. "Water Magic in the Poetry of James Dickey." *English Language Notes*, 8 (Dec. 1970), 131–37.

124. Gunn, Thom. "Things, Voices, Minds." Rev. of *Drowning with Others*. *Yale Review*, 52 (Oct. 1962), 129–38, passim.

125. Gustafson, Richard. "The Peace of a Good Line." *Poet and Critic*, 6, no. 3 (1971), 29–33.

126. Guttenberg, Barnett. "The Pattern of Redemption in Dickey's *Deliverance*." *Critique: Studies in Modern Fiction*, 18, no. 3 (1977), 83–91.

127. Hadžiselimovic, Omer. "Iskupljenje kroz iskutvo: Izbavljenje Džemza Dikija." *Izraz*, 40 no. 5 (1976), 780–90. ["Redemption through Art: James Dickey's *Deliverance*"; cited in *PLMA International Bibliography*.]

128. Harrison, Keith. "Disappointments." Rev. of *Helmets*. *Spectator*, 213 (18 Sept. 1964), 375.

129. Heilbrun, Carolyn. "The Masculine Wilderness of the American Novel." Review of *Deliverance*. *Saturday Review*, 55 (29 Jan. 1972), 41–44.

130. Heyen, William. "A Conversation with James Dickey." *Southern Review*, 9 (Jan. 1973), 135–56.

131. ———. Rev. of *Sorties*. *Saturday Review*, 55 (11 Mar. 1972), 70–71.

132. Hochman, Sandra. "Some of America's Most Natural Resources." *New York Herold-Tribune Book Week,* 20 Feb. 1966, pp. 4, 11.

133. Holley, Linda Tarte. "Design and Focus in James Dickey's *Deliverance.*" *South Carolina Review,* 70, no. 2 (1978), 90–98.

134. Houston, Gary. "Where Do the Deep Rivers of Meaning Run in *Deliverance?*" *Chicago Sun-Times Showcase,* 1 Oct. 1972, pp. 1, 7.

135. Howard, Richard. "Five Poets." Rev. of *Drowing with Others. Poetry,* 101 (Mar. 1963), 412–18.

136. ———. "Five Poets." Rev. of *Drowning with Others. Poetry,* 121 (Oct. 1972), 54–59.

137. ———. "On James Dickey." *Partisan Review,* 33 (Summer 1966), 414–28, 479–86.

138. ———. " 'Resurrection for a Little While.' " Rev. of the *Eye-Beaters. Nation,* 210 (23 Mar. 1970), 341–42.

139. Howes, Victor. "Dickey's World and Welcome to It." Rev. of *Sorties. Christian Science Monitor,* 13 Jan. 1972, sec. 2, p. 11.

140. ———. "Genuine and Bogus." Rev. of *The Suspect in Poetry. Christian Science Monitor,* 3 Dec. 1964, sec. B, p. 8.

141. ———. Rev. of *The Strength of Fields. Christian Science Monitor,* 20 Feb. 1980, p. 17.

142. Huff, Robert. "The Lamb, the Clocks, the Blue Light." Rev. of *Buckdancer's Choice. Poetry,* 109 (Oct. 1966), 44–48.

143. Ignatow, David. "The Permanent Hell." Rev. of *Buckdancer's Choice. Nation,* 202 (20 June 1966), 752–53.

144. "An Interview with James Dickey." *Eclipse,* 5 (1966), 5–20.

145. Italia, Paul G. "Love and Lust in James Dickey's *Deliverance.*" *Modern Fiction Studies,* 21 (1975), 203–13.

146. Jameson, Fredric. "The Great American Hunter, or, Ideological Content in the Novel." *College English,* 34 (Nov. 1972), 180–97.

147. "Journey into Self." Rev. of *Deliverance. Time,* 95 (20 Apr. 1970), 92–93.

148. Kael, Pauline. "After Innocence." Rev. of *Deliverance. New Yorker,* 49 (1 Oct. 1973), 113–18.

149. Kalston, David. Rev. of *Sorties. New York Times Book Review,* 23 Jan. 1972, pp. 6, 24.

150. Kauffman, Stanley. "Fair to Meddling." Rev. of *Deliverance.* *New Republic,* 167 (5–12 Aug. 1972), 24, 35–35.
151. Kaye, Howard. "Why Review Poetry?" Rev. of *Babel to Byzantium. New Republic,* 158 (29 June 1968), 28–29.
152. Kennedy, X. J. "Joys, Griefs, and 'All Things Innocent, Hapless, Forsaken.' " Rev. of *Helmets* and *Two Poems of the Air. New York Times Book Review,* 23 Aug. 1964, p. 5.
153. ———. "Sometimes It's the Sound That Counts." Rev. of *Drowning with Others. New York Times Book Review,* 15 July 1962, p. 4.
154. Kizer, Carolyn, and James Boatwright. "A Conversation with James Dickey." *Shenandoah,* 18 (Autumn 1966), 3–28.
155. Knight, Arthur. ". . . And Deliver Us From Evil." Rev. of *Deliverance. Saturday Review,* 55 (5 Aug. 1972), 61.
156. Korges, James. "James Dickey and Other Good Poets." *Minnesota Review,* 3 (Summer 1963), 473–91, passim.
157. Kostelanetz, Richard. "Flyswatter and Gadfly." Rev. of *The Suspect in Poetry. Shenandoah,*16 (Spring 1965), 92–95.
158. Kunz, Don. "Learning the Hard Way in James Dickey's *Deliverance." Western American Literature,* 12 (1978), 289–301.
159. Landess, Thomas. "Traditional Criticism and the Poetry of James Dickey." *The Occasional Review,* 3 (1975), 5–26.
160. "Leaps and Plunges." Rev. of *Poems 1957–1967. Times Literary Supplement,* 8 May 1967, p. 420.
161. LeBlanc, Jerry. "James Dickey Is a Poet and Quickly Lets You Know It." *Chicago Tribune Magazine,* 29 Oct. 1972, pp. 13, 15.
162. Leibowitz, Herbert. "The Moiling of Secret Forces: *The Eye-Beaters, Blood, Victory, Madness, Buckhead and Mercy." New York Times Book Review,* 8 Nov. 1970, pp. 20, 22.
163. Lennox, John. "Dark Journeys: *Kamouraska* and *Deliverance." Essays on Canadian Writing,* 12 (1978), 84–104.
164. Lensing, George. "The Neo-Romanticism of James Dickey." *South Carolina Review,* 10, no. 2 (1978), 20–32.
165. ———. Rev. of *The Eye-Beaters. Carolina Quarterly,* 22 (Spring 1970), 90–91.
166. Libby, Anthony. "Fire and Light, Four Poets to the End and Beyond." *Iowa Review,* 4 (Spring 1973), 111–26, passim.

167. Lieberman, Laurence. "The Expansional Poet: A Return to Personality." *Yale Review*, 57 (Dec. 1967), 258–71, passim.

168. ———. "Notes on James Dickey's Style." *Far Point*, 2 (1968), 57–63.

169. ———. "Poet-Critics and Scholar-Critics." Rev. of *Babel to Byzantium. Poetry*, 115 (Feb. 1970), 346–52.

170. ———. "Poetry Chronicle: Last Poems, Fragments, and Wholes." Rev. of *Helmets. Antioch Review*, 24 (Winter 1964–65), 537–43.

171. ———. "The Wordly Mystic." Rev. of *Poems 1957–1967. Hudson Review*, 20 (Autumn 1967), 513–20.

172. Lindborg, Henry J. "James Dickey's *Deliverance:* The Ritual of Art." *Southern Literary Journal*, 6, no. 2 (1974), 83–90.

173. Logan, John. "Poetry Shelf." Rev. of *Drowning with Others. The Critic*, 21 (Dec. 1962–Jan. 1963), 84–85.

174. Logan, William. Rev. of *Strength of Fields. Library Journal*, 104 (15 Dec. 1979), 2651.

175. Logue, John. "James Dickey Describes His Life and Works as He 'Moves Toward Hercules.'" *Southern Living*, 6 (Feb. 1971); 44–49.

176. Longen, Eugene. "Dickey's *Deliverance:* Sex and the Great Outdoors." *Southern Literary Journal*, 9, no. 2 (1977), 137–49.

177. Love, Glen A. "Ecology in America." Rev. of *Deliverance. Colorado Quarterly*, 21 (Autumn 1972), 175–85.

178. Lucas, Tom. Rev. of *The Eye Beaters. Spirit*, 37 (Fall 1970), 39–42.

179. McGinnis, Wayne D. "Mysticism in the Poetry of James Dickey." *New Laurel Review*, 5, nos. 1–2 (1975), 5–10.

180. Mahon, Derek. "Suburban Arrows." Rev. of *Deliverance. Listener*, 10 Sept. 1970, p. 352.

181. Maloff, Saul. "Poet Takes His Turn as Critic." Rev. of *Babel to Byzantium. Book World*, 30 June 1968, p. 10.

182. Marin, Daniel B. "James Dickey's *Deliverance:* Darkness Visible." *South Carolina Review*, 3 (1970), 49–59.

183. Markos, Donald W. "Art and Immediacy: James Dickey's *Deliverance.*" *Southern Review*, 7 (July 1971), 947–53.

184. Marty, M. E. Rev. of *God's Images. New York Times Book Review*, 18 Dec. 1977, p. 11.

185. Meiners, R. K. "The Necessary and Permanent Revolution." Rev. of *Helmets*. *Southern Review*, 1 (Autumn 1965), 926–44, passim.

186. ———. "The Way Out: The Poetry of Delmore Schwartz and Others." Rev. of *Poetry 1957–1967*. *Southern Review*, 7 (Jan. 1971), 314–37, passim.

187. Meredith, William. "A Good Time for All." Rev. of *Poetry 1957–1967*. *New York Times Book Review*, 23 Apr. 1967, pp. 4, 46.

188. ———. "James Dickey's Poems." *Partisan Review*, 32 (Summer 1965), 456–57.

189. Mills, Ralph J., Jr. "Brilliant Essays on Contemporary Poetry." Rev. of *Babel to Byzantium*. *Chicago Sun-Times Book Week*, 5 May 1968, p. 4.

190. ———. "The Poetry of James Dickey." *Triquarterly*, 11 (Winter 1968), 231–42.

191. Mitchell, Henry. "Dickey: Friend of Bears and Byron." *Washington Post*, 19 Mar. 1974, sec. B, pp. 1–2.

192. Mizejewski. Linda. "Shamanism toward Confessionalism: James Dickey, Poet." *Georgia Review*, 32 (1978), 409–19.

193. Monagham, Charles. Rev. of *Buckdancer's Choice*. *Commonweal*, 84 (15 Apr. 1966), 120–22.

194. Monk, Donald. "Colour Symbolism in James Dickey's *Deliverance*." *Journal of American Studies*, 11 (1977), 261–79.

195. Morris, Harry. "A Formal View of the Poetry of Dickey, Garrigue, and Simpson." *Sewanee Review*, 77 (Spring 1969), 318–25.

196. Morse, J. Mitchell. "Fiction Chronicle." Rev. of *Deliverance*. *Hudson Review*, 23 (Summer 1970), 327–38.

197. Morse, Jonathan. "James Agee, Southern Literature, and the Domain of Metaphor." *South Atlantic Quarterly*, 76 (1977), 309–17.

198. Morse, Samuel French. "A Baker's Dozen?" Rev. of *Drowning with Others*. *Virginia Quarterly Review*, 38, (Spring 1962), 324–30.

199. ———. "Poetry, 1962: A Partial View." *Wisconsin Studies in Contemporary Literature*, 4 (Autumn 1963), 367–80, passim.

200. Nemerov, Howard. "Poems of Darkness and a Specialized Light." *Sewanee Review*, 71 (Jan.-Mar. 1963), 99–104.

201. Niflis, N. Michael. "A Special Kind of Fantasy: James Dickey on the Razor's Edge." *Southwest Review*, 57 (Autumn 1972), 311–17.

202. Norman, Geoffrey. "*Playboy* Interview: James Dickey." *Playboy*, 20 (Nov. 1973), 81–82, 86, 89, 92, 94, 212–16.

203. ———. "The Stuff of Poetry." *Playboy*, 18 (May 1971), 148–49, 230, 232, 234, 236, 238, 240, 242.

204. Oates, Joyce Carol. "Out of Stone, Into Flesh: The Imagination of James Dickey." *Modern Poetry Studies*, 5 (1974), 97–144.

205. O'Neil, Paul. "The Unlikeliest Poet." *Life*, 61 (22 July 1966), 68–70, 72–74, 77–79.

206. Packard, William. "Craft Interview with James Dickey." *New York Quarterly*, 10 (Spring 1972), 16–35.

207. Parente, D. A. Rev. of *God's Images*. *Best Sellers*, 37 (Dec. 1977), 283.

208. Patrick, Richard. "Heroic *Deliverance*." *Novel*, 4 (Winter 1971), 190–92.

209. Pierce, Constance. "Dickey's 'Adultery': A Ritual of Renewal." *Concerning Poetry*, 9, no. 2 (1976), 67–69.

210. "The Poet as Journalist." *Time*, 92 (13 Dec. 1968), 75.

211. Prescott, P. S. Rev. of *The Zodiac*. *Newsweek*, 88 (6 Dec. 1976), 89.

212. Pritchard, William H. "Shags and Poets." Rev. of *The Eye-Beaters*. *Hudson Review*, 23 (Autumn 1970), 562–77.

213. ———. "Why Read Criticism?" Rev. of *Babel to Byzantium*. *Hudson Review*, 21 (Autumn 1968), 585–92.

214. Rev. of *God's Images*. *American Artist*, 41 (Nov. 1977), 26.

215. Rev. of *God's Images*. *Booklist*, 74 (Oct. 1977), 344.

216. Rev. of *God's Images*. *Christian Century*, 94 (14 Dec. 1977), 1173.

217. Rev. of *God's Images*. *Publisher's Weekly*, 212 (15 Aug. 1977), 63.

218. Rev. of *God's Images*. *Theology Today*, 35 (Jan. 1979), 507.

219. Rev. of *God's Images*. *Wall Street Journal*, 192 (11 Dec. 1978), 28.

220. Rev. of *Jericho*. *American Literature*, 47 (Mar. 1975), 144.

221. Rev. of *Jericho*. *Choice*, 11 (Jan. 1975), 1615.

222. Rev. of *The Strength of Fields. Atlantic Monthly,* 245 (Feb. 1980), 98.
223. Rev. of *The Strength of Fields. Bestsellers,* 39 (Mar. 1980), 459.
224. Rev. of *The Strength of Fields. Booklist,* 76 (1 Feb. 1980), 752.
225. Rev. of *The Strength of Fields. Book World (Washington Post),* 9 (30 Dec. 1979), 7.
226. Rev. of *The Strength of Fields. Kirkus Reviews,* 47 (1 Nov. 1979), 1318.
227. Rev. of *The Strength of Fields. National Review,* 31 (7 Dec. 1979), 1566.
228. Rev. of *The Strength of Fields. Village Voice,* 25 (4 Feb. 1980), 40.
229. Rev. of *Tucky the Hunter. Book World (Washington Post,* 12 Nov. 1978*),* E3.
230. Rev. of *Tucky the Hunter. The Listener,* 102 (8 Nov. 1979), 646.
231. Rev. of *Tucky the Hunter. School Library Journal,* 26 (Sept. 1979), 108.
232. Rev. of *Tucky the Hunter. Southern Living,* 14 (Jan. 1979), 68.
233. Rev. of *The Zodiac. America,* 136 (2 Apr. 1977), 297.
234. Rev. of *The Zodiac. American Poetry Review,* 6 (July 1977), 42.
235. Rev. of *The Zodiac. Booklist,* 73 (15 Oct. 1976), 300.
236. Rev. of *The Zodiac. Book World (Washington Post,* 12 Dec. 1976), H6.
237. Rev. of *The Zodiac. Choice,* 14 (May 1977), 370.
238. Rev. of *The Zodiac. Commonweal,* 103 (3 Dec. 1976), 791.
239. Rev. of *The Zodiac. The Hudson Review,* 30 (Autumn 1977), 467.
240. Rev. of *The Zodiac. Kirkus Reviews,* 44 (15 Sept. 1976), 1080.
241. Rev. of *The Zodiac. Library Journal,* 101 (15 Sept. 1976), 1862.
242. Rev. of *The Zodiac. New Republic,* 179 (9 Dec. 1978), 25.
243. Rev. of *The Zodiac. Newsweek,* 88 (6 Dec. 1976), 89.
244. Rev. of *The Zodiac. North American Review,* 262 (Spring 1977), 75.
245. Rev. of *The Zodiac. Partisan Review,* 46 (1979), 470.

246. Rev. of *The Zodiac. Virginia Quarterly Review,* 53 (Summer 1977), 94.

247. Rev. of *The Zodiac. World Literature Today,* 51 (Summer 1977), 446.

248. Ricks, Christopher. "Man Hunt." Rev. of *Deliverance. New York Review of Books,* 14 (23 Apr. 1970), 37–41.

249. ———. "Spotting Syllabics." Rev. of *Helmets. New Statesman,* 67 (1 May 1964), 684–85.

250. Roberts, Francis. "James Dickey: An Interview." *Per/Se,* 3 (Spring 1968), 8–12.

251. Robinson, James K. "From Criticism to Historicism." Rev. of *Babel to Byzantium. Southern Review,* 9 (July 1973), 692–709, passim.

252. ———. "Terror Lumped and Split: Contemporary British and American Poets." Rev. of *Buckdancer's Choice. Southern Review,* 6 (Jan. 1970), 216–28, passim.

253. Rose, Maxine S. "On Being Born Again: James Dickey's 'May Day Sermon to the Women of Gilmer County, by a Woman Preacher Leaving the Baptist Church.'" *Research Studies,* 46 (1978), 254–58.

254. "Rustic and Urbane." Rev. of *Helmets. Times Literary Supplement,* 20 Aug. 1964, p. 748.

255. Samuels, Charles Thomas. "How Not to Film a Novel." *American Scholar,* 42 (Winter 1972–1973), 148–50, 152, 154.

256. ———. "What Hath Dickey Delivered?" *New Republic,* 162 (18 Apr. 1970), 23–26.

257. Scarborough, George. "One Flew East, One Flew West, One Flew Over the Cuckoo's Nest." Rev. of *Two Poems of the Air. Sewanee Review,* 73 (Jan.–Mar. 1965), 138–150, passim.

258. Shaw, Robert B. "Poets in Midstream." Rev. of *The Eye-Beaters. Poetry,* 118 (July 1971), 228–33.

259. Shepherd, Allen. "Counter-Monster Comes Home: The Last Chapter of Dickey's *Deliverance. Notes on Contemporary Literature,* 3 (Mar. 1973), 8–12.

260. Silverstein, Norman. "James Dickey's Muscular Eschatology." *Salmagundi,* 22–23 (1973), 258–68.

261. ———. "Two Modes of Despair." Rev. of *Drowning with Others. Spirit,* 29 (Sept. 1962), 122–24.

262. Simon, John. "More Brass than Enduring." Rev. of *Drowning with Others. Hudson Review*, 15 (Aug. 1962), 455–68, passim.

263. Simpson, Louis. "New Books of Poems." Rev. of *Poems 1957–1967. Harper's Magazine*, 235 (Aug. 1967), 89–91.

264. Skelton, Robin. "The Verge of Greatness." Rev. of *Poems 1957–1967. Malahat Review*, 4 (1967), 119–24.

265. Smith, Dave. Rev. of *The Zodiac. Library Journal*, 101 (15 Sept. 1977), 1862.

266. Smith, Raymond. "The Poetic Faith of James Dickey." *Modern Poetry Studies*, 2 (1972), 259–72.

267. Squires, Radcliffe. "James Dickey and Others." Rev. of *Buckdancer's Choice. Michigan Quarterly Review*, 6 (Oct. 1967), 296–98.

268. Stella, Mario. "James Dickey: dalla poesia alla narrativa." *Trimestre*, 7 (1973), 420–36.

269. Stephenson, William. "Deliverance from What?" *Georgia Review*, 28 (Spring 1974), 114–20.

270. Strange, William C. "To Dream, to Remember: James Dickey's *Buckdancer's Choice." Northwest Review*, 7 (Fall-Winter 1965–1966), 33–42.

271. Strong, Paul. "James Dickey's Arrow of Deliverance." *South Carolina Review*, 11, no. 1 (1978), 108–16.

272. Sullivan, Rosemary. "*Surfacing* and *Deliverance." Canadian Literature*, 67 (1976), 6–20.

273. Thwaite, Anthony. "Out of Bondage." Rev. of *Deliverance. New Statesman*, 80 (11 Sept. 1970), 310–11.

274. Tillinghast, Richard. "Pilot into Poet." *New Republic*, 157 (9 Sept. 1967), 28–29.

275. Tucker, Charles C. "Knowledge Up, Down, and Beyond: Dickey's 'The Diver' and 'Falling.'" *CEA Critic*, 38 no. 4 (1976), 4–10.

276. Tulip, James. "Robert Lowell and James Dickey." *Poetry Australia*, 24 (Oct. 1968), 39–47.

277. Turco, Lewis. "The Suspect in Criticism." *Mad River Review*, 1 (Spring-Summer 1965), 81–85.

278. Untermeyer, Louis. "A Way of Seeing and Saying." Rev. of *Poems 1957–1967. Saturday Review*, 50 (6 May 1967), 31, 55.

279. Verburg, Larry. "Water Imagery in James Dickey's *Deliverance.*" *Notes on Contemporary Literature*, 4 (Nov. 1974), 11–13.

280. Wagner, Linda. "*Deliverance:* Initiation and Possibility." *South Carolina Review*, 10, no. 2 (1978), 49–55.

281. Warren, W. P. Rev. of *The Zodiac. New York Times Book Review*, 14 Nov. 1976, p. 8.

282. Watson, Robert. "Two Books of Criticism." Rev. of *The Suspect in Poetry. Poetry*, 107 (Feb. 1966), 332–33.

283. Weatherby, H. L. "The Way of Exchange in James Dickey's Poetry." *Sewanee Review*, 74 (July–Sept. 1966), 669–80.

284. Weeks, Edward. Rev. of *Jericho. Atlantic Monthly*, 234 (Dec. 1974), 125.

285. Williams, Miller. "Merrill, Smith and Dickey." Rev. of *Buckdancer's Choice. Shenandoah*, 17 (Spring 1966), 100–113.

286. Willig, Charles L. "Ed's Transformation: A Note on *Deliverance.*" *Notes on Contemporary American Literature*, 3 (Mar. 1973), 4–5.

287. Willson, Robert F., Jr. "*Deliverance* from Novel to Film: Where Is Our Hero?" *Literature/Film Quarterly*, (Winter 1974), 52, 54–55, 57–58.

288. Wimsatt, Margaret. Rev. of *Self-Interviews. Commonweal*, 93 (19 Feb. 1971), 501–3.

289. Winchell, Mark Royden. "The River Within: Primitivism in James Dickey's *Deliverance.*" *West Virginia University Philogogical Papers*, 23 (1977), 106–14.

290. Wright, James, "Shelf of New Poets." Rev. of *Into the Stone. Poetry*, 99 (Dec. 1961), 178–83, passim.

291. Yardley, Jonathan. "A Colossal Ornament?" Rev. of *Jericho. New Republic*, 171 (3 Nov. 1974), 43.

292. ———. "More of Superpoet." Rev. of *Self-Interviews. New Republic*, 163 (5 Dec. 1970), 26–27.

293. Zweig, Paul. Rev. of *The Strength of Fields. New York Times Book Review*, 6 Jan. 1980, p. 6.

Dissertations

294. Arnett, David Leslie. "James Dickey: Poetry and Fiction." *DAI* 34: 1889.

295. Baughman, Ronald Claude. "The Poetry of James Dickey: Variations on Estrangement." *DAI* 36: 7416A–17A.

296. Berry, David C., Jr. "Orphic and Narcissistic Themes in the Poetry of James Dickey, 1951–1970." *DAI* 34: 505A.

297. Brookes, Philip James. "Mythic Continuities in the Poetry of James Dickey." *DAI* 37: 305A.

298. Butts, Leonard Culver. "Nature in the Selected Works of Four Contemporary American Novelists." *DAI* 40: 6277A.

299. Cleghorn, James D. "Preservation of the Wilderness: A Contemporary View of Nature Poetry." *DAI* 35: 2982A–83A.

300. Elliot, David Lindsey. "The Deep Image: Radical Subjectivity in the Poetry of Robert Bly, James Wright, Galway Kinnell, James Dickey, and W. S. Merwin." *DAI* 39: 3577A.

301. Finhalt, Richard David. "The Murder of Moby Dick: Mad Metaphysics and Salvation Psychology in American Fiction." *DAI* 36: 7420A.

302. Fismer, Clyde H. "The Element of Myth in James Dickey's Poetry." *DAI* 35: 2265A.

303. Goodwin, Gayle. "Contemporary Deep South Poetry: A Classification of Subjects." *DAI* 39: 1566A.

304. Harrington, Jane Gouwens. "Animal Imagery in Modern American and British Poetry." *DAI* 39: 1549A.

305. McHughes, Janet Ellen Larsen. "A Phenomenological Analysis of Literary Time in the Poetry of James Dickey." *DAI* 33: 2942A.

306. McKenzie, James Joseph. "A New American Nature Poetry: Theodore Roethke, James Dickey, and James Wright." *DAI* 32: 2698.

307. Meeker, Michael William. "The Influence of the Personal Element on the Language, Form, and Theme in the Poetry of James Dickey and Galway Kinnell." *DAI* 37: 312A.

308. Moore, Robert Nelson, Jr. "Aggression in the Poetry of James Dickey." *DAI* 34: 5195A.

309. Passey, Joel Craig. "An Interpretive Analysis of the Interaction of Illusion and Reality in Selected Verse of James Dickey from 1951 to 1971." *DAI* 36: 5638A.

310. Robbins, Fred Walker. "The Poetry of James Dickey, 1941–1967." *DAI* 32: 6450A.

311. Royden, Mark. "One Foot in Paradise: The American Adam in the Modern World." *DAI* 39: 2935A.

312. Schechter, Harold George. "The Mysterious Way: Individuation in American Literature." *DAI* 36: 6691A.

Notes on Contributors

DAVID C. BERRY teaches at the University of Southern Mississippi; his books of poetry include *saigon cemetery*.

ROBERT DUNCAN's many books of poetry include *Bending the Bow* and *The Truth and Life of Myrtle*. He has published numerous books of prose, including *Fictive Certainties: Five Essays in Essential Autobiography*.

T. R. HUMMER teaches at Oklahoma State University; his books of poetry include *The Passion of the Right-Angled Man*.

HERBERT LEIBOWITZ lives in New York, where he edits *Parnassus* and teaches at the College of Staten Island, CUNY.

LAURENCE LIEBERMAN is the author of *Unassigned Frequencies: American Poetry in Review*, and of numerous books of poetry, including *Eros at the World Kite Pageant*.

JANE BOWERS-MARTIN teaches at the University of Georgia; she has published criticism and poetry in such magazines as *South Carolina Quarterly*, *Kansas Quarterly*, and *Quarterly West*.

RALPH J. MILLS is a distinguished critic whose books on contemporary American poetry include *The Cry of the Human*.

LINDA MIZEJEWSKI teaches at Wheeling College, Wheeling, West Virginia.

HOWARD NEMEROV's books include *Sentences* (poetry) and *Figures of Thought* (essays); he is a recent recipient of the Bollingen Prize for Poetry. Mr. Nemerov lives in St. Louis, where he teaches at Washington University.

N. MICHAEL NIFLIS lives and teaches in Tillamook, Oregon. He has published poetry and criticism in many magazines, including *Partisan Review*, the *New Republic*, and the *Literary Review*.

JOYCE CAROL OATES is one of America's best-known fiction writers; she is also a widely published poet. Her criticism is collected in *New Heaven, New Earth: The Visionary Experience in Literature*.

DAVE SMITH's latest books are *Gray Soldiers* (poetry), *Onliness* (a novel), and *Assays* (essays). He teaches at Virginia Commonwealth University.

DENNIS VANNATTA teaches at the University of Arkansas at Little Rock, where he is an editor of *Crazyhorse*.

H. L. WEATHERBY teaches at Vanderbilt University.

BRUCE WEIGL's books of poetry include *A Romance;* he edited *The Giver of Morning: On the Poetry of Dave Smith*. He teaches at Old Dominion University in Norfolk, Virginia.

DISCARD